THE ELECTION OF 1860

American Presidential Elections

MICHAEL NELSON

JOHN M. MCCARDELL, JR.

THE ELECTION OF 1860

"A CAMPAIGN FRAUGHT WITH CONSEQUENCES"

MICHAEL F. HOLT

UNIVERSITY PRESS OF KANSAS

Published by the University Press of Kansas (Lawrence, Kansas 66045), which was organized by the Kansas Board of Regents and is operated and funded by Emporia State University, Fort Hays State University, Kansas State University, Pittsburg State University, the University of Kansas, and Wichita State University

Names: Holt, Michael F. (Michael Fitzgibbon), author.
Title: The Election of 1860: "A Campaign Fraught with Consequences" / Michael F. Holt.
Description: Lawrence, Kansas : University Press of Kansas, 2017. | Series: American presidential elections | Includes bibliographical references and index.
Identifiers: LCCN 2017026682
ISBN 9780700624874 (hardback)
ISBN 9780700624881 (ebook)
Subjects: LCSH: Presidents—United States—Election—1860. | United States—Politics and government—1857–1861. | Lincoln, Abraham, 1809–1865—Political career before 1861. | Republican Party (U.S. : 1854-) | BISAC: HISTORY / United States / Civil War Period (1850–1877). |HISTORY / United States / 19th Century. | POLITICAL SCIENCE / Political Process / Elections.
Classification: LCC E440 .H65 2017 | DDC 324.973/068—dc23
LC record available at https://lccn.loc.gov/2017026682.

British Library Cataloguing-in-Publication Data is available.

Printed in the United States of America

10 9 8 7 6 5 4 3 2 1

The paper used in this publication is recycled and contains 30 percent postconsumer waste. It is acid free and meets the minimum requirements of the American National Standard for Permanence of Paper for Printed Library Materials Z39.48-1992.

For my grandchildren:

Avis Fitzgibbon Abel,

Juniper Gentry Abel,

and

Winslow Ingalls Sloane

CONTENTS

EDITORS' FOREWORD

Writing in 1936 on the topic "Has the Lincoln Theme Been Exhausted?" James G. Randall answered the question emphatically in the negative. The noted Lincoln scholar pointed to opportunities for new interpretations of a seemingly familiar story. "To interpret," he stated, "will be to avoid merely looking for the familiar. It will mean seeing things anew, judging not by what secondary writers have said, but by a fresh viewing of sources."

In this impressive study of the momentous election of 1860, Michael F. Holt has done just that. He avoids the familiar: Lincoln is "de-centered"; his opponents, who among them won 60 percent of the popular vote, become the focus. Holt sees things anew: the real issue in this election, he persuasively argues, was not slavery but rather the fate of the Union; the campaigns of John Bell and Stephen A. Douglas, in particular, stressed that the election of either John C. Breckinridge or Abraham Lincoln would put the future of the Union at grave risk. Holt judges not by what secondary writers have said. Instead, informed by a thorough mastery of the historiography of the topic, he contends that the Republican campaign—waged in an era when party mattered far more than candidate—focused more on the incompetence and corruption of the Democratic (Buchanan) administration than on the issue of slavery in the territories. And he views his sources freshly. Newspapers, some obscure, allow for a broader and deeper and likely also more reliable probing of what the electorate in 1860 actually was thinking.

Contemporary readers will also be prompted to ask present-minded questions. Is the election of 1860 a case for, or against, the Electoral College? Is it a reminder of the benefits of a two-party system? Is a successful negative campaign that cannot come close to garnering a majority of the popular vote a fundamental threat to national unity? Are there moments, albeit rare moments, in American history when "the center cannot hold," and catastrophe results? Is such catastrophe avoidable?

To pose these questions is to be reminded not only of the critical importance of the election of 1860 but also of the enduring value of historical study. In *The Election of 1860*, Michael F. Holt recasts a familiar narrative and brings to it the freshness that comes, in Randall's words, from "seeing things anew."

PREFACE

Without question, the election of 1860 was the most consequential presidential contest in all of American history. The victory of Republican candidate Abraham Lincoln quickly triggered the secession of seven Deep South states and led, six weeks after Lincoln took office on March 4, 1861, to a horrific four-year Civil War in which over 700,000 young men (the equivalent of 7 million in today's population) died. No other American presidential election has come close to engendering such a catastrophic outcome.

Because of that result, but also, I think, because the election of 1860 elevated Lincoln, the greatest of all American presidents, to the White House, it has also probably been the most chronicled presidential contest in our history. "Done to death," I told Fred Woodward of the University Press of Kansas several years ago when I reluctantly accepted his request that I take on this assignment for the press's series on American presidential elections. So much had already been written about this election, especially from the perspective of Lincoln's nomination and subsequent victory, that finding something new or different to say about it seemed then—and still seems now—a particularly challenging task.

Even before I began to study the election more closely, however, it struck me that compared to the Lincoln saga, the story of this election in the South and especially the campaign of the newly minted Constitutional Union Party had been relatively understudied. Also improperly discounted in previous studies, it seemed to me, was that a large majority of American voters in 1860 opposed the Republican Party because they feared and/or loathed it. Why they did so was a crucial part of the election's story. Thus, I decided at the outset to de-center the Lincoln tale and give his competitors equal billing with the Republican campaign.

Most American voters in 1860 opposed the Republican Party, not so much for what it did or said in 1860 itself but because of its overtly anti-South rhetoric and seemingly unstoppable rise to power in the North from its emergence in 1854 until that election year. Thus I devote a longish chapter to telling that pre-1860 story. Similarly, the problems that Democrats faced in this election culminated in 1860 but had their roots in the Buchanan administration. Hence, I also devote a chapter to the pre-1860 Democratic saga.

I began to study antebellum political history when I entered graduate school in 1962, and I taught college courses on the coming of the Civil War from 1965 until I retired in 2012. But I had never focused very closely on the 1860 election itself, other than reading secondary accounts about it. Once I began to do so by examining the appeals to voters the contesting parties made in 1860, I was surprised to discover that the common understanding of what that election was actually about seemed mistaken. Or perhaps it's more accurate to say that southern secessionists' interpretation of what the election was about—slavery and the Republican Party's purported threat to it—had become our common understanding, regardless of what other actors in 1860 said. Republicans were indeed committed to stopping slavery's extension into the western territories, and Lincoln had indeed famously said, or at least implied, on a few occasions that doing so would put slavery "on the road to ultimate extinction." As well, southern proponents of disunion who seized on Lincoln's triumph as justification for secession did indeed despise Republicans as both dangerous to their propertied interests and insufferably insulting.

Of the four groups who appealed to the electorate for support in 1860, however, only the southern Democrats backing John C. Breckinridge insisted that slavery extension was the election's central issue. John Bell's Constitutional Union supporters in both the North and South, where the largest slaveholders usually backed him, consistently declared that territorial slavery extension was a mooted question, a phony issue, since slaveholders had no interest whatsoever in moving into any of the remaining territories of the United States. They stressed instead the danger that both Republicans and Breckinridge Democrats posed to the preservation of the Union. Nor did the supporters of Democratic candidate Stephen A. Douglas emphasize the slavery extension question, though they took a decidedly different stand on it than did Breckinridge men in the South. Their emphasis instead was on the treasonous disunionism of the Breckinridge crowd and their responsibility for shattering the Democratic Party as well as the dangerous antislavery extremism of Republicans. Ultimately, the Douglas camp, like the Constitutional Union Party, maintained that the fate of the nation, not the fate of slavery or slavery extension, was what was at stake in the 1860 race.

Finally, while every Republican campaigning for Lincoln's election did indeed repeat his party's opposition to slavery's extension beyond the states where it legally existed, Republicans did not focus their campaign on that issue. Instead, they primarily railed and ran against the record and especially the corruption of the incumbent administration of Democratic president James Buchanan. Ousting Democrats from power and restoring honesty to the federal government—not stopping slavery's spread, let alone demanding its abolition—was the central theme of the Republican campaign and, so far as campaign issues determined the election's outcome, by far the major reason why Abraham Lincoln was elected.

Closer examination of the 1860 campaign revealed another misleading aspect of its traditional portrayal. This is the notion that it was fundamentally two separate campaigns—Lincoln versus Douglas in the northern free states and Bell versus Breckinridge in the southern slave states. This characterization distorts how the dynamic of the election developed. It especially effaces the nationwide revulsion of non-Democrats at the sleaze they identified with Democratic governance. The demand in 1860 to throw the Democratic rascals out was a national, not a sectional, passion.

Readers who come to this book unfamiliar with nineteenth-century political culture and practice should know that they differed from politics today. For one thing, people usually voted for or against political parties rather than for or against presidential candidates, who were tellingly referred to as the parties' standard bearers. It was the standard, not its bearer, that usually attracted or repulsed voters. Presidential candidates did not personally campaign in those days, although in 1860 Stephen Douglas would break that rule while Lincoln would win Republicans' nomination because party insiders considered him more electable than any other potential nominee. There is no evidence, however, that the hundreds of thousands of men—and only adult men voted in those days—who supported electors pledged to John Bell or John Breckinridge did so because of any personal attraction of the candidates themselves. And the same was true of the vast majority of men who supported Lincoln.

Presidential candidates then were also utterly dependent on their party organizations to have any chance of election. Until the very end of the nineteenth century, there were no state-printed ballots for voters to mark. Instead, parties had the obligation of printing their own ballots and then distributing them to thousands of polling places so that voters could hand them to election judges for deposit in ballot boxes. If for no other reason, that crucial party responsibility was why the election of 1860 pitted parties, not just candidates, against each other.

An important result of this situation is that, quite unlike the case today, parties' national platforms were deemed to be all-important in 1860. They were so central to the story of that election that I have included all four of the party platforms in Appendix B so readers can easily consult them.

Readers familiar with my previous books will note that this one is based far more on evidence drawn from newspapers and much less on private manuscript sources than those earlier efforts. Here I was interested primarily not in behind-the-scenes strategy-making but in how the campaign was presented to the electorate. Newspapers seemed the best source to explore that matter.

I have relied primarily on newspapers available digitally through the University of Virginia's Alderman Library and other sites. One of these sources—a collection entitled Nineteenth Century U.S. Newspapers at Alderman—gathered what will strike readers as some awfully obscure papers while omitting some far better known ones like, say, Horace Greeley's *New York Tribune*. For me, however, its geographical reach mattered more than its seemingly bizarre selection criteria.

Let me alert readers to one other thing about my use of newspapers. For those whose editor-owners' names I knew, such as James Gordon Bennett of the *New York Herald* and Henry J. Raymond of the *New York Times*, I sometimes attribute editorials in those papers to those individuals even when I did not know who actually wrote the specific editorials in question. My thinking here was that, as owners of the papers, those men would not allow editorials with which they disagreed to appear in their sheets.

The quotation in my title is taken from an address issued by New York Republicans' state convention in April 1860. That address alerted New York's voters that they were entering "a campaign fraught with consequences of the most momentous import."[1] The consequences it referred to were emphatically not the abolition of slavery within the South or the Civil War that it took to achieve that abolition. Rather, it was the opportunity, at long last from Republicans' perspective, to oust a venal Democratic Party regime, and with it the domineering southern Slave Power, from its control of the executive branch of the national government. Republicans would achieve that goal in 1860, but that achievement's concomitant price was a far more momentous consequence—southern secession and a disastrous four years of war.

Let me close by thanking the people who helped me bring this book to conclusion. The staff at the University Press of Kansas was wonderfully prompt and efficient in its preparation. That preparation has occurred under the aegis of three different editors. Fred Woodward initially signed me up for the project. Before I even began to write, he informed me that he was retiring and passing me on to the sure hands of Chuck Myers, who succeeded him as head of the press. Then, before I had finished writing, Chuck informed me that he was leaving to move to the University of Chicago Press. Before he did so, he generously read and passed on most welcome encouraging words about the seven chapters I had then completed. Finally, Joyce Harrison has overseen the completion of the project. I am also deeply indebted to her assistant Cole Anneberg for help in readying the illustrations for publication. The two editors for the presidential election series at the press, Michael Nelson and John McCardell, offered helpful suggestions for revision, most of which I heeded. Chuck Calhoun, who read the manuscript for the press, alerted me to an important factual error in my chapter on the Republican national convention, and I am grateful for his heads-up. But two longtime friends and fellow historians of nineteenth-century America were most helpful of all, even though both were striving to complete book projects of their own. William W. Freehling, who is writing an exciting fresh study of Lincoln, read the two chapters in which he most prominently figures and offered both astute commentary and welcome encouragement. William J. Cooper Jr. read the entire manuscript with characteristic acuity, and he too was most generous in his assessment. "The two Bills," as my one-time editor Thomas LeBien once called them, are true pals indeed.

1

REPUBLICAN STORM RISING?

In early April 1860 a worried Democratic congressman from Pennsylvania warned his party's main Washington newspaper that "State after State in the North" had been inundated by "the swelling tide of Black Republicanism." Democrats probably now lacked a popular majority in every free state save Oregon, he wailed, with little "prospect of reversing, at present, the disastrous current."[1] Three months later, Democratic congressman James Jackson told his fellow townsmen in Athens, Georgia, that a Republican cloud covered the entire North. "It is black and ominous," he warned, "and threatens to discharge its flood of fury—its storm of hail and lightning upon you at any moment." Republicans, he explained, were motivated by "hostility, uncompromising enmity to you and to your great property interests." "Can this tide of fanatical enmity to you, thus swelling every day, be stopped before it engulfs us and our children?" he asked. "It must be arrested," he insisted, "or your peace is at an end—your property destroyed—your land now blooming like a garden, left desolate as a desert."[2]

Divergent reactions to the seemingly inexorable growth of the Republican Party since its emergence in 1854 shaped the presidential election of 1860 more than anything else. Among less astute Republicans, its apparently unstoppable expansion across the North created overconfidence about winning the White House in November. Among the great majority of American voters who regarded Republicans as a hostile and dangerous force, that growth engendered fear and resentment. Union-loving conservatives in both the North and South dreaded that a Republican victory would rend the nation. Meanwhile, southern Democrats, Republicans' primary political target, raved that they would indeed disrupt the Union rather than submit to the victory of a party they deemed abolitionist fanatics. To boot, they howled, Republicans had repeatedly and outrageously insulted white Southerners' honor by insisting that those Southerners were a minority of the nation's population—that is, an inherently unequal portion of it—who must submit to the rule of the northern majority.[3]

However unstoppable the growth of the Republican Party appeared, it had not, in fact, been as irresistible as an incoming tide. Instead, it was fueled by Northerners' indignant reactions to a series of contingent events that Republican propagandists persuasively portrayed as slaveholder or Slave Power aggressions against their rights, interests, and liberties. So dependent were Republicans on events, rather than the institutional loyalty that more mature political organizations like the Democrats could rely on to mobilize voters, that Republican leaders constantly felt the need to justify the very existence of a party whose support was confined almost totally to one section of the nation. In early January 1860, for example, the New Hampshire Republican state platform insisted that only "the continued aggressions of the Slave Power upon the rights of free labor and free men . . . force upon us, in common with the people of the Free States, the necessity of renewed and united efforts in behalf of freedom, free labor, and the Union as our fathers framed it."[4] It was that undeniably sectional nature of the party, indeed, that made it seem so dangerous to the great majority of white Americans. After all, the greatest of the Founders, George Washington himself, had warned against the specter of such a political party.

The event that precipitated the formation of the Republican Party was passage of the Kansas-Nebraska Act in May 1854. That law had opened up the remainder of the Louisiana Purchase territory west of Missouri, Iowa, and Minnesota Territory—from which slavery had been "forever prohibited" by the Missouri Compromise of 1820—to possible settlement by slaveholding Southerners. It had declared that thirty-four-year-old ban "inoperative and void." The vast majority of Northerners, regardless of partisan affiliation, opposed slavery's expansion into western areas where it did not yet legally exist. A Free Soil Party that denounced slavery's possible extension into western territories had garnered 14 percent of the North's popular vote in the 1848 presidential election, but the Nebraska bill outraged a far larger portion of the northern electorate. Mass protest meetings erupted across the North almost from the moment that Democratic senator Stephen A. Douglas's Nebraska bill was introduced in January 1854. As Democratic responsibility for the bill and the unanimous opposition of northern Whigs and Free Soilers in Congress to it became clearer, these meetings increasingly took on an anti-Democratic hue. So great was the hostile uproar in the North, in fact, that when the House of Representatives finally voted on the bill in May, northern Democrats split down the middle, with 44 supporting the measure and 43 opposing it.

Upon passage of the bill, the Free Soil paper in Washington urged all northern congressmen who had voted against it to call "upon the people to disregard obsolete issues, old prejudices, mere party names, and rally as one man for the reestablishment of liberty and the overthrow of the Slave Power."[5] In the fall of 1854 fusion anti-Nebraska coalitions contested the state and congressional elections in most Midwestern states, ousting sitting Democratic congressmen from office. (In the congressional elections of 1854 and 1855, as a whole, northern Democrats lost 66 of the 91 House seats they held in 1854.) In only two states, Wisconsin and Michigan, however, did those coalitions dub themselves Republicans. Elsewhere in that region, anti-Nebraska coalitions seemed to be temporary ad hoc alliances intent simply on restoring the recently repealed Missouri Compromise line, rather than building the foundation for a permanent new anti-Democratic party.

Adopted in July 1854, the Michigan Republican state platform spelled out the rationale for a longer-lasting party in memorable language. After denouncing "the Institution of Slavery" as "a great moral, social and political evil" and as "a relic of barbarism," it insisted that Congress prohibit slavery expansion to check the "unequal representation" of the South in Congress. The fundamental purpose of the Nebraska Act, it declared, was to "give to the Slave States such a decided and practical preponderance in all measures of government as shall reduce the North . . . to the mere province of a few slaveholding Oligarchs of the South—to a condition too shameful to be contemplated." It then included a ringing justification for the name *Republican*. "That in view of the necessity of battling for the first principles of republican government, and against the schemes of aristocracy the most revolting and oppressive with which the earth was ever cursed, or man debased, we will co-operate and be known as Republicans until the contest be terminated."[6]

Republican editors and speakers rang changes on these themes for the remainder of the decade. Some denounced slavery as immoral, and the party's initial national platform in 1856 labeled it "a relic of barbarism." Moreover, up through the 1860 election, virtually every Republican reaffirmed that stopping the extension of slavery beyond the boundaries of the existing slave states was a fundamental purpose of the party. Only a tiny minority of Republicans, however, demanded the immediate abolition of slavery in the South.[7] To the contrary, virtually every public pronouncement by the party denied that Republicans would interfere with slavery where it legally existed. Many Republican spokesmen in fact claimed absolute indifference to the fate of slaves or voiced racist contempt for them. In 1856 the Republican Hartford *Courant* defended the party's free-soil principles as follows: "The Republicans mean to preserve all of the country they can from the pestilential presence of the black man." That same year a Republican orator, who would be named Pennsylvania's sole representative on the Republican National Committee in 1859 and then become a well-regarded Radical Republican congressman during Reconstruction, told his Pittsburgh audience that "he cared nothing for the 'nigger'; it was not the mission of the Republican party to preach rebellion—he had a higher mission to preach—deliverance to the white man."[8] By 1860 the nation's leading Republican, New York senator William H. Seward, admitted that "the motive of those who have protested against the extension of slavery [has] always been concern for the welfare of the white man, not an unnatural sympathy with the negro."[9]

With regard to the fate of western territories, the welfare of northern white men required the exclusion of slaves and slaveholders, lest their presence preclude the migration of northern farmers and laborers to those territories. Yet the Michigan Republican platform makes abundantly clear that the welfare of northern white men was also inextricably bound to the balance of sectional power in the national government and that white southern slaveholders, not African American slavery, constituted Republicans' main target. To Michigan's Republicans, the Nebraska Act was a naked attempt to increase white Southerners' power in Washington by creating more slave states. They—and many other Republicans—found it outrageous that a tiny oligarchy of some 400,000 slaveholders, "the most revolting and oppressive [aristocracy] with which the earth was ever cursed," could, through its control of the national Democratic Party, dictate the fate and welfare of 20 million northern people. The first principle of republican government they meant to defend was majority rule by the nation's majority—that is, the North. As a Republican speaker rhetorically asked a New York rally in 1856, "Shall . . . an arrogant oligarchy of slave masters rule as with a plantation whip, twenty million of American citizens?"[10]

From the founding of their party through the 1860 election, Republicans continually portrayed Northerners as victims of political and even physical assaults by white Southerners, the hated Slave Power, who would politically rule them "as with a plantation whip." Events during the remainder of the decade would provide fresh evidence of an aggressive and bullying slavocracy that, Republicans insisted, only they could resist, for, as Seward averred in 1858, "The Democratic party . . . is identical with the Slave Power."[11]

Despite the forcefulness of Republicans' anti-Southern rhetoric and the widespread northern outrage at the Kansas-Nebraska Act, in 1854, as noted, Republicans as a distinct party planted roots in only two Midwestern states. Elsewhere in that region, Whigs or fusion People's Party coalitions battled Democrats that year. East of Ohio, the existing Whig Party capitalized on anger at the legislation and often refused flatly to fuse with Free Soilers or anti-Nebraska Democrats. In 1854 most northern Whig leaders, who had unanimously opposed the Nebraska measure both inside and outside Congress, were determined to preserve the Whig Party, not fold it into a broader anti-slavery-extension coalition, because they believed that straight-out Whigs could win both the congressional elections of 1854–1855 and the presidential election of 1856.

Two of the men who would vie for the Republican presidential nomination in 1860 were among these initial Whig holdouts. In Illinois, Abraham Lincoln rejected attempts by Chicagoans to put him on a fledgling Republican committee and instead ran for the state legislature in 1854 as a Whig. More important, New York senator Seward, the leader of Senate opposition to the Nebraska bill, clung to the Whig Party while his alter ego, state Whig boss Thurlow Weed, editorialized in his *Albany Evening Journal* that only the Whig Party had ever done anything effective to stop slavery's expansion and that therefore "it is best, now and ever, 'for the Whig party to stand by its colors.'"[12] Until the leaders and followers of that party consigned it to the scrapheap, the Republican Party had no prayer of surviving its birth pangs, let alone growing to maturity.

Far more worrisome to early Republican organizers than northern Whig holdouts during 1854 and 1855 was the astonishing spread of the rival anti-Catholic, anti-immigrant, and anti-politician Know Nothing movement. Organized initially as a secret nativist fraternity, its members answered queries about it by saying, "I know nothing about it." Hence the popular sobriquet. By mid-1855 Know Nothings publicly called themselves the American Party. Most northern Know Nothings undoubtedly shared other Northerners' outrage at the Nebraska Act and at the apparent aggressions by an autocratic Slave Power that legislation seemed to prove. Nonetheless, to incipient Republicans' dismay, Know Nothings clearly placed priority on smashing the political influence of foreigners and Catholics as well as any politicos who sought those groups' support. Know Nothings gravely complicated the task of putting together an antislavery, anti-southern Republican coalition precisely because they seemed capable of defeating Democrats and capturing control of local, state, and congressional offices on a nativist, not an anti-slavery-extension, platform. They scored stunning successes in New England and the Middle Atlantic states in 1854 and 1855, often stymieing attempts even to launch Republican parties there, and they were crucial components of the opposition parties in Ohio, Indiana, and Michigan as well.

However irrepressible the rise of an anti-southern Republican Party appeared to some observers by 1860—and to some contemporary historians today, Republican leaders in 1854 and 1855 knew all too well that many northern voters worried more about Catholics, immigrants, and booze than they did about slavery extension. They also knew that those priorities inhibited the growth of the Republican Party. "This election has demonstrated that, by a majority, Roman Catholicism is feared more than American slavery," wrote a New Yorker in 1854. The following year a frustrated Massachusetts Republican complained that "the election is most disastrous. . . . The people will not confront the issues at present. They want a Paddy hunt & on a Paddy hunt they will go."[13]

By the time the Thirty-Fourth Congress opened in December 1855, however, some of the Northerners elected as Whigs or Know Nothings in 1854 and 1855 stood ready to embrace the new Republican organization. One reason was that the extent of Know Nothing victories in the North's 1854 elections destroyed northern Whigs' hopes that their party could survive intact. Congressmen who, just like Lincoln and Seward, had refused to join the Republicans in 1854 were now ready to do so. Probably more important, however, was how the Kansas-Nebraska Act actually played out in Kansas. Stephen Douglas and other northern Democrats had argued that under Douglas's popular sovereignty formula settlers from northern states were bound to control the first territorial legislature and that it would bar the entry of slaveholders into the territory. When the first Kansas election for a territorial legislature occurred on March 30, 1855, however, proslavery Missourians, soon notorious as Border Ruffians and led by former senator David R. Atchison, poured across the border, stuffed ballot boxes with fraudulent votes, and elected a proslavery majority to the legislature. Then, when the legislature met in the summer of 1855, that majority passed a series of draconian proslavery laws that forced legislators elected by Northerners who opposed slavery in Kansas to resign and, ultimately, set up their own so-called Free State territorial government. In short, other incidents that could be interpreted as Slave Power aggressions against Northerners' rights turned more men to the Republican Party, which portrayed itself as the paladin of the North against the South.

Of vast political importance to Republicans, who began as an anti-Democrat opposition party, Democratic president Franklin Pierce, who had helped write the Kansas-Nebraska Act and pronounced it an administration measure, defended the legitimacy of the proslavery territorial government in Kansas and labeled the Free State government an outlaw regime, which he was prepared to put down with federal troops. Fear and anger at purported Slave Power aggressions fueled the initial growth of the Republican Party, but because Republicans ran candidates almost exclusively in the North, and not directly against southern Democrats, they had to portray northern Democrats as lackeys of the Slave Power. Pierce's stance made that task much easier.

Nonetheless, it was a series of events in 1856 that determined that the new Republican Party, not the old Whigs or the rival Know Nothing Party, would be Democrats' primary foe for the rest of the decade—and, as it has turned out, up to the present day. When the Thirty-Fourth Congress opened in December 1855, it was clear Democrats were a minority in the House, but it was not clear who held the majority. Anti-Nebraska Northerners, Know Nothings, and even former Whigs could reasonably claim that position, although the latter two groups would require cooperation between Northerners and Southerners to achieve it. In the end, after a titanic two-month struggle, most non-Democrat Northerners rallied behind Massachusetts' Nathaniel P. Banks, a former Democrat elected in 1854 as a Know Nothing, to make him the Republican Speaker of the House. "The importance of this victory cannot well be overestimated," rejoiced Maine's Republican congressman Israel Washburn, for it demonstrated, in the words of a different Maine Republican, that "there is a North."[14] Banks's triumph, in sum, convinced Northerners that they could control the federal government without any help from Southerners if they held together as Republicans.

A successful first national meeting of Republicans in Pittsburgh on February 22, 1856, that stressed opposition to slavery extension and to the Pierce administration as the party's twin principles furthered the new party's momentum. Moreover, simultaneous with that Republican meeting in Pittsburgh, a presidential nominating convention of Know Nothings, who now called themselves the American Party, split along sectional lines in

Philadelphia. Most northern Know Nothings refused to accept the nomination of former president Millard Fillmore, whom Southerners and a few Northerners supported. Angry northern American Party members bolted the convention, but they were not yet ready to join the incipient Republican organization. Instead they called for a North American Party convention to nominate its own presidential candidate in New York City on June 12, five days before Republicans would hold their own national nominating convention in Philadelphia. These American Party men hoped they could pressure the Republicans into accepting their nominee. In the end, however, most of the former supported the Republicans' presidential candidate, John C. Frémont.

Some trickery at the New York convention and horse-trading between Know Nothings and Republicans on subpresidential candidate slates and platforms facilitated the merger. Nonetheless, Northerners' outrage at a series of explosive events with sectional ramifications in May 1856 primarily caused it. On May 21 a federal posse that included many Missouri Border Ruffians invaded the "Free State" town of Lawrence, Kansas. They destroyed two free-soil newspapers, burned a few buildings, and fired on one particularly stout edifice with cannons in an attempt to raze it. Although no one was killed, this armed assault by proslavery Southerners on Northerners helped cement the image of Northerners as victims of southern aggressions. Thus "Bleeding Kansas" became one of the pillars of the Republican campaign in 1856.

The national platform the Republicans adopted in Philadelphia stressed the assaults on Northerners' rights in Kansas. It invited the support of everyone, regardless of previous partisan affiliation, who opposed slavery extension and the Democrat Pierce's presidential administration, and it insisted on "both the right and the imperative duty of Congress to prohibit in the Territories those twin relics of barbarism—Polygamy and Slavery." But its longest sections focused on the fraudulent and violent deprivation of "the dearest Constitutional rights of the people of Kansas." After listing a litany of such assaults, it added "that all these things have been done with the knowledge, sanction, and procurement of the present National Administration." "For this high crime against the Constitution, the Union, and humanity," the platform continued, "we arraign the Administration, the President, his advisers, agents, supporters, apologists, and accessories . . . before the country and before the world."[15] That this direct attack on Franklin Pierce was written after he had failed to win renomination and was not the Democratic presidential candidate in 1856 is noteworthy. In

1860 Republicans would again attempt to make the election a referendum on the incumbent Democratic president's record even though he too was not a candidate that year.

Surprisingly, the 1856 Republican national platform made no mention of two events in Washington in May of that year that arguably did more than anything else to expand the Republican electorate. On the morning of May 8, Philemon T. Herbert, a Democratic representative from California and the son of a slaveholding family in Alabama, got into a brawl with an Irish waiter named Thomas Keating at Willard's Hotel and shot and killed him. Far more notorious and politically consequential than this assault, precisely two weeks later South Carolina representative Preston S. Brooks caned Massachusetts Republican senator Charles Sumner into bloody unconsciousness on the Senate floor. Both events showed southern slaveholders brutally treating northern freemen like slaves, and both became fodder for the Republican presidential campaign against Democratic candidate James Buchanan. "Mr. Buchanan is the candidate not only of Pierce and Douglas, but of Herbert who shot the Irishman [and] of Brooks, who assaulted Sumner," Republican John Jay told a New York Republican rally. "The Murder of Keating Approved by the Democratic Party in Congress and out" was part of the title of a Republican campaign pamphlet distributed in Michigan. By allowing Herbert to resume his House seat, it huffed, "the Slave Power has not only justified the infamous act, but has invited its repetition upon all Northern men."[16]

It was the combination of "Bleeding Kansas" and "Bleeding Sumner"—that is, events, not Republicans' free-soil platform—that did the most to help Republicans build a broad electoral base in the North in 1856. "The feeling all over our State, in relation to Kansas affairs and the assault on Sumner, is more intense and determined than I thought it would be," testified a New York Republican at the end of May. By June, Republicans exulted that "the outrage upon Sumner & the occurrences in Kansas have helped us vastly." At the same time, southern Know Nothings recognized that Northerners' anger doomed all chances of maintaining the national American Party at full strength. Thus a Virginian despaired to a northern Fillmore loyalist, "Recent events in Kansas and Washington seem to be driving the masses of your people into the arms of the Republican party." Nor would many northern Whigs, once friendly to Fillmore, support him after the events of May. As one Vermonter lamented in July, "The outrage upon Mr. Sumner and upon the people of Kansas has strengthened [Republicans] as a party and placed it out of our power to carry this State unless

Congress settles the Kansas question soon." Another one-time Whig from Vermont told the hapless Fillmore much the same in October. That state's Whigs had gone as a "body" to the Republicans because of the "deep & extensive revulsion of feeling at the present state of things."[17]

Various Republicans' private correspondence clarifies the substance of that revulsion better than Republicans' public statements. Their letters indicate that Republicans were far more concerned about their own potential political enslavement by southern tyrants than they were about the bondage of African Americans or even slavery's potential spread. What seemed at stake to these writers were the precious legacies of the American Revolution—republican self-government and white men's political liberty. "Did you ever see such infernal, outrageous, liberty-crushing, persecuting, tyrannical, I can't find any word to express it but damnable, proceedings as those engineered by Pierce & Douglas in Kansas?" fumed Indiana's Schuyler Colfax on May 21, 1856, the day before Sumner was caned. "It makes my blood boil." In July a Massachusetts Yankee wrote about the Kansas and Washington attacks: "The Missouri savages seem determined to prevent Northern settlement in the Territory except as servants or slaves of the South. . . . What has taken place in Kansas and at Washington within the last few months is a disgrace to the country and a reproach to our republican form of government." A month later, an Ohioan echoed, "It is high time that the people of the whole country should know and understand, that the degraded negro is not the only class of *slaves* among us, but that the arrogance of the *slave power* tramples ruthlessly upon *all* who pretend to fix the limits of its dominion." A different Republican expressed a similar complaint a year later. "The Slave Power will not submit. The tyrants of the lash will not withhold until they have put padlocks on the lives of freemen. The Union which our fathers formed seventy years ago is not the Union today. . . . The sons of the Revolutionary fathers are becoming *slaves* or *masters*."[18]

In late August 1856, a surviving veteran of the Revolutionary War made a similar connection between that war and Republicans' struggle against the Slave Power. The comment appears in a remarkable letter written for him to Vermont congressman Justin Morrill, who had been elected as an anti-Nebraska Whig in September 1854 but was by the summer of 1856 firmly in the Republican camp. Morrill had sought a relief bill for the veteran, who then asked an acquaintance to write Morrill to express his thanks. "The old man . . . has always been a democrat but he says he shall vote for Frémont if God spares his life and that if a few years younger he would go to fight the Border Ruffians in Kansas," wrote his scribe. "He says he fought for liberty eighty years ago and that Republicans are struggling for the same principles which he then maintained through a long and bloody war. He is now in the second century of his life, but may he never live to see the principles of the Revolution die before him."[19] Quite clearly, the emancipation of African American slaves is not what this aged New England veteran thought he had been fighting for in the 1770s.

Fueled by northern indignation at what seemed like repeated Slave Power aggressions and reinforced by most northern Know Nothings after May's events, Republicans scored what their ablest historian aptly calls a "victorious defeat" in the three-candidate presidential election of 1856.[20] Democrat James Buchanan won the electoral vote handily, with a majority of 174 out of a total of 297. He also led in the national popular vote, with a total of 1,832,955, or a plurality of 45.3 percent. Frémont ran second, with 115 electoral votes and 1,340,537 popular votes, 33.1 percent of the national total. Fillmore, the American Party candidate, carried only Maryland for 8 electoral votes; his popular vote of 871,731 constituted 21.6 percent of the whole. Yet it was the skewed sectional distribution of the votes that was pregnant with implications for the future. Frémont carried eleven of the sixteen free states with 45.2 percent of their popular vote whereas Buchanan won only 41.4 percent of the North's popular vote and carried only five northern states—California, Illinois, Indiana, New Jersey, and, most important, Pennsylvania, which together had 62 electoral votes, slightly more than a third of Buchanan's total. Far, far more important, Republicans' popular vote in the North more than tripled Fillmore's, signaling that Republicans, at least temporarily, had bested Know Nothings in the contest to replace Whigs as Democrats' major opponent. As Table 1 in Appendix A shows, Fillmore's northern support was concentrated in only a few states. Had that vote been thrown to Frémont, he would have carried California, New Jersey, and Illinois and come within a whisker of carrying Indiana and Pennsylvania as well.

Combining Frémont's and Fillmore's votes in northern states to calculate the size of the anti-Democratic vote in the region is the way historians most often look at the results. By that measure almost three-fifths of the section's voters opposed Buchanan. Thus, historians correctly point out, Republicans would have to do better in the Lower North to aggregate that anti-Democratic vote in order to win the election of 1860. With regard to the 1860 contest, however, it is equally revealing to combine the Fillmore and Buchanan votes as an index of hostility to Republicans in the free states. By this measure, a majority of northern voters opposed Republicans in eight states, not just five, for Republicans were also a minority in Iowa, New York, and Ohio, all states that they won with a plurality of the popular vote. In other words, of the five most populous states in the North, Republicans had an absolute majority only in Massachusetts (see Table 1 in Appendix A). Because both the Fillmore and Buchanan campaigns in 1856 had stressed that their candidates were the safest bets to preserve the Union and that a Republican victory made southern secession inevitable, the combined Fillmore and Buchanan vote was interpreted as representing Northerners, to say nothing of Southerners, who regarded the Republican Party as far too dangerously sectional to merit support. All politically aware men in both sections understood that fact. As a result, one of the key themes of the 1860 election would be that all campaigns in that four-candidate race tried to assume the mantle of being the "national" party for themselves while pillorying their various opponents as being too "sectional."

Outside of New England, where states held gubernatorial elections annually, the elections of 1857 provided little evidence of further Republican penetration across the North, although they did signal a substantial drop in the Know Nothing vote in most states. Voter turnout fell everywhere from its 1856 levels, so what those elections portended for the next presidential contest was unclear. Nonetheless, Republicans failed to carry a single free state in 1857 that they had lost in 1856, and Democrats recaptured two of Connecticut's four House seats. In those states holding gubernatorial elections, the Republican proportion of the total vote ebbed everywhere except Iowa, where it edged above the 50 percent level; and Pennsylvania, where David Wilmot, running as a Union candidate, not a Republican, secured two-fifths of the vote, compared with Frémont's meager 32 percent. Still, 40 percent was hardly a majority; nor were Wilmot's 146,000 votes any match for the 231,000 Buchanan had rolled up in 1856. Additional evidence that the supposedly inexorable spread of the Republican Party had in fact stalled in 1857 came from Ohio. There the Republican Salmon P. Chase, with the help of many Know Nothings, had won the governorship in 1855 by almost 16,000 votes. Running for reelection in 1857, he eked out victory with only a 1,400-vote margin over his Democratic opponent, a plurality that was less than a tenth of that won by Frémont in Ohio in 1856 and one still shy of a popular-vote majority.

Most alarming to Republicans, they lost New York's few statewide races to resurgent Democrats. As a panicked Republican editor in Buffalo saw it, "This result shows that there is no Republican party, and that what appeared to be such one year ago was a sort of mirage which was thrown upon the public view by a peculiar condition of the atmosphere and which disappeared when a change of wind came."[21] Put differently, the outrage at Slave Power aggressions that had fueled Republican gains in 1856 had apparently dissipated.

The meaning of the 1857 results was clear. Despite the Supreme Court's notorious *Dred Scott* decision that year, to extend their base in the North Republicans needed further evidence of Democrat-aided Slave Power aggressions against Northerners' rights. An attempt to force Kansas's admission into the Union as a slave state in 1858, and especially James Buchanan's support for that effort, provided that evidence while at the same time so splitting his Democratic Party that it lacked the will, as well as the votes, to resist Republican gains. Indeed, anti-administration Democrats often assisted those gains in 1858's important congressional elections.

Buchanan's top priority upon taking office as president in March 1857 was to reverse the growth of the Republican Party, which, he correctly perceived, jeopardized the Union. That goal is why he persuaded Robert Grier, a Pennsylvanian associate justice on the Supreme Court, to join five southern justices in support of the *Dred Scott* decision, which by clear implication ruled Republicans' most concrete policy proposal—congressional prohibition of slavery from all federal territories—unconstitutional. But Buchanan also recognized that so long as Kansas remained in a disputed territorial phase, Republicans could exploit the turmoil there for partisan gain. Thus, he tried to facilitate statehood for Kansas as soon as possible. To achieve that goal he recruited a Democratic heavyweight to the thankless position of territorial governor.

Born and raised in Pennsylvania, Robert J. Walker had moved as a young man to Mississippi, where in the late 1830s the legislature chose him as one of the state's U.S. senators. As senator, Walker played the lead role in making annexation of the proslavery Republic of Texas a central Democratic issue in the presidential election of 1844. As reward for the help that program gave his candidacy in the South, newly elected president James K. Polk made Walker his treasury secretary in a cabinet where James Buchanan was secretary of state. When Polk's term ended in 1849, Walker did not return to Mississippi. Instead he moved to New York to speculate in stocks, and during the Civil War he helped the Union cause by trying to sell its bonds in England. Walker, in sum, was no proslavery zealot despite his service as a Mississippi senator.

When accepting Buchanan's request, Walker told the president that he could probably bring Kansas in as a Democratic free state, but never as a slave state. The great majority of settlers in Kansas opposed slavery. More important, he insisted that Buchanan guarantee him in writing that the president would back up his determination that any constitution drafted for statehood by Kansans be submitted in its entirety to a vote by all the legitimate adult male residents of Kansas. Buchanan gave him such a written pledge, and that pledge would be publicized widely by the anti-Buchanan press during the 1860 election.

When the diminutive Walker reached Kansas in the late spring of 1857, the proslavery territorial legislature had already called for a June election of delegates to a September convention in the town of Lecompton, Kansas. That body was to write a constitution with which Kansas could apply to Congress for statehood. Walker tried frantically to persuade the heavy free-state majority of settlers to participate in the June election, but they refused because the hated proslavery legislature had called it. As a result, only 2,000 out of approximately 28,000 potential voters came out in June, and they chose an overwhelmingly proslavery constitutional convention. Walker, however, did persuade the free-state men to participate in an October election to choose a new territorial legislature, and along with Walker's rejection of fraudulent ballots cast by Missourians, Northerners gained control of the official territorial legislature for the first time.

Angered by Walker's actions in October, delegates to the Lecompton constitutional convention refused to submit the entire constitution they composed to a public referendum. That document specified that the 200 or so slaves already in Kansas and their descendants would remain slaves in perpetuity, and it prohibited any revision of that constitution before 1864. The convention gave voters a choice only on the question of whether additional slaves would be permitted into or prohibited from Kansas once it became a state. They were denied a direct vote on accepting or rejecting the entire constitution, that is, the procedure upon which Walker insisted and that Buchanan had endorsed in his letter to Walker.

Walker denounced this violation of popular sovereignty, but, after hesitating for several months, Buchanan refused to back him up. Free-state settlers thus boycotted the December 21 referendum on the Lecompton constitution, and it passed with the clause allowing additional slaves by a vote of 6,153 to 569. Free-state men, however, did vote in another referendum on the constitution scheduled by the new antislavery majority of the territorial legislature on January 4, 1858. With loyalists of the former territorial legislature boycotting the election this time, over 10,000 votes were cast against the Lecompton constitution in its entirety. A clear majority of

Kansas' voters, in sum, opposed its admission as a new slave state. Just as clearly, James Buchanan was aware of that fact.

Even before the December 21 referendum in Kansas, Stephen Douglas told Buchanan in the White House that he would oppose the Kansas constitution on the Senate floor because the Lecompton convention did not represent the wishes of the majority of Kansans either in its composition or in the rules it set for the constitution's ratification. Determined to achieve statehood for Kansas no matter what, Buchanan took umbrage at Douglas's challenge. Thus began a titanic battle between the two men that split the Democratic Party until the ballots were cast in the 1860 presidential election. Its ramifications for the Democratic Party will be discussed in the following chapter.

Starting in January 1858 Buchanan sent three messages to Congress urging it to admit Kansas as a slave state under the terms of the Lecompton constitution. If free-state men had failed to vote in the original election of delegates to Lecompton or in the December 21 referendum, he argued, that was their own fault and they would have to live with the results of their abstention. In a February message, before a single vote on Kansas statehood had been taken in Congress, Buchanan proclaimed that "Kansas is at this moment as much a slave state as Georgia or South Carolina."[22] Buchanan, in sum, appeared committed to helping Southerners make Kansas another slave state.

Despite vigorous attacks by Douglas against this proposal, it easily passed the Senate, where Democrats loyal to Buchanan held an unassailable majority. The House with its heavy majority of Northerners was another matter, for most northern Democratic members, who had doubled their numbers in the congressional elections of 1856–1857, had to face the electorate in the fall of 1858. Buchanan used every weapon at his disposal to twist the arms of reluctant northern Democrats, as later congressional investigations would reveal—threats or promises about federal jobs and federal contracts in members' districts, the lure of wine and women, and ultimately outright cash bribes. Nonetheless, prodded by the furious Douglas, enough rebellious northern anti-Lecompton Democrats joined Republicans to defeat the statehood measure and substitute one calling for yet another referendum on the Lecompton constitution in Kansas. A conference committee dominated by Democrats worked out a compromise to save face for Buchanan. It called for another vote on Lecompton in August, packaged with a warning that should Kansans reject that constitution it could not be admitted as a state until it had 93,000 verifiable residents, the population of the then least-populated congressional district. On August 2, 1858, the voters of Kansas rejected entry as a slave state by a vote of 11,300 to 1,800. Thus, over two full years before the 1860 presidential election, the last credible possibility that another slave state would be admitted from land then belonging to the United States was dead.

Within a few months Republicans would realize the political problems inherent in that fact. Initially, however, the fight over the Lecompton constitution seemed enormously beneficial to them. Not only had another Democratic president thrown his weight behind the Slave Power's mistreatment of northern settlers in Kansas, but northern Democratic divisions clearly helped Republicans in the North's congressional elections of 1858 and 1859. It was in those elections, not those of 1857, that Republicans' sway, at first blush at least, appeared to expand further across the North.

In twenty-two congressional districts in five northern states in 1858 anti-Lecompton or anti-Buchanan Democrats ran candidates against party regulars, and eight of those dissidents, usually with overt Republican backing, won House seats. Elsewhere anti-Lecompton men sat out the election or supported Republicans, allowing Republicans to carry the districts. When one includes the 1859 contests in calculations, administration loyalists among northern Democrats shrank from 53 to 26 while the number of Republican seats in the House swelled to 112—a plurality but, significantly, not a majority, of the chamber's 231 seats.

In those 1858 congressional elections Republicans won a majority of the popular vote for the first time in the crucial Lower North states of Indiana, Ohio, and Pennsylvania while reducing Democrats' margin to fewer than 700 votes in Illinois.[23] Understandably, Republicans rejoiced in and Democrats bemoaned these results. For several reasons, however, they hardly guaranteed that Republicans could sweep the North in 1860. Anti-Lecompton Democrats clearly voted to punish the Buchanan administration; they might easily support a Democratic candidate more to their liking in 1860, especially if that candidate were Stephen A. Douglas, the leader of the revolt against Buchanan. The customary lower turnout in off-year elections should have cautioned people not to make confident predictions based on these off-year results. As Table 2 in Appendix A demonstrates, in both Indiana and Pennsylvania the anti-Democratic vote lagged behind the totals Buchanan had achieved in 1856. In both, indeed, Democrats had suffered significant drop-off since 1856, and Democratic stay-at-homes might well return to the Democratic column in a presidential year. Finally, it is vastly important that the party that contested Pennsylvania's elections against

Buchanan's supporters was *not* the Republican Party. To effect a coalition between Americans who had supported Fillmore and Frémont's 1856 supporters, these men called themselves "the People's Party" precisely because they considered the very name "Republican" too radical to carry Pennsylvania. Republicans' antislavery, anti-Southern rhetoric simply seemed too dangerous to too many Pennsylvanians for Democrats' foes in the Keystone State to embrace the Republican name. Indeed, the People's Party state platform in 1858 primarily stressed not the Lecompton fiasco but instead the need for a higher tariff to protect American workers from foreign competition, a position that of course was viewed quite favorably by one-time Fillmore voters.

The People's Party coalition was more than an effort to improve on the 40 percent of the vote David Wilmot had won as a Union Party gubernatorial candidate in 1857. It was also an attempt to ward off an appeal from a new conservative party to Fillmore's 1856 supporters and perhaps others who had supported Frémont in 1856 only because of outrage at Bleeding Kansas and Bleeding Sumner, outrage that had demonstrably waned by 1857, to say nothing of 1858. This threat grew out of the Buchanan administration's mishandling of the Lecompton constitution and a depression ignited by the economic Panic of 1857. It constituted the biggest challenge the new Republican Party faced between 1856 and 1860. Perhaps more than anything else, it gave the lie to the supposed inevitability of a Republican storm rising. It exposed instead a popular perception of plasticity or malleability in the tumultuous political circumstances that had replaced the predictability of the competition between Whigs and Democrats.

In early 1858 Republicans and northern anti-Lecompton Democrats were not the only ones outraged by Buchanan's efforts to bring Kansas into the Union as a slave state. So too were the remaining southern Whigs still serving in the Senate, most of whom had supported Fillmore in 1856. Of these, the most important were John Bell of Tennessee and, especially, John J. Crittenden of Kentucky. They saw in Buchanan's actions an opportunity to build a new bisectional party that could displace the fledgling Republicans as Democrats' primary political opponent. Crittenden gave two major Senate speeches in the spring of 1858 to define the basis for the new party he and Bell envisioned. The first flayed Buchanan's Kansas policy, demanded another referendum on the Lecompton constitution in which all eligible Kansans participated, and insisted on majority rule in all territories, even if it produced free soil. The second speech denounced the fiscal extravagance of Buchanan's administration, which had resorted to deficit financing in response to the Panic of 1857, and demanded instead an increase in tariff rates to generate more federal revenue and protect American workers from hard times, an increase Democrats had theretofore steadfastly opposed. Together with nativism and assaults on official corruption, these themes would provide the platform for a new party that all opponents of Buchanan, and not just Yankees, might support.

Congratulations inundated Crittenden from around the country along with predictions that he would win the presidency in 1860. Fillmore's northern supporters from 1856 rejoiced that Crittenden's anti-Lecompton stance had given them new life, for it eradicated the stigma of cooperating with Southerners under which they had labored in 1856. "You can have no conception of the importance of your position," hymned Washington Hunt from New York. "It gives assurance to the whole country that patriotism and love of justice do not belong to North or South, but both sections have men true to the Union, and to the principles of constitutional liberty." From Buffalo a correspondent predicted that American Party members and Republicans would unite in a "new party" behind Crittenden and elect him president. A resident of Erie, Pennsylvania, echoed: "I look to a reorganization of parties within the next year on a basis similar to the principle embodied in your great speech."[24]

A Kentuckian concurred that "this Lecompton Business" presented "a field for a new organization of parties, or rather the organization of a new party with a new name." It would have "the principles of truth and justice of the old Whigs, the national principles of the Americans, without their fanaticism and proscription, and some of the best features of the National democracy." In it, "all the Americans, all the national [anti-Lecompton] Democrats North, all the old line Whigs, and the soundest portion of the Republicans could unite."[25]

That last possibility gave Republican politicians the willies. With the final defeat of the Lecompton constitution on August 2, 1858, and with it the last realistic possibility of slavery expansion into existing territories, the justification for an exclusively northern party like the Republicans had seemingly disappeared. A new conservative party based on bisectional opposition to Buchanan's administration, rather than northern resentment of Slave Power aggressions, could prevent Republicans from absorbing the northern Fillmore voters in the Lower North they needed to win in 1860. But it might also draw off 1856 Frémont voters who now no longer saw the need for the sectional paladin Republicans had portrayed themselves as being.

In 1858 and 1859, in fact, Republican leaders like national committee chairman Edwin D. Morgan of New York and Ohio governor Salmon Chase received many letters worrying that free-soil sentiment was receding, that voters were becoming less fearful of the South, and that a new polyglot opposition party like the one envisioned by Crittenden's correspondents might consign the Republican Party to an early grave. "The object is to break down or override the Republican party & elevate John Bell or some other Old Line Tariff Whig to the Presidency or in other words the object is to reestablish the old Whig party under a new name & crush out all 'Slavery agitation,'" an anxious Philadelphian informed Morgan. Similarly, some Ohioans complained to Chase that the political comeback of the exceptionally conservative former Whig Thomas Corwin as a Republican congressional candidate in 1858 was meant "to bring down our doctrines and position to the Fillmore level in order to make Corwin our leader and Senator and Crittenden our President in 1860."[26]

Republicans reacted to this perceived threat in different ways. Some, like those in Pennsylvania, redoubled efforts to merge with Know Nothings to prevent their decamping to the envisioned new party. Much to the dismay of Seward, who had despised anti-Catholic bigots throughout his life, for example, New York's Republicans included two planks in their 1858 state platform that were obvious concessions to Know Nothing demands that Irish Catholic immigrants be stopped from voting. New Jersey's anti-Democrats, like those in Pennsylvania, stressed the tariff issue rather than antislavery to court Know Nothings. To woo Know Nothings in Massachusetts, where they had once been dominant, Republican state legislators passed a state constitutional amendment that barred immigrants from voting until two years after they were naturalized.

Other Republicans took a different tack to stifle a potential new bisectional anti-Democratic party that might displace them. In 1854 Michigan's Republicans had vowed to battle against Slave Power aggressions "until the contest be terminated." Thus, some Republicans in 1858 sought to convince voters that the battle against the Slave Power had not yet ended despite the August 2 referendum in Kansas and that therefore the Republican Party remained indispensable to the North. This effort explains the two most famous Republican speeches delivered in 1858, speeches that infuriated Southerners worried about a gathering Republican storm because both, willfully or not, were misinterpreted as saying that Republicans sought control of the federal government in order to achieve the abolition of slavery in the South. In 1860 both were frequently cited by southern Democratic newspapers as the reason why a Republican victory in the presidential election would be intolerable. Indeed, southern Democratic newspapers treated the speeches as interchangeable, even though they were given by men who competed against each other for Republicans' presidential nomination and were not in fact interchangeable.

On June 16, 1858, Abraham Lincoln gave his now-well-known "House Divided" speech to a Republican convention meeting in the statehouse in Springfield, Illinois. The background for this speech is crucial to understand. An important Illinois Whig leader for twenty years who had served but a single term in Congress in the late 1840s, Lincoln had dearly hoped to capture a U.S. Senate seat that came open in 1855. Anti-Nebraska men, most of whom like Lincoln were Whigs, won control of the state legislature in the elections of 1854. But a minority of the anti-Nebraska men were Democrats who refused to support Lincoln precisely because he was a Whig. Thus, that Senate seat went to the anti-Nebraska Democrat Lyman Trumbull; in this case, the Democratic tail absolutely wagged the Whig dog. Lincoln next set his ambitious sights on Stephen Douglas's Senate seat that would be filled by the state legislature elected in 1858. In a move that was highly unusual for the day, the Republicans Lincoln addressed in June had publicly committed the party to support him when the next legislature decided the fate of Douglas's Senate seat.

By June it was apparent antislavery forces would win the next referendum on the Lecompton constitution in Kansas and that Republicans needed new ammunition. By then it was also apparent that Douglas's opposition to the Lecompton constitution had neutralized much of the antagonism his authorship of the Nebraska Act had earned. Indeed, some eastern Republicans, led by Horace Greeley—editor of the *New York Tribune*, the most influential Republican newspaper in the country—urged Illinois Republicans to reelect Douglas by acclamation rather than run a Republican for the seat. Anger at that outside meddling in part explained why some Republicans named Lincoln as their Senate candidate five months before the legislative elections. Still, because those elections would be a referendum on the Senate seat, it was incumbent upon Lincoln to articulate why he would be a better choice for it than Douglas. That was the purpose of the "House Divided" speech.

"A house divided against itself cannot stand," Lincoln intoned near the start of his remarks. "This government cannot endure, permanently half *slave* and half *free*." He did not expect the Union to dissolve, "but I *do* expect it will cease to be divided." Slavery would legally exist everywhere or nowhere in the United States. Either its opponents would stop its spread and "place it where the public mind shall rest in the belief that it is in the course of ultimate extinction, or its *advocates* shall push it forward, till it shall become alike lawful in *all* the States, *old* as well as *new—North* as well as *South*."[27]

The "ultimate extinction" phrase is what caught the attention of Southerners, and in 1860, after Lincoln won the Republican nomination, Southerners repeatedly pointed to this speech as evidence that Lincoln, if elected, would use federal power to hasten the eradication of Negro slavery. But the gist of Lincoln's speech was not about the extinction of slavery, however "ultimate." It was the danger that slavery would be legalized in all northern states, from Maine through the Midwest to California. And it was that danger—the extension of slavery not just to western territories but to existing northern states—that necessitated the continued efforts of an exclusively northern Republican Party.

No historian of the antebellum South has unearthed any evidence that Southerners had any intention of trying to foist slavery on northern states, but Lincoln argued that the logic of recent events pointed to that conclusion. Together the Kansas-Nebraska Act and Roger B. Taney's *Dred Scott* decision proved that there was a conspiracy involving Douglas, Franklin Pierce, Taney, and James Buchanan to spread slavery to Kansas. All it would take to legalize slavery in northern states was another Supreme Court decision by Taney holding it just as unconstitutional for a state to prohibit slavery within its borders as it was unconstitutional for Congress to prohibit it from federal territories. Douglas's recent break with the Buchanan administration and battle against admitting Kansas as a slave state meant little, Lincoln averred. Douglas had repeatedly insisted that he did not care whether or not slavery expanded, only that a majority of the people in a territory make the decision. That "care not" posture, Lincoln argued, was meant to soften Northerners' opposition to the spread of slavery so that they would meekly acquiesce in Taney's next decision legalizing slavery in Illinois and other northern states. That was why Douglas did not merit reelection to the Senate. Lincoln's pitch almost worked. The popular vote that fall in Illinois was exceptionally close, but Democrats held onto enough legislative seats in a joint session to frustrate Lincoln once again and return Douglas to the Senate.

The northern public focused on the Illinois Senate race, and thus on the opening section of Lincoln's opening speech, because it was so unusual to have rival parties' candidates for a U.S. Senate seat debating each other prior to the election of the legislature that would pick the winner. In 1858, however, far more attention was paid to a speech by the Republican Party's foremost national spokesman, New York's William H. Seward. As noted earlier, in 1858 Seward was deeply incensed by the willingness of other New York Republican leaders to make concessions to Know Nothings, whom Seward loathed, in the party's 1858 state platform. His anger in large part explains the radical tone of the speech he gave at Rochester, New York, on October 16, 1858, an oration thereafter notorious as the "Irrepressible Conflict" speech. As Seward informed a friend after he spoke, it "was needful to stay and brace up the Republican party" in the face of the conservative renaissance that year and to "justify its purpose to lead, not to follow, to exact concessions not to make them under any circumstances."[28] In short, it was necessary to stress again that the Slave Power and the Democratic Party it controlled, not Irish Catholics, constituted Republicans' target.

Free labor and slave labor were vastly different systems, Seward maintained. The impending collision between them in the West was "an irrepressible conflict between opposing and enduring forces, and it means that the United States must and will, sooner or later, become either entirely a slaveholding nation, or entirely a free-labor nation." Here Seward sounded like Lincoln, and in 1860 southern newspapers labeled Lincoln an exponent of the "Irrepressible Conflict" dogma. But Seward did not harp on the prospect that the country would become "entirely a slaveholding nation." Instead, his speech, if people read published versions of it carefully, exuded confidence that free labor was vastly superior to slave labor. Southerners would eventually recognize this superiority and abolish slavery through amendments to their state constitutions. Seward explicitly insisted that he contemplated no federal action dissolving slavery whatsoever. Southerners, indeed, would have abolished slavery by state action decades earlier, he maintained, except for one thing—Democrats' long-time control of the federal government. Democrats used that control to perpetuate and expand slavery. Only that Democratic support explained why slavery had not disappeared years ago.

A critique of the Democratic Party formed the core of this misunderstood speech. "The Democratic party must be permanently dislodged from the Government" for "the Democratic party is inextricably committed to the designs of the slaveholders." Seward repeated this charge at least five times in this relatively short speech. Democrats bore responsibility for slavery's spread with the annexation of Texas, the Mexican War and the abrogation of Mexico's antislavery laws in the Mexican Cession, the deplorable Kansas-Nebraska Act, and the despicable attempt to force Kansas into the Union as a slave state. And Democrats were not yet finished, for now Seward insisted there was a movement by southern Democrats in Congress to reopen the African slave trade, which had been banned since 1808. That new threat, rather than Lincoln's imagined legalization of slavery within northern states, was the bugaboo that Seward identified as requiring the perpetuation of the Republican Party as an exclusively northern, overtly anti–Slave Power party. It is "high time," Seward concluded, "for the friends of Freedom . . . to dismiss the Democratic party from the administration of the Government." No other party—that is, enthusiasts for Crittenden's bisectional anti-Buchanan party—could be trusted. "Everyone knows that it is the Republican party or none, that shall displace the Democratic party. . . . I know that the Democratic party must go down and that the Republican party must rise into its place."[29]

Despite Republicans' impressive performance in the 1858 elections, talk of folding the party into a bisectional anti-Buchanan party and thus surrendering Republicans' anti-southern impetus did not abate, especially as it appeared that Opposition Party elements loyal to Bell and Crittenden would do well in the Upper South's congressional elections of 1859. Thus Republican leaders again found it necessary to defend the mission of the Republican Party. In the spring of 1859 Edwin D. Morgan, chairman of the Republican national committee, distributed a circular specifically to rejustify the Republican Party's existence and to scotch any appeal a bisectional anti-Buchanan party might have for its northern supporters. "The republican party had its origin in the obvious necessity for resistance to the aggressions of the slave power," it began. Although some of the problems forcing the party's organization in 1856 had been resolved by early 1859, it admitted, "The attitude of the slave power is persistently insolent and aggressive. . . . It is not content with its well-known influence, always pernicious over the legislature at the national capital, but it demands fresh concessions from a free people." Here the circular cited some Southerners' demands that the African slave trade be reopened. It also pointed to the demands of some southern Democrats in early 1859 to have Congress impose upon all federal territories a federal slave code that would make Southerners' property rights in slaves inviolate until those territories became states. "Upon no organization, except the republican party," Morgan's circular concluded, "can the country rely for successful resistance to these monstrous propositions, and for the correction of the gross abuses which have characterized the present national administration."[30]

A month after Morgan's circular was printed, Lincoln rejected overtures to fold the Republican Party into a new bisectional anti-Buchanan organization even more emphatically. Lincoln's performance against Douglas in 1858 and his 1859 campaign speeches for Republicans in Indiana and Ohio had established his visibility as an important regional Republican leader. Thus Nathan Sargent, who had been the Whig sergeant-at-arms in the House of Representatives when the Whig Lincoln served his single term there, sought Lincoln's blessing for a merger of Republicans with southern Opposition men like Bell and Crittenden. Identifying himself as an "Old Whig" and "an American" rather than a Republican, Sargent urged Lincoln from Washington on June 13, 1859, to help unite the opposition to Democrats' "misrule and corrupt rulers." "We must have the South as well as the North, with us," he argued. Couldn't Republicans be content with combining with those southern anti-Democrats on a platform "simply declaring opposition to the opening of the slave trade, & eternal hostility to the rotten democracy"? If so, "there will be no obstacle to a union of the opposition."[31]

The answer Lincoln penned to Sargent on June 23 was an unmistakable no. Sargent's suggested platform, Lincoln complained, said nothing about resisting the western spread and nationalization of slavery. "Whenever this object is waived by the [Republican] organization . . . the organization itself will dissolve into thin air." Such a combination on the platform Sargent proposed could not carry any northern, let alone southern, state, except perhaps Maryland. "If the rotten democracy shall be beaten in 1860," Lincoln insisted, "it has to be done by the North; no human intervention can deprive them of the South."[32] In 1859, in sum, Lincoln opposed any attempt to create a national anti-Democratic party because that attempt would require Republicans to surrender their opposition to slavery's expansion. Looking ahead, one sees here the main reason—dissolution of the Republican Party—why Lincoln staunchly opposed any relaxation of that opposition in the winter of 1860–1861 after he was elected.

Lincoln underestimated the strength of the anti-Buchanan opposition in the South, or at least in the Upper South that summer. In August anti-Buchanan candidates carried 16 of the 28 House seats at stake in Kentucky, Tennessee, and North Carolina. In no slave state, however, did the opposition, by whatever name it used, win a statewide race, and the political atmosphere in Dixie was on the cusp of changing dramatically. Lincoln's confidence that Republicans did not need southern aid because they could sweep the North, in contrast, seemed borne out by the 1859 results. Republicans won the governorship in every free state that held a gubernatorial contest.

Of these, two were most notable for Republicans and worrisome for their polyglot opponents. Salmon Chase had won the Ohio governorship in 1857 with only a 1,400-vote plurality, but in 1859 the Republican William Dennison swept to victory with a margin of more than 13,000 votes on a platform that demanded repeal of the 1850 Fugitive Slave Act. Republicans in New Jersey were hardly as aggressively anti-southern as those in Ohio. Probably because they were not, they carried the state for their gubernatorial candidate with a statewide popular-vote majority, the first the party ever achieved. More than likely, it was these statewide results in 1859 that engendered nervous Democratic fears about Republicans sweeping the North in 1860.

Aside from New Jersey and Massachusetts, however, all of the Republican Party's gubernatorial victories occurred before news of John Brown's October 16 raid on Harper's Ferry reached the North. Instantly Republicans' political opponents, who were, it bears repeating, a large majority of Americans, charged either that Republicans had helped Brown plan his raid, which they had not, or, more plausibly, that Republicans' antislavery, anti-southern rhetoric had inspired Brown—that his criminal assault on the federal armory in Harper's Ferry was the inevitable result of Republicans' hostility to slavery and slaveholders. Those charges instantly ended any chance that southern opponents of Buchanan's administration could cooperate with Republicans in the upcoming 1860 presidential election. Instead, they would have to vent their deep-seated disdain and disgust for Democrats in a separate organization.

Precisely because Brown's raid could be interpreted as the inevitable consequence of Republicans' anti–Slave Power message, it threatened Republicans' attempt to drop or at least dilute the party's sectionalist identity, which had been so central to their effort to woo Fillmore's northern supporters after 1856. On December 10, 1859, a week after Brown had been hanged in Virginia, the Republican *New York Times* announced that the Republican Party would need a new platform for the 1860 election. The demand for congressional prohibition of slavery from federal territories was moot, for now "there is no territory so exposed to the danger as to demand its exercise." Indeed, the principle of popular sovereignty "has been established in fact" by the resolution of the Kansas question. It "will hereafter settle all disputes that may arise concerning slavery in new territories of the United States. The controversy upon this point is over."[33]

If Republicans shifted their focus to other slavery-related issues, like repeal of the Fugitive Slave Act, warned the *Times*, the party stood in danger of becoming "openly a sectional Anti-Slavery, Abolition party."[34] That would be disastrous, *Times* owner and editor Henry J. Raymond warned, given that Brown's raid had reawakened Know Nothings' fears that Republicans were far too "sectional" to merit support. Raymond, who took southern threats of disunion more seriously than most other Republican newsmen, was at the conservative end of the Republican spectrum. The far more rigidly anti-southern *Chicago Press and Tribune*, for example, once called Raymond's paper "the most thoroughly detestable of all American journals" even though it had incontestably the best stable of news reporters of any paper in the United States.[35]

Nonetheless, Raymond had a point. Republicans needed a new platform to run on now that the danger of slavery extension to the territories had receded. Congressional prohibition of slavery in those areas was no longer necessary; besides, the Supreme Court had ruled it unconstitutional. So what would the thrust of Republicans' campaign in 1860 now be?

The call that the Republican national committee issued on December 22, 1859, for a national convention to be held in Chicago in June 1860 suggested a cornucopia of possibilities. It solicited support from all who, among other things, "are opposed to the policy of the present Administration, to Federal corruptions and usurpations, to the extension of Slavery to the Territories, to the new and dangerous" call for a federal slave code, and to the reopening of the African slave trade.[36]

That policies of Buchanan's administration and federal corruption preceded anything to do with slavery on this list is significant. In 1859 Lincoln had called the Democratic Party "rotten," and in early 1860 the Republican *Chicago Press and Tribune* contended that Buchanan's annual message exposed that "from the byways and highways of the Government the rottenness of corruption sends forth an insufferable stench."[37] In the 1860 campaign Democratic corruption would replace congressional prohibition of slavery extension as Republicans' primary issue. They would focus on the putrid stench of the rotten—and now rent—Democracy. They could make the election a referendum on the Buchanan administration. They would insist that its woeful record made it imperative to throw the Democratic rascals out. Yet, spotlighting the Democratic Party resurrected what to do about slavery in the territories as an issue of the 1860 campaign—and, ominously, what ensued after that campaign. For it was primarily the quarrel between feuding Democrats that made slavery extension a salient issue in the presidential election of 1860.

2

DEMOCRATS' TRIALS AND TRIBULATIONS

"Open and unblushing corruptions and usurpations constitute the very existence of the Administration policy," declared a meeting of Baltimore's Opposition Party in early January 1860 in response to Republicans' recent call for their national convention. Hence, "the only way to save our institutions from positive and final destruction is to drive the dynasty out of power with a universal shout of indignation. It has earned the wages of political sin" and should "be consigned speedily to the political death it merits."[1] Simultaneously New Hampshire's Republicans declared in their state platform "that the corruption and extravagance of the present National Administration, exhibited in its frequent attempts to bribe members of Congress" and "in its fraudulent sale and fraudulent purchase of public property, for the enrichment of partisan favorites . . . demand a change of rulers."[2] A week later, Rhode Island's Republican state convention chorused: "By its enormous expenditures" and "its extravagant and corrupt use of the public treasury . . . the Federal Administration has justly forfeited the confidence of the people, and shown itself unworthy of the high trust that has been committed to it."[3]

Widespread disgust with the widely rumored dishonesty of Buchanan's administration—a revulsion shared by many Democrats themselves—and a determination among all non-Democrats to oust the Democratic "dynasty" from its eight-year control of the federal executive branch constituted another powerful force shaping the presidential campaign of 1860. Among other things, the intensity of anti-Democratic animosity explains why all the groups who feared a Republican triumph could not unite against them while that fear of a Republican triumph explains why all who loathed Democrats would not, at least in 1860, combine against them.

These countervailing dislikes were not the only things that fragmented politicians and produced a four-candidate race in 1860. Equally important was the increasingly bitter split in the Democratic Party between Stephen Douglas and James Buchanan along with virtually all southern Democrats who fumed about Douglas's opposition to the admission of Kansas as a slave state. Together, non-Democrats' intensifying disgust with the Buchanan administration's malodorous record and the increasingly corrosive internal warfare Democrats waged against each other helped Democrats' problems run a close second to Republicans' ominous ascent as the most important factor influencing the election.

That it was Douglas, rather than some other northern Democrat, who challenged Buchanan's handling of Kansas' Lecompton constitution in 1857–1858 was all-important. By then Douglas was not just the senior U.S. senator from Illinois. He was, arguably, the most consequential Democratic politician in the country and, in many minds (including his own), the Democrat who most deserved to succeed James Buchanan in the White House.

Born in Vermont in April 1813, Douglas had moved through upstate New York and northern Ohio before settling in Illinois in 1833. There he served several terms in the state legislature and one on the state supreme court before being elected in August 1843, at the age of thirty, to the first of two terms in the U.S. House of Representatives and then by the state legislature in 1847 to the first of three terms in the U.S. Senate.[4] In Congress, Douglas championed federal support for building transportation infrastructure—canals and railroads—in the Midwest, thus defying traditional Democratic opposition to such support as unconstitutional. In 1850, for example, he was a major author of a bill that gave federal land grants to Illinois and Alabama that were to be used to subsidize construction of the Mobile & Ohio and Illinois Central Railroads.

Douglas was best known, however, for his efforts to finesse sectional strife over slavery expansion into western territories. Those efforts began in 1846 with the introduction in Congress of the Wilmot Proviso. The measure, which would ban slavery from any lands acquired from Mexico as the result of the Mexican War, triggered furious and unanimous southern opposition. At first Douglas sought to negate congressional prohibition by immediately admitting the entire Mexican Cession as a state to avoid a territorial stage upon which a congressional statute could be imposed. But then he settled on popular sovereignty—decision about slavery by the territorial residents rather than by Congress. In 1850 he played the central role in arranging Senate passage of the bills that together constituted the famous Compromise of 1850. Then, in 1854 he substituted the provisions regarding slavery from the Utah and New Mexico laws of 1850 for the Missouri Compromise's ban on slavery in the Kansas and Nebraska Territory bills. And it was his undying commitment to popular sovereignty as he understood it that generated friction between him and southern Democrats in the late 1850s.

To many Illinois residents Douglas remained Judge Douglas for the remainder of his life because of his brief service on the state supreme court. To most, however, he was the Little Giant because of his five-foot-four-inch height, powerful torso, large head, and pugnacious debating style. In 1852 at the age of thirty-nine Douglas had challenged the older Lewis Cass and James Buchanan for the Democrats' presidential nomination. The stalemate among those three had allowed Franklin Pierce to grasp the ring. Then, in 1856, he and the incumbent Pierce contested Buchanan for the party's nod. Douglas's supporters were numerous enough to prevent either of his competitors from gaining the two-thirds majority necessary for a Democratic nomination, but once Buchanan gained an absolute majority, Douglas graciously urged his followers to back the Pennsylvanian. He did so, however, with the tacit understanding of the convention—certainly it was Douglas's own understanding—that the way would be clear for his own nomination in 1860. Douglas's defeat in 1856 was in some ways a blessing, for it kept him clear of the executive branch malfeasance and corruption that would tar Buchanan's name.

Credible allegations that Democrats had bought votes in Indiana and Pennsylvania besmirched Buchanan's victory in 1856. Virginia fire-eater Edmund Ruffin, for example, moaned that he had learned in Washington shortly after that triumph "that enormous sums of money were sent from the city of New York and a good deal also from the democrats of New England to buy votes in Pennsylvania and which turned the vote in that state."[5] Moreover, within a few months of Buchanan's inauguration in March 1857, plausible charges against his administration appeared in newspapers. Such accusations continued for the remainder of his term. The list of shady dealings, malfeasance, and outright theft was extensive. Postmasters like Isaac Fowler in New York and Isaac (Ike) Cook in Chicago stole government and private monies in their charge seemingly at will. Cabinet officers gave sweetheart deals to Democratic insiders on federal contracts. If bids were taken on the jobs, the low bids were usually ignored to give them to a favored Democrat who overcharged or underpaid, depending on the particular deal. Quite often, however, no bids at all were asked. The Navy and War Departments were the worst offenders in this regard, but they were not alone.

The first scandal to receive broad newspaper notice involved Secretary of War John B. Floyd. Without asking for bids or even publicizing that there would be a sale, he sold the 7,500-acre Fort Snelling military reservation in Minnesota Territory to a Democratic appointee who was then the sutler in the fort for $90,000 when, according to local residents, the land was worth between $1 million and $2 million. Floyd signed off on the transfer in Washington on June 10, 1857. Within weeks Republican papers in the North and Opposition papers across the South were howling about "The Fort Snelling Swindle."[6] "The people of the United States, who were the real owners of this soil, were outrageously swindled by Democratic members of Congress [who added a last-minute clause to an army appropriations bill allowing the sale] and territorial U.S. officials, through a private sale at their own prices," railed the Republican *Cleveland Herald* on August 17. "So patent and so outrageous is the fraud that even the Cincinnati *Enquirer*, the leading organ of the Administration calls for action." "The more this locofoco swindle is examined, the worse it looks," echoed the Republican *Milwaukee Sentinel* on September 5. According to a story in a Memphis, Tennessee, paper later that month, "The gigantic fraud perpetrated upon the people by the sale of the Fort Snelling property, is creating a profound sensation through the country."[7]

Democrats' exploitation of public printing contracts for partisan gain also became public knowledge well before the start of 1860. Until Congress passed a law that year establishing the Government Printing Office, House, Senate, and executive branch documents were prepared by private printers at government expense. Printing contracts, too, did not go to the lowest bidder. Instead, they went to printers chosen by the president or by majorities in the House and Senate, which for almost the entire decade of the 1850s were Democratic. Local contracts for printing like lists of letters received at local post offices were usually made by local postmasters—again mostly Democrats in the 1850s. But the contracts for federal printing awarded in Washington were customarily subcontracted, for a percentage of the take, in order to share the wealth among Democratic printers across the country, who almost always published Democratic newspapers. Because there was no competitive bidding, printers bilked the government for scandalously high profits. The recognized "king" of Democratic publishers, Cornelius

Wendell, was said to have made millions through direct contracting and subcontracting between 1853 and 1860. He later admitted to a congressional committee that he had given $100,000 of his profits directly to Democratic campaigns in 1856 and 1858, over and above what he shared with Democratic newspaper editors.

In 1858 a House committee exposed some of the printing abuses. Among other things, it discovered that the official appointed by the president to distribute the executive branch's printing business had consistently extorted bribes or kickbacks from bidders before awarding them government contracts. Appointed by Pierce and retained by Buchanan, that official was indicted and convicted for corruption in office. That committee also persuaded Congress to pass a law forbidding double payment for printing the same document for the House and Senate as well as the subcontracting of printing contracts, although this latter stipulation was easily evaded.[8] More serious revelations would be made by the House Covode Committee in the spring of 1860, and it would be that investigation that directly linked the corruption issue to the Democrats' internal feud over slavery extension into western territories.

That exposure depended upon the outcome of a protracted battle for control of the House Speakership and thus the House machinery in the Thirty-Sixth Congress, a battle that began with the first ballot for Speaker on December 5, 1859, and ended with the forty-fourth ballot on February 1, 1860. Four distinct political groupings could be identified when the House assembled on December 4: Democrats loyal to Buchanan; anti-Lecompton or anti–Buchanan administration Democrats from the North; American Party and other Opposition men, primarily from the South; and Republicans, who held 112 seats, five less than a majority when the House was fully attended. House rules in fact stipulated that a victorious Speaker needed a majority only of members voting on each ballot, rather than an absolute majority of the entire House. Nonetheless, it rapidly became evident that Republicans required some non-Republican votes to win, and for week after week that aid did not materialize.

By the second ballot Republicans coalesced behind John Sherman of Ohio, brother of the soon-to-be-famous William Tecumseh Sherman, and they remained united behind him through the thirty-ninth ballot on January 27, 1860. Sherman came within three or four votes of winning on several occasions, but he failed to get over the top. Anti-Lecompton Democrats scattered their votes or united behind men of their own rather than support Sherman. Their reticence was an important sign that Republicans could not in fact count on support from most anti-Buchanan Democrats in the impending presidential election despite the cooperation between Republicans and anti-Lecompton Democrats in many 1858 congressional races. Nor would southern American Party members back Sherman. They shared Republicans' profound disgust at the corruption of Buchanan's administration as well as their hope of using House committees in this Congress to ventilate its sorry record. But they would not aid in making John Sherman Speaker.

The main reason why is that as soon as it became clear that Republicans intended to unite behind Sherman, Missouri Democrat John Clark introduced a resolution declaring that no man who had endorsed a Republican-printed *Compendium* to Hinton Rowan Helper's *The Impending Crisis of the South: How to Meet It* was fit to serve as Speaker of the House. Sixty-eight Republicans, including Sherman, had done just that. Sherman said that he had no recollection of allowing his name to be used and that he had never read the book or the compendium of it. Nonetheless, he freely admitted that he must have told someone his name could be added to the list of other Republicans touting it. That confession made supporting Sherman a kiss of political death for any southern congressman.

Originally published in 1857, Helper's book sought to mobilize the nonslaveholding majority of white Southerners against the slaveholding minority. Using data from the 1850 census to compare the prosperity and institutional societal development of the South with that of the North, Helper, a native North Carolinian, railed that slavery palpably disadvantaged nonslaveholders like himself who lacked the schools, libraries, factories, and manifold opportunities for upward economic mobility of their northern counterparts. Hence, Helper concluded, nonslaveholders should shun slaveholders. They should not buy from them, go to church with them, or, most significantly, ever vote for them. Nonslaveholders, he urged, must use their latent political power—their numbers—to rid the South of slavery by voting slaveholders out of control of southern state governments. Understandably, slaveholding politicians like John Clark saw Helper's message as a call for class warfare in the South and an attempt to mobilize a proto-Republican electorate in Dixie should that hateful party ever organize there. Thus, to a man Southerners in the House refused to vote for Sherman while on ballot after ballot almost all Republicans supported him. This fight thus increased the sectional animosity between the two groups.

The turning point came on the thirty-ninth ballot on January 27, 1860. In that vote Democrats, including most anti-Lecompton Democrats, threw their support to an Opposition Party man from North Carolina who outpolled Sherman by six votes and came within three of winning the prize. At that point five conservative Republicans, four from Pennsylvania and one from New Jersey, told the party's caucus that they would vote for and elect the North Carolinian on the next ballot unless Republicans replaced Sherman with New Jersey's William Pennington, a former Whig and recent convert to the Republicans who had not signed the Helper compendium. Sherman agreed to withdraw, and Pennington was substituted for him. Scattered votes prevented anyone from obtaining the necessary majority until Pennington won with the precise majority necessary, 117 votes, on the forty-fourth ballot. Four anti-Lecompton Democrats and Maryland Know Nothing Henry Winter Davis provided the votes that put him over the top. Pennington then appointed Republicans to chair twenty-five of the House's thirty-four standing committees. Anti-Lecompton Democrats and southern American Party members would chair seven, the defeated Democrats only two.[9]

On the day after Pennington's victory the Republican *New York Times* spotlighted what was primarily at stake in the long battle. Democrats had prolonged it, maintained the editorial, because they sought "to shelter the Administration from the consequences of the corruption which has grown up under its patronage and encouragement, by raising frivolous objections to the election of any candidate decidedly committed to the Opposition." Pennington was seen more as a Whig than as a Republican because he had not endorsed Helper's book. Still, "we may all rejoice that the corruptions which have grown up under the existing Administration, are as likely to be brought to light in the House under the sway of Mr. Pennington as they could have been under any other Speaker whatever."[10]

Within five weeks of Pennington's triumph, House Republicans demonstrated the leverage it gave them to put the administration on trial for its suspected sins. On March 5, John Covode, a western Pennsylvania Republican, introduced a resolution asking that the Republican Speaker, rather than the entire House membership, appoint a special committee of five. That committee would then investigate "whether the President of the United States, or any other officer of the United States has, by money, patronage, or other improper means, sought to influence the action of Congress, or any committee thereof, for or against any law appertaining to the rights of any State or Territory." That this language alluded to Buchanan's attempts to induce northern Democratic congressmen to support Kansas statehood under the proslavery Lecompton constitution in 1858 was clear to everyone on the floor. The committee would also investigate whether any government official had "prevented or defeated, or attempted to prevent or defeat the execution of any law or laws now upon the statute book, and whether the President has failed or refused to compel the execution of any law thereof," abuses at the Chicago post office and the Philadelphia navy yard, and whether Democrats had used money to buy votes in Pennsylvania's elections of 1856 and 1858, as Buchanan himself had seemed to admit in a public letter to the citizens of Pittsburgh in November 1858. The reference to executing the law clearly targeted the failure of federal officials to award contracts to the lowest bidder, rather than favored Democratic insiders, as federal law required.[11]

Democrats immediately protested that the House had no authority to investigate the president outside of impeachment hearings, that Covode made no specific charge that might warrant an investigation, that any investigating should be done by the standing Judiciary Committee, not an ad hoc body—especially one that Covode, Buchanan's accuser, might chair—and that the whole thing was simply a partisan witch hunt to make fodder for the impending presidential campaign. This last charge possessed considerable merit. Nonetheless, with many members abstaining, the House passed Covode's resolutions 117–45. Pennington then proceeded to appoint three Republicans, including Covode as chair, and two Democrats to what a Democrat labeled "The Executive Corruption Investigating Committee."[12]

Buchanan himself sent a message to the House on March 28 insisting that it had no right to investigate him outside of public impeachment hearings, calling Covode's chairmanship of the committee outrageous, and ominously predicting the subversion of the separation of powers prescribed by the U.S. Constitution. House Republicans responded that they had every right to investigate the administration. One declared that "the House has been insulted by this Napoleonic decree of the present President," and Republican editors mocked "King James' Bull" as an unprecedented "assertion of a kingly prerogative" that "must arouse the indignation of the country."[13]

Throughout the spring the Covode Committee called in witnesses from New York, Philadelphia, and elsewhere. It met in secret sessions that Democrats denounced as "Star Chamber proceedings."[14] From the start it leaked the most damaging testimony against Buchanan to Republican papers while concealing anything said in his defense, as Buchanan would rightly complain in yet another message to the House on June 22, 1860. By then, House Republicans had voted to print and distribute thousands of copies of the Covode Committee's findings, and at their own expense Republicans would print tens of thousands more as Republican campaign documents.

Covode's findings increased the anger and disgust of the non-Democratic press. According to the Republican *Milwaukee Sentinel,* they revealed "an extent of corruption on the part of the Administration that will startle the nation." That paper also wildly charged, before the report was released, that Covode's evidence proved that Buchanan had spent $925,000 in 1858 to get Kansas statehood under the Lecompton constitution passed by Congress. The Richmond, Virginia, *Whig,* a long-time anti-Democratic sheet, gasped that the committee had unearthed "startling evidence . . . of the corruption, depravity and utter rottenness of the great head of the Democratic party—even the President of the United States."[15]

Even before Covode's committee presented its findings, the standing House Committee on Public Expenditures had reported that the new superintendent of printing appointed by Buchanan in 1858 had refused to give contracts for postal printing to the lowest bidder. Examination of those ignored bids revealed that neglected bidders had promised to do for five to ten cents on the dollar what the favored Democratic insider was paid $45,000 of government money to do.[16] Covode's findings proved even more damaging. Claiming an intimate personal friendship with Buchanan, the notorious Cornelius Wendell testified that $30,000–$40,000 of the money he had given the administration in 1858 had been spent to bribe congressmen to support the Lecompton constitution. John W. Forney, a Philadelphia editor who had once been Buchanan's principal lieutenant in Pennsylvania but now supported Douglas, testified that he had been offered $80,000 worth of post office printing in return for endorsing Lecompton. As if this were not enough, the Covode Committee also exposed the peculations of Chicago postmaster Ike Cook, a known thief whom Buchanan had reappointed to that position in 1858 specifically because he was a mortal enemy of Stephen Douglas.

Throughout the spring Democrats in Congress and in newspapers tried to defend Buchanan by denouncing the unfairness of the committee's procedures, producing evidence that Republicans once in office were just as corrupt as their Democratic counterparts, or pooh-poohing the whole investigation as unimportant and irrelevant to the impending presidential contest. Perhaps the most important newsman in this regard was James Gordon Bennett, whose *New York Herald* had the widest circulation of any newspaper in the country. "It is absurd to suppose that the republican committees at Washington can make any issue for the approaching election out of any charges of corruption against the democratic politicians," Bennett editorialized on April 13. "The issue before the country is broader and deeper than corrupt practices of any party." That issue was the threat to the Union posed by Republican antislavery fanatics. "From this great question no petty intrigues of political demagogues like these investigating committees . . . can divert the public mind; or can they convince the people that in the matter of dishonesty, corruption, and fraud, the politicians of all parties do not stand upon an even platform."[17]

With unintentional prescience, the avidly Republican *New Hampshire Statesman* printed a riposte to this claim a week before it appeared. "We embark on this [presidential] campaign," it announced on April 7, 1860, "for the expulsion of the selfish, narrow-minded, unprincipled partisan hordes now entrenched in the seats of power and patronage, and for filling their places with honest, able and candid men and statesmen, who will administer the Government after the fashion of its founders." "More than this," it added, "we do not desire."[18] While the editorial went on to say that it expected any Republican presidential nominee to share the principles adopted by the Republican national convention, the absence of any mention of slavery or slavery extension in this statement is telling. Clearly, this Republican editor expected Democratic corruption, not slavery extension or animosity between Southerners and Republicans, to be the central issue of the election.

What did make slavery extension an issue, instead, was the escalating feud between Stephen A. Douglas and his northern Democratic supporters, on the one hand, and southern Democrats and pro-Buchanan northern Democrats, on the other. Northern and southern Democrats had differed over the meaning of popular sovereignty since the doctrine was first articulated in the late 1840s. They agreed on its basic premise: Congress should neither prohibit slavery from nor establish slavery in any federal territory by a concrete statute. Rather, the actual residents of the territory must make the decision. There, however, consensus ended. Like most northern Democrats, Douglas insisted that territorial residents could decide whether or not to allow slavery as soon as the size of their population justified choosing a territorial legislature. Southerners denounced this idea as "squatter sovereignty" and declared instead that a decision about slavery could be made only by a constitutional convention when the territory applied for statehood—that is, much later in the territorial phase. Until that later decision, Southerners insisted, slaveholders must be welcomed in the territories on equal terms with nonslaveholding Northerners.

Adopted by a national convention in Cincinnati, the Democrats' 1856 national platform, which would be all-important in 1860, seemed to embody both divergent interpretations. One plank declared that "the American democracy recognize and adopt the principles contained in" the Kansas-Nebraska Act as "the only sound and safe solution of the 'slavery question' upon which the great national idea of the people of this whole country can repose in its determined conservatism of the Union—*Non-Interference by Congress with Slavery in State and Territory, or in the District of Columbia.*" But another plank then averred: "That we recognize the right of the people of all the Territories, including Kansas and Nebraska, acting . . . whenever the number of their inhabitants justifies it, to form a Constitution, with or without domestic slavery, and be admitted into the Union upon terms of perfect equality with other States."[19] Although this plank seemed to tilt toward the southern interpretation, a number of Democrats complained at the time that the platform still allowed for divergent interpretations in the North and South. In 1860, determined southern Democrats meant to extirpate an ambiguity they now found intolerable.

Although James Buchanan had endorsed the Cincinnati platform when accepting the Democratic nomination in 1856, he shared southern Democrats' impatience with Douglas's interpretation of it. In his March 1857 inaugural address Buchanan declared that the "appropriate period" for the residents of Kansas Territory to decide about slavery "will be when the number of actual residents in the Territory shall justify the formation of a constitution with a view to its admission as a State into the Union." But this matter was moot, he declared in the same paragraph, for the Supreme Court was about to provide a judicial solution to the whole question of slavery expansion. To that solution, he and "all good citizens" would "cheerfully submit."[20] Buchanan, of course, knew precisely what that decision would be, for a southern Democratic associate justice had already informed him of it.

Buchanan and Douglas would famously split over Douglas's opposition to Kansas statehood under the Lecompton constitution. Ultimately what pitted Douglas and his followers against Buchanan and southern Democrats, however, was Douglas's refusal to accept what appeared to be the plain language of the Supreme Court's *Dred Scott* decision. Southern Democrats regarded Roger B. Taney's ruling in March 1857 as a complete vindication of what they had been arguing about territorial slavery expansion since at least the 1840s. The Court declared congressional prohibition of slavery an unconstitutional deprivation of slaveholders' property rights under the Fifth Amendment. Thus the Court seemingly held that the United States Constitution guaranteed a property right in slaves even outside of slave states, a position that antislavery groups in the North had always damned as anathema. To boot, Taney, without the concurrence of a majority of the Court, added to his decision a codicil saying that if Congress could not prohibit slavery from a territory, then clearly a territorial legislature could not do so either. Congress could not grant to a subordinate government of its creation a power that it itself did not constitutionally possess.

Like southern Democrats, Buchanan applauded the entire decision. In his annual message in December 1857, he declared that the slaves then living in Kansas Territory were "property of their masters" "under the United States Constitution" because all citizens of all the states had a right to take into federal territories "whatsoever is recognized as property by the common Constitution"—that is, and the point is absolutely crucial, by the United States Constitution, not simply individual state constitutions.[21]

Republicans rejected as *obiter dicta* without legal force everything in the *Dred Scott* decision after the Court held that Scott was not a citizen and thus had no legal standing to sue in federal courts. But they were especially incensed by this claim of a federal constitutional right to property in slaves, for they and earlier antislavery groups had constantly held that only state and local laws, not the U.S. Constitution, established property rights in slavery. Thus, the call Republicans issued for their national convention in December 1859 invited all who, among other things, rejected "the new and dangerous doctrine that the Constitution, on its own force, carries Slavery into all the Territories of the United States."[22]

Stephen Douglas meanwhile rejoiced that the Supreme Court had held congressional prohibition of slavery from territories to be unconstitutional. But he rejected Taney's further stipulation about territorial legislatures as well as the contention that the U.S. Constitution established a right to slave property in federal territories until those territories entered the Union as full-fledged states. He passionately insisted instead that local majorities through the instrument of territorial legislatures could bar slavery long before those territories had a population sufficient to apply for statehood. He also recognized that letting Taney's ruling stand unchallenged would obliterate Democrats' electoral prospects in the North, allow Republicans to sweep that section, and, quite probably, precipitate the disruption of the Union and a bloody civil war. As he later wrote a Democratic editor in Connecticut, "The Democratic party is the only political organization which can preserve the peace and harmony of the Union," and only an explicit commitment to popular sovereignty could preserve "the integrity and ascendancy of the Democratic party."[23] Both principle and political necessity, in sum, prompted Douglas to challenge parts of Taney's holding. That challenge put Douglas at odds with southern Democrats as well as with Buchanan. It led ultimately to a disastrous division of the national Democratic Party in 1860.

Whereas Republicans immediately denounced Taney's decision after he issued it in March 1857, Douglas held his fire until giving a public address when he arrived home in Chicago in late May of that year. Rather than reject Taney's logic whole cloth, he maintained that it was perfectly compatible with popular sovereignty as he understood it. A master's right to slave property in any territory, he contended, "necessarily remains a barren and worthless right, unless sustained, protected and enforced by appropriate police regulations and local legislation, prescribing adequate remedies for its violation." Those "regulations and remedies" depended upon the "will and wishes of the people of the territory" as expressed through their "local legislatures."[24] What Douglas left unsaid explicitly here but was clearly implicit in what he did say was that despite Taney's ruling, the people of a territory, while it was still a territory, could bar slavery from it simply by refusing to enact the local laws and police regulations necessary to sustain it.

Douglas provided no written version of his speech to newspapers until some months after he gave it, and it is not clear that many southern Democrats then read it. Without question, his opposition to admitting Kansas as a slave state under the Lecompton constitution is what aroused their enmity during the first half of 1858. They regarded Douglas's stand as the ultimate betrayal not only of them, but of his own popular sovereignty principles. Kansas residents, they protested, had played by Douglas's rules. The very first territorial legislature had ruled on slavery, but it had ruled that slavery should exist in Kansas. Then a constitutional convention had allowed Kansas residents to decide if Kansas should be a slave state, and they had said yes. It made no difference that the convention denied a referendum on the entire constitution because a constitutional convention was sovereign. It had every right to make its own rules about how, if at all, a constitution should be popularly ratified. Indeed, from their perspective what was outrageous was that territorial governor Robert J. Walker, a mere federal appointee, had tried to dictate to a sovereign convention what it had to do. What was still more outrageous was that Douglas worked to deny the South the representation of another slave state in Congress that they had won fair and square—at least as they defined fair and square. From the moment Douglas came out against Lecompton, therefore, many southern

Democratic politicos angrily determined that he must not be Democrats' presidential candidate in 1860.

For the furious James Buchanan that retaliation against Douglas was insufficiently prompt. He set out to prevent Douglas's reelection to the Senate by the Illinois legislature to be chosen in November 1858, a contest for legislative seats that occasioned the legendary debates between Douglas and Abraham Lincoln. As early as February 1858 Douglas wrote political allies that "the administration are determined to crush every public man who dissents from their policy of forcing a constitution on the people of Kansas against their will" and that it was "more anxious for my destruction than they are for the harmony & unity of the Democratic Party."[25] By the summer Buchanan was openly supporting pro-administration, anti-Douglas Democrats in Illinois who backed Democrat Sidney Breese for Douglas's Senate seat. To that end, Buchanan replaced a Douglas ally in the Chicago post office with Douglas's arch foe Ike Cook, who along with other patronage holders managed to run anti-Douglas Democratic candidates for the state legislature in most districts.[26] Douglas men referred to these anti-Douglas dissidents as Buchaneers or Danites, but they called themselves "Illinois National Democrats." A platform they adopted in January 1860 lavishly praised Buchanan's administration and repudiated Douglas's claims that territorial legislatures could still bar slavery by doing nothing to bulwark it.[27]

Prior to 1860, Douglas's most widely publicized statement of that position occurred in his joint debate with Lincoln at Freeport, Illinois, on August 27, 1858. Urged by Republican allies to put Douglas on the spot, Lincoln asked him if, given the *Dred Scott* decision, a territorial legislature could ban slavery from a territory. Douglas declared, correctly, that the full Supreme Court had never ruled that a territorial legislature could not bar it. But even if a future Court decision so ruled, he contended, the people had "lawful means" to exclude it by refusing to pass the local police regulations necessary to sustain the institution. "Slavery cannot exist a day or an hour anywhere, unless it is supported by local police regulations," he maintained. Refusal to enact those regulations would effectively bar it.[28] As Lincoln well knew, Douglas had made this argument previously on several occasions within Illinois. It was not news to him. It was apparently news, however, to most southern Democrats reading newspaper accounts of the Lincoln-Douglas debates. That news infuriated many of them. Douglas had not only aided Republicans in blocking Kansas' admission as a slave state. Now he averred that the constitutional guarantee of property rights in slaves in all territories was meaningless because local residents, mere squatting clodhoppers, could nullify the United States Constitution simply by neglecting to enact local laws in accordance with it.

However unsettled some southern Democrats were by Douglas's so-called Freeport Doctrine, unlike Buchanan in 1858 they did not aid the Illinois pro-administration Democrats who ran anti-Douglas candidates for the state legislature and statewide offices. Braking the Republican Party's growth by defeating Lincoln's senatorial bid was far too important to them. Hence, many southern Democrats—including Georgia's Alexander Stephens, South Carolina congressman James Orr, Virginia governor Henry Wise, and Mississippi senator Albert Gallatin Brown—urged Douglas's election. Once the Little Giant was safely returned to the Senate, however, it was another matter.

When the second session of the Thirty-Fifth Congress opened in December 1858, Douglas had not yet reached Washington. In his absence, a lightly attended caucus of Democratic senators (only twenty-four of the total forty-four) took the opportunity to punish him for his alleged heresies. They stripped Douglas of his cherished chairmanship of the Senate Committee on Territories. Mississippi senator Jefferson Davis and California senator William Gwin, a native of Tennessee, orchestrated this purge, although Buchanan may have been the mover behind the scenes. Nonetheless, seven of the senators in attendance voted against Douglas's decapitation. One of them was Davis's Mississippi colleague and intraparty rival Albert Gallatin Brown, who had earlier endorsed Douglas's reelection to the Senate despite Buchanan's obvious hatred of him.

Brown's inclusion among Douglas's defenders was ironic, for on February 23, 1859, Brown, along with Davis, would introduce resolutions specifically intended to rebut Douglas's argument at Freeport that territorial residents could prohibit slavery regardless of what Taney had held in the *Dred Scott* decision. Brown agreed with Douglas that slave property required positive local legislation to protect it and that the Constitution's recognition of property rights in slaves did not suffice. But precisely because of that constitutional guarantee, insisted Brown, Congress must pass federal laws to protect property rights in slaves in any territory whose residents refused or neglected to enact the positive local laws necessary to do so. Southern Democrats, Brown added, would insist that a provision requiring such congressional legislation be included in Democrats' 1860 national platform. If it was not, Brown warned in February 1859, Southerners would bolt the Democratic convention and refuse to support its nominee. Thus the gauntlet that would wreck the Democratic Party was thrown fourteen months before the party's national convention gathered in Charleston, South Carolina, in late April 1860 and twenty months before voters went to the polls to choose the sixteenth president of the United States.

Brown did not use the term, but what he demanded quickly became known as a "federal slave code." Even that February, some people recognized that this demand was wholly an abstraction since, after the decision in Kansas on August 2, 1858, there was no territory within the existing area of the United States into which slaveholders had any interest of moving. Brown's threat, wrote one newspaperman, was "one of the most unprofitable, barren and impracticable abstractions of the day."[29] Abstract it might be, but Douglas and his northern Democratic supporters rejected it instantly. They would continue to do so up through the day votes were cast on November 6, 1860. The reason was clear. Even before that session of Congress opened, John Forney, the Philadelphia Democratic newsman who had backed Douglas in his revolt against Buchanan, had warned him that if a "platform of Congressional intervention for the protection of slavery" should be imposed on the North, "there will be no help for us."[30]

Douglas needed no advice from Forney to understand how calamitous any acquiescence in a pro-slavery-extension stance would be for northern Democrats in 1860, especially as he himself expected to be the Democratic presidential nominee that year. But more than realistic political calculation motivated Douglas. What Brown and other southern Democrats now demanded violated the Cincinnati platform of 1856, to which Douglas was deeply committed emotionally and ideologically. In accordance with popular sovereignty as Democrats had understood it since the 1840s, that platform insisted that there must be no federal intervention concerning slavery in federal territories. That was precisely what Brown, Davis, and other southern Democrats were now insisting might be necessary. "Might" is the critical qualifier here. Southern Democrats did not demand that federal slave codes instantly be imposed on existing territories into which slaveholders had zero interest of moving. Rather the demand referred to possible additional new federal territories. For several decades, indeed, many southern Democrats had demanded the acquisition of Cuba, but to no avail. Nonetheless, their well-known expansionist designs made their insistence on a possible federal slave code especially corrosive.

Douglas made his defiance of southern demands emphatically clear by publishing a lengthy article in *Harper's* magazine in September 1859. Entitled "The Dividing Line between Federal and Local Authority: Popu-

Stephen A. Douglas, ca. late 1859 or early 1860. The photograph brutally reveals the physical toll his battles with fellow Democrats and his heavy drinking had taken on him. Courtesy of the Chicago Museum of History.

lar Sovereignty in the Territories," Douglas's essay argued that Congress had always clothed territorial legislatures with authority over things with which Congress itself lacked authority. Those were domestic or local concerns that were beyond Congress's constitutional purview. Slavery in the territories, he maintained, was one such local issue. Hence, the United States Constitution could not and did not establish property rights in slaves in federal territories. Despite the *Dred Scott* decision, territorial legislatures could prevent slavery from entering either by passing prohibitory laws or by refusing to enact the positive police regulations necessary to sustain it.[31]

A state convention of Douglas's Illinois Democratic supporters in early January 1860 iterated Douglas's defiance. Its platform "affirm[ed] the Cincinnati platform in . . . the meaning with which the same was adopted, and utterly repudiates all such new issues and tests such as the revival of the African slave trade, or a Congressional slave code for the Territories, and denies that slavery derives its validity where it exists in State or Territory from the Constitution of the United States." The Cincinnati platform, it further applauded, "pledged to banish forever the question of slavery from the halls of Congress, and leave the people of the States and Territories free to settle all domestic questions in their own way."[32]

Douglas's Democratic enemies were quick to rebut his position. Buchanan's Annual Message of December 19, 1859, declared that the Supreme Court had given a "final settlement" to the question of slavery in the territories. "Every citizen" had a "right" "to take his property of any kind, including slaves, into the common Territories . . . and have it protected there under the Federal Constitution." Neither Congress, nor a territory legislature, nor "any human power" had authority "to annul or impair this vested right." "Thus has the status of a Territory during the intermediate period from its first settlement until it shall become a State been irrevocably fixed by the final decision of the Supreme Court." And, Buchanan added, if the judiciary failed to protect that constitutional property right in slaves, "it will be time enough to strengthen their hands by further legislation."[33] Buchanan only alluded indirectly to his potential support for a federal slave code. Two days after Buchanan submitted his message, in contrast, Vice President John C. Breckinridge explicitly told a crowd in Frankfort, Kentucky, that he favored a federal slave code, an endorsement that in turn was quickly denounced by pro-Douglas Democratic newspapers like the *Cincinnati Enquirer*.[34] Breckinridge's speech, contended the Republican *Chicago Press and Tribune*, "indicates a purpose on the part of the Administration to crush out the little life there is still left in 'popular sovereignty' and its twin brother 'unfriendly legislation.'"[35]

Southern Democrats in the Senate also angrily repudiated Douglas's stance. Senators Brown and Davis of Mississippi reintroduced resolutions calling for a congressional slave code on January 18 and February 2, 1860, respectively. Both averred that the U.S. Constitution recognized a property right in slaves that must be protected, exactly what Douglas had denied in his *Harper's* article. But then they differed. Brown's insisted that the "Committee on Territories be instructed to insert in any bill . . . for the organization of new Territories, a clause declaring it to be the duty of the Territorial Legislature to enact adequate and sufficient laws for the protection of" slavery and all other property. And if the territorial legislature refused to do so, "it is the admitted duty of Congress to impose and pass such laws." In short, Brown demanded that the Senate take action on the very next territory formally organized by Congress. Davis called only for a prospective passage of a federal slave code if—and it was a big if—the United States acquired new territory to which slaveholders wished to go. The relevant part of his resolution read: "That neither Congress nor a Territorial Legislature, whether by direct legislation or legislation of an indirect and unfriendly nature, possess the power to annul or impair the constitutional right of any citizen of the United States to take his property into the common Territories." The federal government had a "duty" to protect that property in those territories. Hence, "if experience should at any time prove that the judiciary does not possess the power to insure adequate protection, it will become the duty of Congress to apply such deficiency."[36] Davis, in sum, here took a stance quite similar to Buchanan's, although in other speeches he made clear that he opposed trying to force slavery on any territory whose residents obviously did not want it.[37]

In his speech defending his resolutions, Albert Gallatin Brown openly savaged Douglas, whom he had previously defended. "The Senator from Illinois," he complained, "first promulgated the idea that non-action and unfriendly action" by a territorial legislature "would be effective for the exclusion of slavery." That doctrine explained why there were few slaves left in Kansas Territory (the 1860 census counted only two). Complaints that demands for a federal slave code violated the noninterference doctrine of the Cincinnati platform were baseless since the Supreme Court in 1857 had decreed that the U.S. Constitution guaranteed property rights in slaves and therefore the federal government must protect those rights. As for the supposed agreement by all Democrats that Congress must never interpose about slavery in a territory, "I have never agreed to any such thing. . . . I never considered at any time . . . that the people of a Territory had a right to exclude slavery. I never yielded the point that Congress was bound to interpose everywhere . . . for the protection of my property and the property of my section, of my State and of my people." As if his point were not clear enough, Brown iterated, "What I demand is protection—that protection which you admit we are entitled to by the common Constitution. Give it to us now; do it at once."[38]

Here Brown claimed to speak for all Southerners—but not all southern Democrats, to say nothing of Opposition men, agreed with him about the pressing need for a federal slave code in the territories. While Brown and southern Democrats like him reviled Douglas for his supposed treachery to slaveholders' interests, other prominent southern Democrats openly endorsed him for the 1860 presidential nomination. "*The South has now no issue with the Federal Government on the Slavery question—not one,*" Mobile, Alabama, editor John Forsyth wrote in a public letter to the Montgomery *Advertiser* in February. "They are all settled with Southern concurrence and consent. The only issue left is . . . whether, with the aid of the constitutional men of the North and West, we have the voting strength to defeat the Black Republicans in a Presidential contest."[39] The admitted power of Congress to protect slavery in the territories, chimed former Alabama senator Jeremiah Clemens, "is at present a mere abstraction, and I consider it doubtful whether it ever will assume a practical form. We have no Territory into which slavery can go."[40]

"The issue of protection to slavery in the Territories, and a Congressional slave code, which is so warmly agitated by the Southern portion of the Administration Democracy, really seems to us destitute of any prominent practical bearing," editorialized the pro-Douglas *New Orleans Bee*. At the same time, "the opinions of Mr. Douglas, which are deemed absolutely heretical, and at war with the dearest interests of the South, are justly viewed by many as innocent abstractions."[41]

Such voices were a minority, at least of vocal southern Democrats. On February 25, for example, a caucus of Senate Democrats passed resolutions that not only adopted Davis's language about a potential need for congressional action if territorial legislatures failed to protect property rights in slaves, but also insisted, in a direct slap at Douglas, that no territorial legislature could by direct legislation or "indirect action" impair the rights of "any citizen of the United States to take his slave property into the common Territories, and to hold and enjoy the same while the Territorial condition remains."[42]

By March it seemed clear that southern Democrats would insist upon inserting the demand for a federal slave code into the Democratic national platform when the party's national convention met in late April. Democratic state conventions, even in Upper South and border states like Arkansas, Missouri, Kentucky, and Maryland, denounced Douglas's new position, stridently opposed his nomination, and endorsed a federal slave code should it prove necessary to protect slaveholders' rights. By then as well, it was clear that Douglas and his northern allies who were choosing delegations pledged to him in state after northern state in the early months of 1860 had no intention of allowing such a modification of the Democratic platform. Nor would they abandon their insistence that Douglas be the party's nominee. In short, by March newspapers around the country were, correctly, predicting a sectional donnybrook at the Democratic national convention that might possibly result in the party's smash-up.

Battles between pro-Buchanan and pro-Douglas men at northern Democratic state conventions held in the run-up to the April national convention indicated that anticipated fights there would not be strictly sectional clashes. Just as some southern Democrats opposed a federal slave code and/or endorsed Douglas, so some northern Democrats clung to the administration's position and echoed its hostility to the Little Giant. The rival Democratic state conventions in Illinois both sent delegations to Charleston, one instructed to win re-adoption of the Cincinnati platform and to secure Douglas's nomination, the other determined to stop his selection and to repudiate his defiance of Buchanan's insistence on the finality of the *Dred Scott* decision. In Ohio's Democratic state convention, the pro-Douglas majority hooted down a platform plank praising Buchanan, reaffirmed the Cincinnati platform's insistence on absolute noninterference by Congress in territorial matters, and instructed Ohio's delegates to the Charleston convention to vote for Douglas as a unit. Indiana's closely divided convention, in contrast, praised Buchanan's interpretation of the *Dred Scott* decision while endorsing the Cincinnati platform and sending pro-Douglas delegates to Charleston. Minnesota, Michigan, and Wisconsin Democrats all endorsed Douglas's position, but the hostile Buchanan clearly had more clout among northeastern Democrats. A district convention in Maine denounced Douglas and his refusal to accept the finality of the *Dred Scott* decision, Connecticut's state convention pointedly refused to endorse both his nomination and his Freeport Doctrine, and Pennsylvania's Democratic state convention, over the strident opposition of a pro-Douglas minority, lavishly praised Buchanan's record as "eminently pure, patriotic, conservative and just," and endorsed John C. Breckinridge as its choice for the presidential nomination.[43]

By March, southern Democrats' aggressive demand for a federal slave code also caused the moderate Republican *New York Times* to modify its declaration of the preceding December that slavery extension would not be an issue in the 1860 presidential election. Editor Henry Raymond still maintained that Republicans no longer demanded congressional legislation barring slavery from the territories because such a positive ban was no longer necessary. But now, he added, Republicans must be elected to prevent southern Democrats from enacting a congressional statute protecting the right to hold slaves in territories in which slavery had never previously existed.[44] Stopping congressional action about slavery, not achieving it, was now Republicans' mission.

If only indirectly, the *Times* here made a crucial point. Throughout the 1860 campaign Republican speakers and editors declared that their party opposed the extension of slavery into federal territories. But they did not insist that Congress must bar it by federal statute or that slavery extension was the most important, let alone the only, issue at stake in the contest. As Oliver P. Morton, the Republican candidate for lieutenant governor in Indiana, told a rally in Fort Wayne, "The mission of the republican party is to prevent the further extension of slavery, and to rescue the government from the corruption and abuses of the party in power."[45] Many Republicans, as this chapter suggests, would reverse the order of those priorities. But the important point here is that Republicans understood correctly that events in Kansas had demonstrated that a decision by local residents would prevent slavery extension into federal territories if slavery were not imposed upon them by federal law. For that reason, when Congress formally organized new territories in the West during the second session of the Thirty-Sixth Congress after Lincoln's election, Republicans made no attempt to bar slavery from them by congressional statute.

Nor did southern Opposition parties want to make slavery extension a central issue in 1860. In January the state committee of Mississippi's Opposition Party announced that slavery extension "has lost much of its practical importance and tends to nothing but mischief." Indeed, their address complained, "A sectional party has arisen upon it, and continues its organization, though, substantially, it has achieved its professed objective."[46] Throughout the remainder of the 1860 campaign southern opponents of the Democrats denounced slavery extension as a phony issue that their Democratic enemies had trumped up to no practical purpose whatsoever.

Not Republicans, southern Opposition men, or even pro-Douglas Democrats insisted on the centrality of slavery extension in the 1860 campaign. Rather, it was southern Democrats who did. They continued to do so even when they admitted that the question was an abstraction with no practical significance with regard to the existing land area of the United States. So why did they do so? In part, one suspects, it was a determined defense of equal rights in angry response to Republicans' demand that the minority

South must submit to northern majority rule. One of the resolutions adopted by that southern-dominated Senate Democratic caucus on February 25, for example, asserted that "the Union of these states rests on the equality of rights and privileges among its members" and that in relation to slavery in the territories the Senate must resist any action that gave "advantages to the citizens of one State which are not equally assured to those of every other State."[47] Similar language about preserving the "equality" and the "rights" of southern states characterized virtually every set of local or state Democratic resolutions adopted in slave states prior to and beyond Democrats' Charleston convention. As an Alabama Democratic presidential elector publicly vowed even before the Charleston convention met, when Southerners "are left to the degradation of an unequal and unjust position in the Union, I shall advocate an effort to reclaim our rights at the sacrifice of the Union."[48] Any attempt to treat the South as the minority it was, in short, meant secession.

Given the unreality of the extension issue, however, it is difficult to resist the conclusion that southern Democrats stressed the territorial question primarily because they now so despised Douglas that they were determined to renounce and repudiate his cherished doctrine of congressional noninterference. In other words, many southern Democrats' hatred of Douglas injected slavery extension into the 1860 race. Their intransigence assured that starkly conflicting sectional attitudes toward Douglas and Southerners' preferred platform would shape almost everything that Democrats did when they assembled in Charleston for the party's national nominating convention.

3

DEMOCRATS' NOMINATIONS: ACT I

The Democrats were the first party to hold a national presidential nominating convention in 1860. They would be the last, however, to choose their candidates that year. Their convention opened in Charleston, South Carolina's, Institute Hall on Monday, April 23. Charleston had been designated its site at the Cincinnati convention in 1856 as a consolation prize to southern delegates, most of whom had far preferred the renomination of President Franklin Pierce to the selection of James Buchanan. Salving the disappointment of Pierce's supporters also primarily explains why the convention chose Kentucky's John C. Breckinridge, a close Pierce ally, as Buchanan's running mate that year. Precisely because Breckinridge was deemed Pierce's friend, Buchanan had treated him with the coldest of cold shoulders for the first three years of his administration. Only a few months before the Charleston gathering convened did Buchanan decide that Breckinridge might be the Democrats' best stop-Douglas candidate. Upon learning of this conversion, Kentucky's Robert P. Letcher wrote that he knew that Buchanan "*hates him* [though] perhaps not as much as he does Douglas."[1]

A city of considerable physical charm, Charleston was a dreadful place to host the Democrats' 1860 convention and one that was particularly off-putting to Stephen A. Douglas's northern supporters. One could sail or steam there from Atlantic and Gulf ports, but most delegates and the party faithful who accompanied them had to transfer between at least six different railroad lines to get there. Charleston, moreover, lacked sufficient hotel rooms and beds to accommodate the hordes who descended on it. Innkeepers, restaurateurs, and barkeeps jacked up prices, while pickpockets and faro dealers had a field day fleecing outsiders. Democrats were well aware of the lodging inadequacies and anticipated price gouging weeks before the convention met. In March many made a concerted, but unsuccessful, attempt to get the national committee to switch the convention from Charleston to Baltimore. Cramped quarters and stratospheric prices hardly ended the disadvantages of Charleston for Northerners. The early spring had been unusually cold in Washington and in most of the North, but when woolen-clad Yankees reached Charleston they sweltered in an early heat wave replete with the Low Country's notorious humidity. A sudden cloudburst on the very afternoon the convention opened reduced the torrid temperatures somewhat but did little to reduce delegates' discomfort.

For Northerners determined to nominate Douglas on the Cincinnati platform of 1856, Charleston was as politically forbidding as it was climatically enervating and monetarily depleting. Since the 1820s Charleston had been a hotbed of secessionist sentiment. Its most prominent fire-eaters, who would prod South Carolina into leaving the Union after the election, were contemptuous of the Democratic Party, which they considered an obstacle to, rather than a catalyst for, southern separatism. They had no intention of attending its national convention as delegates or even as spectators. Charleston's residents, who by 1860 had dined on a diet of secessionist rhetoric for years, loathed virtually all things Yankee. "The people of the Southern States constitute, for all practical purposes, the Democratic Party," they had declared at a public meeting in February. Hence, "no constitutional right or principal [*sic*] which they unite in demanding, can be ignored or refused." And the right Southerners should unite behind at the impending national convention was "the constitutional right" of slaveholders "to an equal enjoyment of the Territories" and "the constitutional duty" of the federal government "in all its departments to protect them in that as in all their other rights."[2]

Threats of a rupture at Charleston had mounted outside of Congress as well as in it since the beginning of the year. The Alabama Democrats' January state convention especially alarmed those hoping to preserve party unity. There William Lowndes Yancey, perhaps Dixie's shrewdest and most compelling proponent of secession, had persuaded its members to instruct the state's delegation to Charleston, on which Yancey himself would sit, to bolt the national convention if it refused to adopt a national platform that "in substance" committed the party to the adoption of a federal slave code.[3] In 1848 Yancey had ostentatiously departed the Democrats' convention hall when they nominated Lewis Cass, a well-known proponent of popular sovereignty. Only one other delegate had then accompanied him in protest. Such was the commitment of most Deep South Democrats to a federal slave code in 1860, however, that all knew that if Yancey left this time, far more than a single fellow traveler would join him.

In response to the Alabama convention, the pro-Douglas *New Orleans Bee* warned that if other southern delegations at Charleston joined Alabama in demanding "federal protection of slavery and a Congressional slave code for the Territories," something that "the Democracy of the North will never sanction, . . . a national Democratic nomination will be rendered impractical." The certain rejection of Alabama's platform by "the majority of the Convention" would "be the signal for the withdrawal of most of the Southern delegations." Any nomination the remaining delegates might make would be "sectional." This result would be not simply "lamentable" but "absolutely ruinous." "If the Democratic party breaks to pieces, we can discover no bulwark to the encroachment of [Republican] fanaticism, and therefore no safety to the South."[4]

This frightened prediction was eerily accurate. It also pointed, if only indirectly, to the key rules that governed Democratic national conventions. Each state had a number of votes at Charleston equal to its electoral votes, though most states sent much larger delegations than the floor votes allotted to them. Georgia, for example, had 10 votes but sent a delegation of thirty-seven men. The eighteen free states represented at Charleston had a total of 183 floor votes, or 61 percent of the total, while the fifteen slave states had 118 votes, or 39 percent. Since 1832 Democratic conventions had required a two-thirds majority to select their presidential and vice presidential nominees. Hence, 202 votes would be required in 1860. Even if all the northern delegates supported Douglas—and all of them did not—Southerners had the votes to block his nomination. Yet Douglas's supporters, about half of the total delegate votes, also clearly had the power to stop anyone else. They made clear from the moment the convention opened that they would do so. How long that resolve might hold up was an imponderable. Some Democrats from both North and South believed that Douglas would reluctantly step aside if necessary to preserve the party's national unity.

The national platform the convention would adopt required a different arithmetic and generated far more unity among northern delegates about terms they could accept than did the selection of a nominee. By tradition, each state had one representative on the committee that wrote the platform. Thus, Northerners would outnumber slave state men 18 to 15. Since their admission as states, however, California (1850) and Oregon (1859) had sent pro-southern Democrats to Congress. At Charleston their men would vote to give the slave states a working 17–16 edge on the platform committee. Many Southerners at Charleston openly avowed their aim of making whatever platform the committee wrote so obnoxious to Douglas and his supporters that he would withdraw his candidacy for the nomination rather than run on it. That tactic, in fact, may have been their only hope of getting Douglas delegates to relent their opposition to a nominee other than Douglas. The problem with this tactic was that once the committee adopted a platform, it had to be approved by all the voting delegates. As the *New Orleans Bee* perceived so unerringly in January, whatever they thought of Douglas there was no way that the three-fifths majority of northern delegates would submit to a platform that seemingly pledged the Democratic Party to enactment of a federal slave code. Even a hint of such a pledge was a death warrant for Democrats in the North. Thus, they would more than likely adopt a different platform that embraced the ambiguity of popular sovereignty as Douglas hoped, an ambiguity that most southern Democrats now loathed as a cheat and a fraud since Douglas had seized on it to nullify the proslavery rulings of the *Dred Scott* decision.

To stop Northerners from winning the anticipated platform fight, in March the Virginia Democrats' state convention as well as the state's leading Democratic newspaper, the *Richmond Enquirer,* urged the Charleston gathering to change the rules to require a two-thirds majority for the party's platform as well as its candidate. The *Enquirer* also insisted upon the "extreme importance of deciding once and for all that it is only at statehood that residents of a territory can prohibit slavery."[5] That position was precisely what Douglas's supporters at Charleston were determined to keep out of the party's platform. They were no more receptive to changing the rules for platform votes.

Democratic delegates to Charleston were usually chosen in state conventions where all the delegates picked the at-large state representatives but only the delegates from individual congressional districts selected the men representing those districts. Alternatively, separate congressional district party conventions, not the men at the state convention from those districts, chose the district delegates. The upshot was that not all southern Democrats sent to Charleston opposed Douglas or his desire to retain the Cincinnati platform's ambiguous language and, as noted, not all Northerners were committed to him. Many delegates from northeastern states that the Democrats had little chance of carrying, in fact, cared most about finding a winner who could continue to award them federal patronage plums. If that goal required dumping Douglas and his desired platform, so be it.

As noted in the preceding chapter, Illinois sent rival pro- and anti-Douglas delegations to Charleston. New York's delegation chosen at the Democrats' Syracuse state convention was challenged by one that New York City mayor Fernando Wood had organized. The former was not formally committed to Douglas, but it had endorsed his version of popular sovereignty. The latter unabashedly opposed Douglas. A credentials committee had to decide which delegations to seat, and in both instances it rejected the anti-Douglas men.

Not all intrastate feuds among Democrats occurred in the North. Georgia is an important case in point. In December 1859 a quasi-official state convention at Milledgeville chose a delegation to Charleston that it instructed to support the nomination of Howell Cobb, the Georgian then serving as Buchanan's treasury secretary. It also passed a platform pledging that it would make no concessions to northern Democrats "for the sake of party harmony" but would instead "demand a firm, strict, and unqualified adherence to the doctrines and principles" concerning slavery in the territories "recently declared by the Supreme Court of the United States." Douglas's many supporters among Georgia Democrats blanched at both the Cobb endorsement and a platform plank intentionally hostile to Douglas's position. They successfully demanded that a more fully attended state convention be held in March, which they very narrowly controlled. To the horror of the anti-Douglas Athens *Southern Banner*, the Douglas men rejected the platform plank adopted earlier and sent an uninstructed delegation to Charleston with no platform statement about territorial slavery at all. The *Banner* found this action cowardly, "humiliating," and contrary to "the feelings of the masses of Georgia" and "we believe . . . the feelings of a majority of her delegates to Charleston." That majority were "Cobb men first, for a Southern man next, and anybody else but Douglas last."[6] This contention was probably true, but it is equally true that a minority of the Georgia delegates, like those in some other southern delegations to Charleston, were in the Douglas camp.

By the time the convention opened, anti-Douglas men had failed to unite behind a single challenger. The Virginians Henry Wise and Robert M. T. Hunter, the Kentuckians James Guthrie and John C. Breckinridge, the New Yorker Daniel S. Dickinson, Mississippi's Jefferson Davis, and Cobb, among others, all had fans at the convention. In its first few days, moreover, the convention made crucial decisions that made the contest for the nomination even murkier. To the delight of Douglas's supporters, the rules committee decided that all individual delegates from states whose conventions had not imposed a unit rule on their delegations could vote as they wished, regardless of how the majority of their delegations felt. This ruling meant that the minority of Douglas men in southern and some northern delegations, like Pennsylvania's, could vote for the Little Giant if they had the chance. In a floor vote considered a test of Douglas's strength, an attempt to defeat this rule lost 101 to 198. Four-fifths of the losing aye votes came from slave states. To counter-balance this victory, the Douglas men lost their attempt to make a pro-Douglas Arkansan the convention's permanent chairman. Instead, by a vote of 17 to 11, the committee on permanent organization chose Caleb Cushing of Newburyport, Massachusetts, for the post. Eleven of Cushing's 17 votes came from slave states, including Alabama, and ultimately Cushing's decisions as chair would quash any chance that Douglas could be nominated at Charleston.

Largely forgotten today, Cushing, whose handsome brick home on Newburyport's High Street now houses the local historical society, could not have been more different from Newburyport's other most famous native son, William Lloyd Garrison. A one-time Whig friend and admirer of Daniel Webster, Cushing had followed John Tyler out of the Whig Party in the early 1840s. He served as an officer in the Mexican War, where he met and befriended Franklin Pierce—whose nomination he helped secure in 1852 and in whose cabinet he served as attorney general. In the early 1850s Cushing also headed a conservative minority faction of Massachusetts Democrats who strenuously, if vainly, opposed the majority's coalition with Free Soilers that sent the stridently antislavery Charles Sumner to the U.S. Senate. There were good reasons, in short, why southern delegations at Charleston supported his selection as chairman over a pro-Douglas Arkansan.

On the convention's very first night, a caucus of most of the southern delegations lobbed another shell at the pro-Douglas camp. After it adjourned, a correspondent for the Republican *New York Tribune* telegraphed, the delegations from Alabama, Mississippi, Florida, Arkansas, Texas, and Louisiana "announced emphatically that they will go out of the Convention unless their platform was adopted."[7] The following day, the convention made its most pivotal decision. By a large majority that included both the Douglas men and the Deep South Douglas haters, it voted to adopt the party's new national platform before holding any votes on its nominee.

Why Southerners took this position is easily explained. Their top priority was to force upon the party the Alabama platform, which, as one southern newspaper put it, "negatives Douglasism in all its forms."[8] That platform demanded a congressional slave code for any territories whose residents failed to protect slave property and, in addition, flatly denied that those residents could by any means prohibit slavery before they applied for statehood. They hoped that their threatened bolt would force Northerners to acquiesce to Southerners' demands concerning slavery in order to preserve party unity as they had so often done in the past. That is, these men, including Yancey, did not seek intentionally to split the Democratic Party so that Republicans won the election and fire-eaters could then seize on that victory as a rationale for secession. They instead hoped to bend the national party to their will.

Douglas's northern supporters eagerly welcomed a platform fight to show that southern Democratic senators who had tried to dictate the party's platform in Washington with their February caucus resolutions did not in fact speak for the party's rank and file. They knew—and repeatedly asserted—that the Alabama platform meant political suicide for northern Democrats. But they also knew that they could defeat it on the convention floor, if not in the platform committee itself. Many of them, indeed, welcomed a walk-out of southern delegates if it were confined to the six states that had proudly announced their intention to bolt, because they thought it would make Douglas's nomination easier to achieve. Those six states together controlled 33 votes, slightly more than one-tenth of the total. Their departure would reduce the convention's total to 268, meaning that Douglas would need 180 rather than 202 votes to take the prize. Their gamble here, of course, was that only the delegates from at most those six states would leave if Southerners lost the platform fight. This turned out to be a bad bet.

As soon as this decision was reached, the individual state delegations chose their representatives on the platform committee, if they had not previously done so, and the committee then left the convention hall to undertake deliberations in private. Presumably for strategic reasons, Yancey did not represent Alabama on this committee. Nor did former congressman William A. Richardson, Douglas's floor leader at the convention, represent Illinois. H. B. Payne, Douglas's most determined and intransigent supporter in Ohio, instead provided leadership for Northerners on that committee. The key southern member turned out to be Senator James A. Bayard from Delaware. Delaware barely qualified as a slave state; most of its black residents were already free. But Bayard, like some other U.S. senators who had traveled to Charleston from Washington, was a Buchanan loyalist whose top priority was denying Douglas the nomination. Thus he would draft a platform intended to do just that.

Appointed on Tuesday, April 24, Northerners and Southerners on the platform committee would argue without reaching any consensus until late Thursday night, when they agreed to present not one but three versions of a platform to the convention on the morning of Friday, April 27. All three reendorsed the Cincinnati platform, and the two main alternatives also advocated the construction of a transcontinental railroad to the Pacific Coast, denounced northern states' personal liberty laws that thwarted enforcement of the Fugitive Slave Act, pledged to defend the rights of foreign-born citizens, and urged the annexation of Cuba, long a target of Democratic expansionists. Then they diverged.[9]

Adopted eventually by a vote of 17 to 16, with the California and Oregon representatives joining those from all fifteen slave states against representatives of the remaining northern states, Bayard's majority platform encapsulated the Alabama platform by annexing the following provisions regarding slavery in the territories to the Cincinnati platform: they denied that either Congress or a territorial legislature could abolish slavery in or prohibit slavery from a federal territory. They also denied that territorial legislatures had "any power to destroy or impair the right of property in slaves by any legislation whatsoever." By itself this language flatly repudiated everything Douglas had argued since 1857 and was certain to be opposed by his supporters on the convention floor just as it was in the platform committee. But the slaveholders did not stop there. Another provision insisted "that it is the duty of the federal government to protect, when necessary, the rights of person or property on the high seas, in the territories, and wherever else its constitutional jurisdiction enters." The committee's majority, in short, offered a platform on which Stephen A. Douglas could not possibly run.[10]

When the editors of the Republican *New York Times* saw this platform, indeed, they declared that the South wanted a "distinct declaration" by the entire Democratic Party that "slaves are recognized as property by the Federal Constitution." No Northerner, they exaggerated, could possibly support that position.[11] Stephen A. Douglas certainly could not.

In the platform committee, those same seventeen states defeated the preferred platform of the remaining sixteen northern states. In what the Douglas men considered a major concession to the South, it would annex to the reendorsement of the Cincinnati platform the following language: "That all questions in regard to the rights of property in States or Territories arising under the Constitution of the United States, are judicial in their character; and the Democratic party is pledged to abide by and faithfully carry out such determination of these questions as had been or may be made by the Supreme Court of the United States."[12] Because Douglas had publicly denied that the *Dred Scott* decision had settled this question and argued that no matter what the Supreme Court eventually ruled, territorial residents could still effectively bar slavery by refusing to enact the local laws necessary to protect it, Southerners hardly considered this sop a concession at all.

When Northerners' preferred platform was defeated by that 17–16 vote in the platform committee, Massachusetts committee man Benjamin F. Butler determined to present a platform of his own to the full convention the following morning. It simply reendorsed the Cincinnati platform with no additional language concerning slavery.

Although the platform committee jousted in private sessions, word of their arguments leaked out days before it reported to the full convention. And those leaks provoked dissension in both the New York and Pennsylvania delegations. On a preliminary vote in committee, New York's representative Edwin Crosswell, a longtime Albany newspaper editor, had voted with the California and Oregon men in support of the majority—i.e., the anti-Douglas—platform to give it a majority of 18 to 15. Crosswell had then immediately reversed himself and joined the other northern representatives in support of the minority platform that lost 16–17. According to a reporter for the pro-Democratic *New York Herald*, a caucus of New York's delegates and alternates then voted 48 to 22 against Crosswell's support for the majority platform. So admonished, Crosswell ultimately signed on to the minority platform.[13]

Meanwhile the vote of Pennsylvania's Hendrick Wright for the minority platform infuriated the majority of the Pennsylvania delegation who were Buchanan men and wanted Wright to support the majority platform, which would, in the words of one reporter, "dispose of Douglas." Wright had not been instructed how to vote, but some Buchanan men—including incumbent U.S. senator William Bigler, who headed the Pennsylvania delegation; a congressman; and Philadelphia's customs collector—went to the extent of forging spurious caucus instructions about how Wright should vote on the committee. When Wright refused to accept the bogus instructions or to change his vote, the incensed customs collector, a much younger man, punched him in the mouth while heaping curses upon the venerable former congressman.[14]

The three platforms were not read to the convention until 11 a.m. on

Friday morning. North Carolina's William Avery and Ohio's Payne, respectively, defended the majority and minority platforms. Payne's speech was particularly impassioned. Do not saddle us with more weight, he warned Southerners. As for popular sovereignty, "We will never recede from that doctrine, Sir; *never, never, never,* so help us God."[15] When Payne finished, Ben Butler, who would win notoriety as a Union commander in the subsequent Civil War, immediately pointed out flaws in the other two platforms. Southerners complained that the Cincinnati platform maddeningly invited divergent interpretations; true, he admitted, but all platforms invited divergent interpretations. Indeed, so did the Bible! The majority platform's language about the duty of the federal government to protect slave property on the high seas, for example, could be interpreted as committing it to protect the heinous African slave trade. But the minority platform's commitment to supporting future Supreme Court decisions concerning slavery was equally dangerous, for it pledged southern Democrats to support any slavery decisions a future Republican majority on the Court might make. The other two platforms' endorsement of federal support for construction of a Pacific railroad, he jeered, was meaningless since the Democratic Party had long held federal subsidization of internal improvements to be unconstitutional. Far, far better, he contended, simply to readopt the Cincinnati platform of 1856 that had then won unanimous approval.

Butler's pointed gibes ended the morning session, and the convention recessed until four o'clock so the delegates and spectators could have dinner. The debates following its reconvening occasioned the convention's two most memorable speeches. After an elderly Missouri delegate rousingly lauded Douglas while criticizing the majority platform as guaranteeing the electoral demolition of northern Democrats, Alabama's Yancey took the floor in rebuttal. Everyone knew that Yancey was behind the threats to bolt the convention if the majority platform was rejected, but thus far he had said nothing of consequence within Institute Hall itself. Yancey asked for and got an extra half hour added to the standard hour-long limit for speeches. His was, in the words of an astute northern reporter, "captivating," and it repeatedly drew thunderous applause from Southerners in the spectator gallery. He minced no words, attacking Douglas, blaming northern Democrats' losses on their failure to defend slavery openly, and boasting that southern Democrats were indeed demanding that northern Democrats go further than they ever had in endorsing Southerners' constitutional rights.[16] For Yancey, all knew, that endorsement was the price of Southerners' willingness to remain in the convention.

Yancey was still talking when Ohio's George E. Pugh, an incumbent though lame-duck U.S. senator and staunch Douglas ally, took the platform to respond. Yancey and other Southerners were asking northern Democrats to eat dust, he protested. "Gentlemen of the South," he thundered, "you mistake us—you mistake us—we will not do it." If the only way Southerners would remain in the Democratic Party was for Northerners to submit to their preferred platform, then the Southerners must go—and good riddance. Northerners would no longer bow to "the beck and bidding of the South."[17]

After Pugh's speech the convention descended into pandemonium as scores of men shouted to gain recognition from the chair and angrily shook fists at each other. Cushing finally regained enough control to obtain an adjournment until the following morning. To astute observers like the Cincinnati reporter Murat Halstead, it was apparent that delegates did everything they could to avoid platform votes that would precipitate the expected explosion. Southerners were especially desperate to avoid a final confrontation. The first action of Saturday morning, for example, was to approve a motion from Pennsylvania's Bigler to send all three proposed platforms back to the resolutions committee for reconsideration. On a separate vote, however, the convention resoundingly defeated Bigler's attempt to instruct that committee to report back within an hour with a compromise platform that Bigler himself had written. Instead, it was 4 p.m. when the committee reported on its efforts.

All three proposed platforms were modified, though only slightly. The majority platform now added "the following explanatory resolutions" to its reaffirmation of the Cincinnati platform. The first averred that territorial governments were "provisional and temporary" and that during their existence "all citizens of the United States have an equal right to settle with their property in the Territory without their rights, either of person or property, being destroyed or impaired by Congressional or Territorial legislation." The second dropped all language about high seas and now read: "That it is the duty of the Federal Government, in all its departments, to protect, when necessary, the rights of persons and property in the Territories, and wherever else its constitutional authority extends." The third insisted that residents of a territory became sovereign—i.e., able to make their own laws regarding slavery—only upon its admission to statehood and then it must be admitted with or without slavery as its state constitution provided.[18]

The pro-Douglas minority now modified the language concerning slavery it would annex to the reaffirmation of the Cincinnati platform in a way that directly addressed the party's sectional divide over territorial slavery.

It now read: "Inasmuch as differences of opinion exist in the Democratic party as to the nature and extent of the powers of a Territorial Legislature, and as to the powers and duties of Congress, under the Constitution of the United States, over the institution of slavery within the Territories; Resolved, That the Democratic party will abide by the decisions of the Supreme Court of the United States on the questions of constitutional law."[19]

After these reworded platforms were read, a tedious and inconclusive debate followed until the convention once again adjourned without any action, this time until Monday morning. The Democratic convention, in sum, had sat for six days without producing either a platform or a candidate. Observers noted that the Douglasites wanted to force a vote on the platforms on Saturday night, but Southerners, aware of the momentous step—that is, disrupting the Democratic Party, perhaps permanently—they might be forced to take, successfully warded off any action until Monday morning.

Saturday and Sunday saw a major exodus of northern hangers-on from Charleston. Many were flat broke; some had exhausted the whiskey supplies they had brought with them. Their mass departure meant that rabidly pro-Southern Charlestonians would monopolize the convention hall's spectator seats. On Sunday rumors circulated that at least some southern delegates, including Yancey himself, were reconsidering their vow to secede from the convention should it not adopt the majority platform. Goaded by taunts from Midwesterners that their departure would simply make Douglas's nomination surer, they apparently considered remaining in the hall despite a defeat on the platform so they could assure that Douglas was stopped.

By Monday morning, most, but not all, Deep South delegates had regained their appetite for a showdown. The first substantive vote that morning was on Butler's platform, reendorsement of the Cincinnati platform with no further language about slavery. It showed clearly who wanted to avoid that disrupting confrontation. Adoption of Butler's platform, which was anathema to Deep South Douglas haters like Yancey, was defeated 105–198. The minority who wanted to avert the anticipated explosion included the majority of the Massachusetts delegation, the pro-Buchanan majority of the Pennsylvania delegation, twenty of the twenty-four delegates from Tennessee and Kentucky, the entire North Carolina delegation, four-fifths of the Virginia delegation, and, most strikingly, all 10 of Georgia's votes. In sum, the Deep South states, let alone all slave state delegations, were far from unanimous. Altogether, slave state men cast 47 votes for Butler's attempted compromise and 50 votes against it.[20]

Now came the dreaded up-or-down vote to substitute the pro-Douglas minority platform for the anti-Douglas majority platform. That motion carried 165–138, with 105 of 112 slave state votes in the defeated minority along with majorities of those from Pennsylvania and Michigan and 6 of the 13 votes Massachusetts cast. The other free states, save for Oregon, California, and New Jersey, were solidly in the majority. The old majority platform had been replaced, but the replacement required another vote to win formal adoption from the delegates. Butler moved successfully to vote on each plank separately, beginning with the opening reendorsement of the Cincinnati platform, which an angry Mississippi delegate denounced as "a miserable swindle." This carried 237 to 65, with all but 3 of the negative votes coming from slave-state delegates. An attempt to lay the remaining planks on the table without a vote lost, and then Deep South states began to withhold their votes as the other planks were first adopted and then defeated as Northerners switched their aye votes to nays in an attempt to conciliate Southerners. In the end, indeed, only the plank reendorsing the Cincinnati platform was formally adopted. After an insulting anti-southern speech from a Michigan delegate, the chairman of the Alabama delegation, LeRoy Pope Walker, read a carefully drafted protest against the convention's proceedings and announced that the Alabamians were withdrawing from it. Mississippi, Louisiana, South Carolina, Florida, Texas, and Arkansas followed them out of the hall in that order. So did Delaware's Bayard, author of the original anti-Douglas majority platform. They could never, declared Louisiana's chairman, accept a platform capable of "a double construction."[21] The reporter Halstead described the speech of a Mississippian justifying their departure as "one of the most impassioned and thrilling" he had ever heard. The Mississippian climbed on a chair, turned around, and directly addressed the Ohio delegation seated behind him. "We say go your way and we will go ours," he declared. "The South leaves not like Hagar in the wilderness." Rather "in less than sixty days they [the Ohioans] would find a united South, standing shoulder to shoulder."[22]

Notably, Georgia did not join the other Deep South states in their walkout even though Senator Robert Toombs had telegraphed the delegates from Washington to do so. Instead, they announced they would determine what to do at a caucus. The following morning twenty-six of Georgia's thirty-seven delegates joined the other southern bolters. With the exception of Delaware's Bayard and the Arkansas men, delegates from the Upper South and border states, the most heavily populated slave states with the most electoral votes, remained in the convention.

The following day, Tuesday, May 1, with the bolters absent, a Tennessee delegate introduced a supposed compromise platform that might lure southern bolters back to Institute Hall. Actually written by New Yorkers who had huddled with the Tennessee and Kentucky delegations the preceding night, this platform declared that according to the Supreme Court's "correct exposition of the Constitution" citizens' property rights in the territories could not "be destroyed or impaired by Congressional or Territorial legislation." Known thereafter as the Tennessee platform, this motion, which dropped all references to a contingent federal slave code, was never adopted by the convention. Far more important, in fact, was the same Tennessean's motion that nomination by those who remained in Institute Hall would require a two-thirds majority of the original 301 floor votes, not just two-thirds of the number of the remaining delegates who could vote. This motion, too, was primarily the work of New Yorkers, who hoped to stop Douglas and find some compromise candidate the dissident Southerners could back. A Virginian then warned that his state's delegation would join the bolters unless Cushing ruled that the motion was in order—that is, that it would require a minimum of 202 votes to win the nomination. Cushing so ruled, virtually making Douglas's nomination at Charleston an arithmetical impossibility. Illinois' William Richardson, Douglas's floor manager, tried to resurrect his chances by moving to table the Tennessean's motion. That move lost 111 to 141. Massachusetts and Pennsylvania together supplied 25 of the negative votes, and Oregon and California 7, but it was the solid 35 votes in the nay column from New York that killed Douglas's chances. Only 7 votes from the remaining slave states supported the failed motion to table while 61 Southerners opposed it. The vote formally adopting the Tennessean's motion was identical. Cushing's rulings and New Yorkers' hopes of finding a different candidate who could bring the Deep South men back into the party doomed Douglas to defeat.

Subsequent votes on the nomination proved fruitless. On the first ballot Douglas garnered 145 votes, far shy of the necessary total. Virginia's R. M. T. Hunter ran second with 42, Kentucky's James Guthrie third with 35, and the rest scattered. Altogether 57 ballots were held, with Douglas peaking at 152 votes, a majority of the original convention but still far from the mandatory two-thirds, and with Kentucky's Guthrie ultimately emerging as his strongest challenger. Strikingly, New York's Democrats, having assured that Douglas could not win at Charleston, unanimously supported him on many of those ballots.

One other incident of note occurred during the fruitless balloting. On the thirty-sixth roll call, the lone Arkansas delegate remaining in the convention cast his vote for Vice President Breckinridge, the first time his name was publicly mentioned in Institute Hall. A Kentuckian immediately stressed that Breckinridge did not want his name entered into the competition for the nomination, and the Arkansan changed his vote in compliance with Breckinridge's wishes. The next time Breckinridge's name arose at a Democratic gathering, delegates would ignore his reluctance to be a candidate.

By the convention's ninth day, it was clear that no one could get the necessary 202 votes. As a result, on the tenth day, Thursday, May 3, the convention voted to recess until June 18 when it would reconvene in Baltimore. The same motion advised "the Democratic party of the several States to make provision for supplying all vacancies in their respective delegations to this Convention when it shall reassemble."[23] This apparent call to Democrats in states whose delegates had bolted to send different men to Baltimore was a ticking time bomb.

The decision to recess the national convention until June 18 gobsmacked the southern bolters, most of whom had hoped to rejoin the convention after it nominated someone other than Douglas. They had dubbed themselves the Constitutional Democratic Convention, met in a series of halls, and chosen the respected Delaware senator Bayard as their chairman. The numbers attending their meetings varied, but the great majority hailed from the seven Deep South states—South Carolina, Georgia, Florida, Alabama, Mississippi, Louisiana, and Texas. They unanimously adopted the majority platform reported to the national convention as their statement of principles. Despite the wishes of a few hotheads, however, they did not nominate a presidential ticket of their own. Bayard, the Buchanan operative who had joined the bolters to prevent rash actions, strongly opposed any nomination. Yancey also advised against that step, for, he argued, it would make them seem disunionists when their real goal was to unify the Democratic Party around candidates and a platform to their liking. Instead, they invited all Democrats who endorsed the majority platform that the Douglasites had replaced to send delegates to a new convention in Richmond, Virginia, on June 11, a week before the recessed national convention met in Baltimore. Even so, some of the bolters made clear even then that they would do whatever was necessary to prevent new, presumably pro-Douglas delegates, from representing their states in Baltimore. Thus it was left unclear whether these anti-Douglas, anti–popular sovereignty Southerners would travel to Richmond or Baltimore or both. Those decisions would occasion considerable dispute in the coming weeks.

Douglas had followed these proceedings from Washington, where Congress remained officially in session and where a stream of telegrams kept him informed. He was surprised by the Deep South bolt and appalled by the depth of those delegates' hatred for him. But he knew that he had supporters in most of the bolting states and remained confident he could carry them if he got the nomination in Baltimore. Thus he refused to withdraw his candidacy or to accept any weakening of the party's 1856 commitment to popular sovereignty.

Republicans reacted to the Charleston stalemate in different ways. Newspapers such as the *Milwaukee Sentinel* gloated that Democrats' disruption at Charleston assured Democratic defeat in 1860 while the platform Southerners had supported "fulfils all the Republican predictions, and abundantly justifies the organization and action of the Republican Party."[24] Others expressed disappointment about the results there. Republicans had rescheduled their own national convention for May 16 in Chicago on the assumption that Democrats would have adopted both their candidate and their platform before they met. Most continued to expect that Douglas would be the Democrats' nominee, but they had hoped that he would be saddled with a federal slave code platform Republicans could eviscerate. The *New York Times* thus considered the defeat of that platform at Charleston a Republican setback. The Deep South bolt, it concluded, would make Douglas a stronger candidate in the North than he would have been with southern support, especially as his supporters had defeated Southerners' favored platform. "Thus far the action at Charleston is not calculated to encourage overweening confidence on the part of the Republicans," it warned. "They will not get the square fight on principle for which they were hoping, and which earlier action of the convention encouraged them to expect. They will have to contend with a dodging foe."[25]

The Democrats' failure to nominate Douglas before the Republicans' own convention met in Chicago on May 16 especially disappointed one group of Republicans. These were friends of Abraham Lincoln, the Illinois Republican leader. As noted earlier, his debates with Douglas in 1858, which had been published in pamphlet form by 1860; his speeches for Republican candidates in Indiana and Ohio in 1859; and the smashing success of his speech in New York City's Cooper Union in February 1860 had catapulted him into the first rank of Midwestern Republican leaders. Thus his name was widely bruited in party circles as a good choice for the vice presidential slot on the Republican ticket. By the spring of 1860, however, his most devoted Midwestern friends thought he deserved the top spot on that ticket. Minnesota Republicans, as one wrote Lincoln on April 24, thought that to win in the fall the Republican ticket should be "Lincoln and some good republican instead of Some good Republican and Lincoln."[26] These friends had hoped that Douglas's nomination at Charleston would alert Republican delegates at Chicago to the likelihood that Republicans would lose the absolutely crucial electoral votes of Illinois and Indiana unless Republicans nominated a candidate who could compete with Douglas on that Midwestern turf. And who better to do so than Lincoln, who had gone toe to toe with Douglas in 1858? Thus, they feared that the indecisive outcome at Charleston might jeopardize Lincoln's long-shot chance of grasping the Republican nomination.

Before Lincoln's backers learned what would happen to Lincoln's fortunes in Chicago, however, another contender entered the presidential sweepstakes who might complicate both Democrats' and Republicans' prospects. That was the ex-Whig John Bell of Tennessee, the nominee of a newly formed Constitutional Union Party, who might potentially keep Millard Fillmore's over 800,000 1856 supporters out of both the Republican and the Democratic columns. For Republicans that threat was especially dire.

4 THE THIRD WAY

Democrats' internal quarrels in early 1860 did nothing to remove the biggest obstacle between Republicans and winning the White House in November. With no chance of carrying any slave state, victory depended on sweeping almost the entire North. To do that, they had to win over conservative ex-Whigs in Illinois, Indiana, and, above all, Pennsylvania with its 27 electoral votes who, fearing that a Republican triumph would trigger southern secession, had supported Millard Fillmore in 1856. Castigating the corruption of Buchanan's administration appealed to such men. If anything, conservative Whigs loathed Democratic malfeasance more intensely than did Republicans themselves. The real problem, however, was how to counteract or dissipate conservatives' fears raised in early 1860 by southern Democrats' cascading threats to dismember the Union rather than allow the inauguration of a Republican president.

To lure Fillmore voters, different Republicans dealt with secessionist threats in different ways. Some—Henry J. Raymond, owner and editor of the *New York Times*, is a prime example—stressed the unionist commitments and lack of anti-southern animus in the Republican Party. They also disassociated the party from abolitionists, whom Raymond called the real instigators of sectional animosity, and called on Republican majorities in northern state legislatures to repeal the personal liberty laws that Southerners found so offensive. In the service of this effort Raymond often used the columns of his paper to denounce other Republican editors, such as Horace Greeley, whom he accused of pushing the Republican Party toward abolitionism.[1]

Rather than soft-soaping their party's anti-southern slant

to reassure conservative Whigs, other Republicans dismissed secessionist threats as empty bluster meant solely to scare Northerners away from voting Republican in November. Thus, one plank of Rhode Island Republicans' state platform declared "that we regard the threat of resisting the inauguration of a Republican President, as an empty threat to subserve the interest of political parties, by deterring the people from exercising freely their constitutional rights."[2] "This is the merest rant," chorused the Republican *Pittsburgh Gazette*, which circulated widely in western Pennsylvania and Ohio. "It is an insulting demand from the minority to the majority to disband and give up their cherished views and purposes. The demand will not be complied with." Editor Russell Errett, a key player in Pennsylvania's People's Party, declared that the North must "assert its independence of Southern influence in defiance of South Carolina cockades and the idle threats of secession which are sent up to us from the cotton plantations."[3]

Errett for one would not relent on his insistence that the minority South must knuckle under to the majority North. The central question "to be settled by the approaching Presidential election is, Shall the majority rule?" he editorialized four days before men went to the polls in November. If Southerners threatening secession "are to be taken at their word and permitted to do as they threaten, the majority does not and cannot rule. . . . Will then the northern majority submit to the dictates of the southern oligarchy—a pitiful minority which has insinuated itself into the control of the government?" Northerners must elect a Republican president, he insisted, "just to show that they *will* rule, in spite of incipient traitors."[4]

Rather than challenge fearful northern conservatives to assert their manhood and defy secessionist bombast, still another Republican tack was to deny that Democratic fire-eaters in fact represented majority opinion in Dixie. The same Rhode Island Republican platform cited above, for example, declared "that we look with indignation upon the persistent misrepresentation of public opinion in the South, as increasing the sectional character of the Democratic party, and weakening the bonds of Union."[5] More important, because of its source, was the reaction of Thurlow Weed's *Albany Evening Journal* to the resolutions of the Baltimore Opposition Party in early January, some of which are quoted at the start of Chapter 2. Weed was the longtime ally—many said the alter ego—of New York senator William H. Seward, the acknowledged frontrunner for the Republican presidential nomination at the start of 1860. His editorial response to the Baltimore meeting clearly attempted to allay conservatives' fears about a Seward candidacy.

That the Baltimore Opposition meeting in January welcomed the call for a Republican national convention, Weed began, "is a significant and gratifying indication" of public opinion in the slave states. "Those who accept the ranting of Disunion Congressmen, and the Democratic press as the true and authorized expression of Southern sentiment egregiously deceive themselves." A "strong conservative sentiment" existed "throughout the Southern States," and, he averred in a flight of fancy, the Republican call "expresses the convictions of a large and daily increasing portion of those in the South." Hence, "the course taken by the Democratic Party is precisely that which is calculated to show Southern men that they can look only to the Republican Party for conservative doctrines and safe constitutional action."[6]

The savvy Weed had been one of the shrewdest political operatives in the nation for over three decades when he wrote these words. He simply could not have believed that anti-Democratic Southerners would vote Republican in the 1860 election, if only because no organization that could distribute Republican ballots existed in any slave state south of the border states. His targeted audience had to have been Northerners who had supported Fillmore in 1856. Even as he wrote this editorial, however, former leaders of the American Party were urging the creation of yet another new conservative pro-Union party that would challenge both Republicans and Democrats for support in 1860.

Since the summer of 1850 periods of acute sectional tension over slavery had evoked efforts to form bipartisan Union parties that stressed intersectional comity rather than partisan exploitation of sectional animosities. In 1850 and 1851 such Union parties won sweeping victories in Georgia, Alabama, and Mississippi, and in the latter year forty-four members of Congress, both Whigs and Democrats, signed a round-robin letter pledging to support no candidate for any political office, including the presidency, who did not accept the Compromise of 1850 as absolutely the final settlement of all disputes over slavery. In the mid-1850s Millard Fillmore's closest Whig allies tried to convert the anti-immigrant, anti-Catholic Know Nothing American Party into an organization that stressed the danger to the Union posed by Republicans and southern Democrats. And starting in the summer of 1859, affiliates of the American Party who had supported Fillmore in 1856 once again urged the creation of a new nationwide pro-Union party. Their hope, as Maryland's Know Nothing U.S. senator Anthony Kennedy put it in June 1859, was "to exclude if possible the slavery question from our union organization."[7] In mid-December 1859, a meeting of Americans in New York City nominated an Independent Union ticket of Winfield Scott for president and the Texan Sam Houston for vice president, and in January 1860 American Party members in Tennessee's legislature nominated former senator John Bell as a Union candidate for president. No national Union party yet existed when these nominations were made, but by January one was in the works. As one enthusiast for a new party put it that month, the thousands who were "indignant at the shams and follies and alarmed at the recklessness of the Democratic and Republican parties" were "anxiously looking for a safe harbor wherein to carry the anchor of their country's hopes."[8]

Kentucky's elderly John J. Crittenden, around whom conservative former Whigs had hoped to build a bisectional, non-Republican anti-Democratic party in 1858, took the lead in organizing the new Union party. He had told the New York meeting that nominated Scott that he himself would accept no nomination because he was in his seventy-third year. But he considered organizing a unionist alternative to the Republicans and Democrats absolutely essential to avert disaster. Thus he called together all the Opposition members of Congress in December 1859 to formulate plans for starting the new party. They urged him to contact the national chairmen of the nearly defunct Whig and American parties for help. The latter appointed Crittenden as chairman of a ten-member American Party committee that would try to recruit supporters for the new party around the nation. They approached a few Democrats, like Tennessee's Andrew Jackson Donelson—Fillmore's running mate in 1856—and former senator Jeremiah Clemens, who had been a critical player in Alabama's Union party movement of 1851 and a signer of the round-robin letter. Clemens also had a young cousin in Missouri later famous as Mark Twain. Nonetheless, the overwhelming majority of the men they contacted were one-time Whigs who had supported Fillmore in 1856. Unlike previous editions of the Union party movement, in short, this one made little pretense of bipartisanship.

Crittenden called on his Whig correspondents to recruit men to local and state Union organizations. Meanwhile he would line up a national executive committee of prominent men and arrange to have a public address that justified a new party prepared. Returns to Crittenden's plea began to arrive in early January, and, with a few notable exceptions, they expressed enthusiasm about launching what Crittenden had called the "National Union Party." A respondent from Delaware, for example, worried that both the Democratic and Republican parties had "become entirely sectional." Hence, Americans needed a party "in opposition to the ultra fire-eating disunion democracy upon the one hand and the Republican fanatics upon the other." Would any Democrats support it?, he asked. And what about Whigs who had "taken shelter" under the Democrats in 1856 because they so feared a Republican victory? "Can you not, in Heaven's name," he concluded, "devise something in the way of a strong and popular organization which will advance the country's deliverance from the corruption, the perils and the thralldom of Locofoco misrule?"[9]

This letter highlights three themes that characterized the third party's appeal to the electorate for the remainder of the year. First, *sectional* was the dirty word of the 1860 campaign. Conservatives aimed it at both of the existing major parties. Feuding Democrats hung that label on each other. And all non-Republicans with some justice tarred Republicans with the slur. Second, the new party always presented itself as in the middle of and an alternative to both dangerous northern Republicans and fire-eating southern Democrats. Third, this "conservative party," as the writer called it, harped on the corruption and dishonesty of Democrats and continually cited them as reasons why Democrats must be ousted from office. As Tennessee's Donelson put it in a speech welcoming a new Union party, Democrats had instilled "corruption, imbecility, and unfaithfulness in the Executive Department" of the national government.[10]

The *Southern Recorder*, an Opposition paper published in Milledgeville, Georgia's state capital, was hardly the only paper to denounce Democratic sleaze, but it did so in especially memorable language. Democrats were a "miserable, rotten, and corrupt party . . . in the throes of dissolution, which we hope will be eternal," the paper railed in May after the breakup of the Charleston convention. "The Augean stable of Democracy needs a thorough cleaning out. . . . The corruption that has crept into the Democratic party since it has been in power . . . is sufficient instigation for the conservative elements of the country to come together, and by a united action to remedy the evil spoken of." People, it continued in July, "see that turning out one Democrat to put in another, does not remedy the evil complained of. There must be a complete, full, and thorough revolution, if corruption and fraud are to be checked; new men must be put in place of those now in office."[11] Buchanan's corruption alone, asserted a speaker at a March Union party rally, was "of itself . . . a sufficient reason why the Democrats should no longer be permitted to remain in power."[12]

James Gordon Bennett of the *New York Herald*, who saw preventing a Republican triumph as the top priority in 1860, admitted that the Unionists were absolutely correct about the corruption polluting Buchanan's administration. But they could never stop a Republican victory by themselves. Instead they must postpone a campaign against Democratic rottenness until a later time. Now conservative Whigs who might be attracted to a new Union party must combine with Democrats against "the revolutionary legions of black republicanism."[13]

For the unionist Whigs targeted by Crittenden and others, however, the "perils of Locofoco misrule" went beyond corruption and militated against any common anti-Republican front with Democrats. For, as one conservative unionist speaker and editor after another declared, Democrats, especially with the Kansas-Nebraska Act and the Lecompton constitution, had caused the birth and nourished the growth of the frighteningly dangerous Republican Party. Only their new third party could be trusted to save the Union. As a Baltimore Opposition paper put it, the Democratic Party could never be relied on to defeat Republicans because "the black Republican party owes its very existence and every stage of its growth to the unwisdom of that very organization."[14] "By repeal of the Missouri Compromise and the attempt to force upon the people of Kansas a constitution which they did not approve," echoed the *Nashville Southern Banner*, Democrats "built up a sectional party in the North, with opposition to slavery extension as the leading article of its creed. . . . This is what the Democratic party, with its slavery agitation hobby, has done for the South and the country." All "who are for renouncing this sectional controversy, in which neither party has a practical issue at stake, will act with the party which declares itself in favor of a cessation of the slavery discussion, for the Union, the Constitution, and the Enforcement of the Laws."[15]

A few of Crittenden's respondents, such as Boston's Amos A. Lawrence, state chairman of the "National Americans" in Massachusetts who had not yet fused with Republicans, and Louisiana's Charles M. Conrad, a member of Fillmore's cabinet along with Crittenden, expressed enthusiasm for the third-party effort. But they also warned that it would have only the remotest chance of carrying their states against Republicans in the former and Democrats in the latter. Others offered advice about where a national convention should be held in order to maximize support for the new party. Harrisburg, Philadelphia, Washington, and Baltimore were all suggested. Still others hyped potential presidential candidates. The early response that most influenced Crittenden, however, came from Virginia's William C. Rives, former U.S. senator from the Old Dominion and twice the American minister to France. Crittenden's initial circular—some called it a "flier"—spoke of organizing a new "*National* Union Party." Rives warned that "the word national in the southern mind has unfortunately come to be very much confounded with *consolidated*." Hence he urged that "National" be replaced by "Constitutional." "Let the new party receive its baptism under the name of the Constitutional Union Party."[16] And so it would be.

Only three of Crittenden's initial respondents doubted the wisdom of launching a third-party campaign, though for different reasons. An Indianan warned him on February 2 that anti-Democrats in his state would go Republican if they thought a vote for "a third ticket" candidate would help Democrats carry the Hoosier State as Fillmore's candidacy had in 1856.[17] Deeply opposed to the Republicans, New Jersey's Joseph A. Randolph, a Fillmore stalwart in 1856, could "not see very clearly how a third party will relieve us or succeed; we tried it in 1856 & N.J. was then the breakwater which saved us & will probably be so again with or without a third party." Republicans at Chicago, he was convinced, could "nominate no Republican who can obtain her vote."[18] "There are most powerful reasons opposed to the nomination of a third candidate by our friends," Hiram Ketchum, long a Whig activist and fund-raiser in New York City, told Crittenden in early May. A third-party nomination would assure that Republicans nominated the dreaded Seward since they would lose all incentive to court northern conservatives' votes. "Besides," he added, he had spent so much effort in 1856 raising money for the fruitless Fillmore campaign that he had not the "courage" to "look some men in the face today whom I persuaded to give large sums of money for the support of Fillmore."[19]

Some Opposition newspapers in the South also had doubts about a third-party effort. "We see no cheering prospect of the successful formation of a new party at the present time," opined the *Savannah Republican* in early February. Nonetheless, "could such a thing be done, on a footing that shall guarantee the rights of every section and put down disunion agitation at the South and anti-slavery agitation at the north," every true patriot in the nation would support it.[20] An Augusta, Georgia, Opposition sheet was more dubious still: "We do not favor a Union party, organized upon generalities and with the simple battle-cry of the Constitution and the Laws." The paper called for specifics, for "we want nobody deceived, and nobody cheated." Among the specifics it demanded were a commitment to uphold the Fugitive Slave Law, repeal of northern personal liberty laws, unqualified acceptance of the *Dred Scott* decision, and a forceful renunciation of Stephen Douglas's version of popular sovereignty. "We shall join in no cry for the Union, for the sake of Union only, nor for the sake of party ascendancy."[21]

In contrast to these equivocations, some former Whig allies of Crittenden worried primarily about the delay in organizing the third party and getting its candidate in the field in order to prevent their fellow Whigs from joining the Democrats as the best way to resist the Republican tide. On January 22 Virginia's Alexander H. H. Stuart, yet another fellow member of Fillmore's cabinet in the early 1850s, wrote from Richmond that getting the address Crittenden had promised out as soon as possible was "a matter of the highest importance." Conservatives needed a "tangible rallying point." If the address were delayed until late February, "it might as well not come out at all." The real "Union men, in the South, are fast falling into the democratic ranks, merely because they have nowhere else to go." Unless the address was out soon, "we will not have a corporal's guard left. All are disheartened by the delay already." Even as he wrote this letter, Stuart added, South Carolina's Christopher Memminger was in Richmond to persuade the Virginia legislature to commit to secession should a Republican win the 1860 election. "For God's sake give us a rallying point or disunion may follow."[22]

Crittenden's long-time Kentucky friend Robert P. Letcher was not quite so dire when he wrote from Frankfort on March 1. If the Union party for some reason failed to run a third candidate, he warned, "our party will be absorbed by the Democratic party in this State. A good many are inclined to Douglas at any rate."[23] Kentucky's Democratic state convention had in fact listed Douglas as one of its two preferences for the Democrats' presidential nomination, along with native son James Guthrie, who had been secretary of the treasury in Franklin Pierce's administration. There was a good reason why Kentucky Americans might be inclined to support Douglas. In 1858 their hero Crittenden had publicly aligned with him against the Lecompton constitution. Indeed, in that year he had written letters to Illinois Whigs urging them to secure Douglas's reelection to the Senate rather than give the seat to Republican Abraham Lincoln. As a result, the talk of forming a new non-Republican anti-Buchanan party behind Crittenden had always included Douglas and like-minded northern Democrats among its potential supporters.

When Letcher wrote on March 1, the promised "Address of the National Executive Committee of the Constitutional Union Party" had already been published on February 22, weeks after Alexander H. H. Stuart had hoped to see it. Crittenden had met considerable frustration in getting it out. He had first asked New York Know Nothing newspaper editor Erastus Brooks to draft the address but then rejected what Brooks produced. Next he approached Baltimore's renowned novelist John Pendleton Kennedy, yet another fellow veteran of Fillmore's cabinet, to write it. Illness delayed Kennedy, and then Crittenden thought his product required revision. Issued under the aegis of the national chairmen of the Whig and American parties, respectively, Francis Granger and Jacob Broome, the address listed twenty-seven well-known Whigs along with Jere Clemens as the executive committee,[24] very few of whom, Crittenden's incoming correspondence makes clear, could possibly have seen it before it was issued. It included men from only twenty-three of the nation's thirty-three states.

People everywhere, the address began, feared "some disastrous crisis."[25] It loomed because Democratic and Republican politicians had tried to "force the country into an organization of parties founded on the question of slavery." Both had deployed sectional agitation of the slavery issue "for the promotion of party purposes" at the expense of "the public welfare." Thus it was "indisputable" that conflict between the existing parties had produced "the present lamentable state of public affairs." Those combatants were "now preparing for a sectional struggle far exceeding in violence any that has yet occurred, the results of which may be disastrous for the country." The violence alluded to, as Crittenden's subsequent campaign speeches made clear, was not physical, let alone armed. Rather, it was the rancorously insulting language northern Republicans and southern Democrats hurled at each other. "Two great political armies are contending for mastery. Both are infuriated with a rage that threatens fearful extremes."

In this situation, the address continued, a number of current and former members of Congress had met in Washington and agreed "that immediate steps should be taken to organize a 'Constitutional Union party' pledged to support 'the Union, the Constitution, and the enforcement of the laws.'" They fully understood how difficult it was to launch a new party at the beginning of a presidential campaign when old party attachments were "heightened by the ardor of expected victory or inflamed by zeal of opposition." By their estimate, however, almost a million men, most of them former Whigs, were prepared to sit out the election rather than vote for either odious existing party but would support a new, nonsectional conservative alternative. Even other ex-Whigs who had joined the Democrats or Republicans after the Whig Party's disintegration in the mid-1850s "will, it is believed, be prompt to join their old comrades in rallying to a conservative field to fight a new battle for the cause of the Constitution and the restoration of lost harmony."

The only way to rescue the country from the calamitous sectional warfare agitated by Republicans and Democrats, it concluded, was "to organize a party whose cardinal principle shall be: To remove the subject of slavery from the arena of party politics and leave it to the independent control of the States in which it exists, and to the unbiased action of the judiciary," to repeal all northern personal liberty laws frustrating the rendition of fugitive slaves, and to "cultivate and expand the resources of the country by such protection to every useful pursuit and interest as is compatible with the general welfare and equitable to all." If the call for a crusade to save the Union was not enough to entice northern Whigs, in short, then an endorsement of protective tariffs might be. The executive committee of Pennsylvania's Constitutional Union Party, indeed, demanded a plank touting tariff protection in whatever national platform the new party adopted.

The address ended by calling on conservative unionists to arrange for state conventions that would choose delegates to a national Constitutional Union Party convention to be held in Baltimore. Those state conventions should also name the two men they thought most deserving of the new party's presidential nomination. The delegates in Baltimore would then choose the man from a list of those so recommended. Notably, the address explicitly instructed the state conventions not to suggest a vice presidential candidate. The national convention would name that individual. Even more notably, the address did not specify a date on which this proposed convention would be held. It instead promised that the executive committee would announce the date later.

Precisely a month later, on March 21, in fact, the committee named May 9 as the day that the national convention would open in Baltimore. That date was hardly a coincidence. It fell between April 23, when the Democrats' national convention would assemble in Charleston, and May 16, when the Republicans' national convention had been rescheduled to meet in Chicago.

In many states the organizational efforts went smoothly. The proposed party "has already enlisted every man of the Opposition" in North Carolina, William A. Graham, yet another former Whig cabinet colleague, informed Crittenden on February 27. Six days later John P. Kennedy exulted from Baltimore, "The Union party throughout the country seems to be so widely aroused to . . . the necessity of the movement that argument is scarcely needed either to confirm personal opinion or stimulate action."[26]

The resolutions adopted by Union state conventions and public letters from some men on the national executive committee also fleshed out the purpose of the new party in the weeks before the Baltimore convention met. Above all else, they emphasized its intention to bury the slavery issue. In a widely reprinted public letter, for example, Jere Clemens declared, "One of the main objects of the Union organization is to get rid of slavery as a political question—to bring back the times when parties were divided upon banks, tariffs, internal improvements, foreign relations, and other legitimate subjects." Territorial slavery extension, he added, was "at present a mere abstraction" since "we have no Territory into which slavery can go." Southern Democrats' insistence upon injecting the extension issue "into the politics of the nation has been fruitful of nothing but evil," dividing "the nation into two great sectional parties" and exciting "jealousy, distrust and ill feeling to an extent which threatens civil war . . . without one single compensating advantage to the South as a section." Nor was Stephen Douglas's interpretation of popular sovereignty any better than the southern Democrats' demand for a federal slave code. Every single member of the Constitution Union Party's national executive committee, Clemens maintained, was appalled at the idea of allowing "a majority" of settlers in a territory to determine whether slavery could exist there.[27]

Meeting in late March, the state convention of the party in Massachusetts also insisted that the party intended "to put an end to the useless, and worse than useless, agitation" over slavery extension. There was no live issue confronting the nation that justified the existence of the "sectional" Republican Party. There "are no Territories where the question of slave labor or free labor is not already effectually settled." All efforts by political leaders "to excite the people of different sections against each other on this issue are misdirected and mischievous." It was far more important, this Bay State convention added, to provide tariff protection for American industry and to "expose the corruption" of the Democratic national administration and the Republican state administration.[28]

Names of possible nominees also sprouted up: Crittenden, despite his public declination; Bell; Edward Everett; John Minor Botts of Richmond, Virginia; Ohio's John McLean, an associate justice on the Supreme Court; Missouri's Edward Bates; and North Carolina's Graham, a member of the national executive committee for the new party and Winfield Scott's running mate on the 1852 Whig national ticket. By far the most intriguing suggestion, however, was Texas governor Sam Houston, a lifelong Jacksonian Democratic nationalist who was at well-publicized and increasingly bitter loggerheads with his state's Democratic fire-eaters. His proponents maintained that he could attract so many traditionally Democratic nonslaveholders in the South that, combined with Whig unionists, he could sweep every slave state.

Instead, developments in Dixie prior to the May convention portended anything but smooth sailing for the new party in Baltimore. Constitutional Union Party state conventions in Georgia, Alabama, and even Tennessee and Kentucky adopted platforms that echoed southern Democrats' case that the *Dred Scott* decision established that the U.S. Constitution recognized property rights in slaves and that the federal government had an obligation to protect those property rights in territories. "The Opposition in both Tennessee and Kentucky have gone quite as far in demanding Federal protection for Slave property in the Territories as the Democrats," carped the *New York Times*.[29] In the widely reprinted public letter cited above, Jere Clemens also insisted that Congress had a duty to protect slaveholders' property rights in territories but that the duty was meaningless since there were no further territories into which slaveholders had any intention of moving. These positions were anathema to Whig Unionists from the North. That was why the address issued on February 22 had spoken of taking the slavery issue out of politics and leaving it to the states and to "the unbiased action of the judiciary," a transparent slap at the proslavery decision of seven Democratic justices in the *Dred Scott* case. If forced into any platform coming out of the Baltimore convention, those southern planks were almost certain to deter northern Whigs from supporting the new party or, even worse, drive them into the arms of the Republicans in order to defy southern demands and defeat the hated Democrats.

The national leaders of the Constitutional Union Party fully understood that no matter how well it might run in the South, averting disunion primarily required stopping a Republican victory. They must either prevent Republicans from winning an electoral-vote majority in the North or somehow defuse the threat that Southerners saw in the Republican Party. That was why scheduling the national convention a week before Republicans met was so strategically important. "The third party movement at the North evidently aims at controlling the Republican nomination," charged the *New York Times* a week after the date of the Baltimore convention was announced.[30] When the organizing state convention of Maryland's Constitutional Union Party met in mid-April, the *Times* correspondent in Baltimore reported that the party's primary newspaper organ evinced the same goal. The third party's "leading doctrine," it asserted, "is that Republicanism must yield to the great opposition Union movement, or fight single-handed and alone, and either suffer defeat, or, through the actions of a third party, have the Presidential election thrown finally into the House for adjustment."[31]

From the beginning of the year, in fact, northern proponents of the new party had suggested ways it could shape what Republicans did at their Chicago convention. An Indianan wrote Crittenden on February 2 that Unionists should preempt Republicans by nominating "an unexceptionable ticket" that Republicans at Chicago would have to adopt "or accept defeat as in 1856. They will see this and I hope take a good national ticket rather than refuse to cooperate with us and thereby perpetuate the reign of Locofocoism."[32]

The best thing the Constitutional Union Party could do in Baltimore, a New Yorker told Crittenden in early April, was to nominate John McLean. Then "let him withhold his acceptance or refusal until after the Chicago nomination. The Republicans will be afraid to refuse him. They will fear even for Ohio and will feel certain of his getting the whole of Fillmore's vote in Penn & N. Jer., which is equivalent to the certain election of a Dem."[33] That same month a Washington correspondent of the *New York Times* speculated that it was "not improbable" that the Republicans in Chicago would accept McLean if the Constitutional Union Party first nominated him.[34] Missouri's Constitutional Union state convention suggested yet another way to influence the Republican ticket. They urged the nomination of Edward Bates, an old Whig from their state who was already being touted by some Republicans, including Horace Greeley, as the best man Republicans could choose as their candidate. What none of this fantasizing about candidates and what one visionary termed "a grand movement against the common [Democratic] enemy" mentioned was the near certainty that Republicans would adopt an anti-slavery-extension platform that would prevent all southern and many northern unionists from supporting their ticket.[35]

McLean, though not Bates, would receive a few votes at the Baltimore convention. On the whole, however, as a Chicago newsman reported, "all idea of nominating him or anyone else with reference to [Republicans in] Chicago is dropped."[36] By the time the Constitutional Union convention met, the fractured Democrats had already failed to nominate any candidate at Charleston and postponed their decision until late June. With the possibility that Democrats would then deny Douglas the nomination in an attempt to reunite their party, enlisting Douglas's disappointed supporters behind the Constitutional Union candidate seemed too tempting to curry favor with Republicans. The pro-Democratic James Gordon Bennett of the *New York Herald*, indeed, later said that the Democratic delegates at Charleston who hadn't bolted the convention should have gone to Baltimore in May to arrange a common ticket with the Union men rather than calling another Democratic convention there in June.[37] In any event, the possibility of attracting support from Douglas Democrats ensured that the convention would reject the planks about territorial slavery that southern state conventions had adopted and that Douglas Democrats abhorred.

Some five hundred delegates and alternates from twenty-three states, most of them elderly and well-off gentlemen, populated the convention floor. The spectator galleries housed an altogether different breed. Baltimore had been chosen as the convention's site not simply because of its central location between North and South but also because Know Nothings had an exceptionally strong presence in the city, which they had dominated politically for years. Thus Know Nothing thugs, or Plug Uglies as the waspishly sarcastic young Cincinnati newspaperman Murat Halstead called them, filled the spectator gallery and cheered raucously at virtually every speech.[38] In one of those speeches, the convention's chairman, Washington Hunt of New York, dismissed the slavery extension issue harped on by Republicans as "a miserable abstraction." A Pennsylvanian labeled it as a "distracting question" that he wanted to shut out entirely from the coming contest "in so far as the Constitutional Union Party is concerned." "The moment that any remark upon the slavery question was made," reported the *New York Herald*'s correspondent, "there was a universal hiss." In another speech, New York's Erastus Brooks, who had taken the first crack at writing the party's February address, declared that the American people were "heartsick and head-sick of what are called, technically, party platforms." They "were invented to deceive the people—to wear one face in the North and another in the South."[39]

The most notable aspect of this convention to the modern observer, in fact, is the remarkable animus it expressed about the inherent duplicity of all party platforms—a theme that Constitutional Union speakers would trumpet throughout the remainder of the campaign. This chorus of denigration was in part—probably in large part—intended to justify the intentional brevity and platitudinous vapidity of the Constitutional Union Party's own national platform. Adopted unanimously to the accompaniment of prolonged cheering prior to any votes for candidates, it began with yet another assault on platforms themselves. Previous experience, it averred, "demonstrated that platform[s] adopted by the partisan Convention[s] of the country have had the effect to mislead and deceive the people, and at the same time to widen the political divisions of the country" by encouraging the creation "of geographical and sectional parties." As patriotic Americans, therefore, the Constitutional Union Party could "recognize" only three "political principles": "The Constitution of the Country, The Union of the States, and The Enforcement of the Laws."[40]

Aside from the loudness of the Know Nothings packing the spectator galleries, what struck Halstead most about this convention were its harmony—he had just come from the Democratic melee at Charleston—the complete absence of Know Nothings' nativist rhetoric, and the age, respectability, and self-evident unfitness for active face-to-face campaigning of the delegates. These "distinguished men," he wise-cracked, "were mostly 'venerable men,' who have come down to us from a former generation of politicians, and whose retirement from the busy scenes of public life have been rather involuntary than otherwise."[41] The only other national political convention that was this fossilized had also been held in Baltimore. That was the final Whig national convention in September 1856.

Certainly the men the convention considered for its nomination were mature, if not downright aged. Ten men received votes on the first ballot for a presidential candidate. None was younger than fifty, and only four were younger than sixty. And three of these comparative youths were fringe candidates who together received only 20 of the 254 votes cast on that ballot. The top three vote-getters on it, Bell, Houston, and Crittenden, were sixty-three, sixty-seven, and seventy-two, respectively. By way of contrast, the three other nominees that vied with Bell for the presidency in 1860 were fifty-one, forty-seven, and thirty-nine.

The convention allowed individual delegates to vote for whom they chose, although the chairmen of the state delegations would report the votes. Ten states were totally unrepresented. Bell, who led with 68½ votes on the first ballot, received support from ten states. Houston, the Texas Democrat, trailed closely with 57 votes, all but 7 of which, somewhat surprisingly, came from northern states. Houston, indeed, won 28 of New York's 35 votes on the first ballot and 29 of 35 on the second. After Bell won the nomination on that ballot despite New Yorkers' preference for the Texan, they complained that picking Bell rather than Houston was a major mistake.

Newspaper reports from the convention suggest two possible explanations for the heavy support the Democrat Houston got from this overwhelmingly Whig gathering. A Georgian touted Houston's record in leading Texans' battle for independence from Mexico in 1836. All the other men mentioned as possible candidates, he complained, "are representatives of a defunct party—the old Whig party. We cannot rally men to . . . support . . . a candidate who has been resuscitated from a dead body." Clay had lost in 1844, but Zachary Taylor had won in 1848 because he was "a man of

John Bell of Tennessee, Constitutional Union candidate for president in 1860. The John Paul Getty Museum, Los Angeles, Whitehurst Gallery, Washington, 1860, Salted Paper Print.

military renown. . . . With the hero of Buena Vista we drove the Democracy from their strongholds, and with the hero of San Jacinto a similar victory may be obtained."[42] Other reporters explained that the split between Bell and Houston represented a division between Whig conservatives who favored Bell and die-hard Know Nothings who wanted Houston. The heavy tilt of New York's delegation toward Houston was attributed to Erastus Brooks's command of its members. Houston in fact got 69 votes on the second ballot, but Bell prevailed with 138, a victory that was then declared unanimous, as was customary at most national nominating conventions.

The favorite of delegates at the convention for the vice presidential slot was its president Washington Hunt, a former Whig congressman from and governor of New York, but Hunt refused to be considered. By acclamation without a roll-call vote the convention then picked Edward Everett of Massachusetts for the spot. Everett, too, did not want it. He had given a letter declining any such nomination to a Massachusetts delegate to be read to the convention should his name come up, but that delegate had kept the letter pocketed. Bell accepted his nomination instantly; the reluctant Everett did not do so until the end of May, after considerable coaxing from an increasingly anxious Crittenden.

Thus the convention had picked an all-Whig ticket of aged, if not antique, men. Bell was sixty-three, Everett sixty-seven. A *New York Times* correspondent reported from Baltimore that "the unmixed Whig character of the ticket does not escape remark. An occasional Democrat suspects that this is little more than a Whig convention."[43] If hardly scintillating or bipartisan, the ticket unquestionably consisted of committed nationalists. Bell had served in both the House and Senate as well as in William Henry Harrison's short-lived cabinet.[44] He had strongly supported the Compromise of 1850, bravely voted against the Kansas-Nebraska Act explicitly on the grounds that it would inevitably produce exactly what it did—a new and powerful anti-southern party in the North—and opposed the Lecompton constitution in 1858. Southern Democrats immediately and continually denounced Bell as a traitor to the South, but their aspersions may only have enhanced his aura as a man who put Union ahead of section.

Everett had not held public office for as many years as Bell. Nonetheless, he served ten years in the House between 1825 and 1835, six months as a U.S. senator in the pivotal Thirty-Fourth Congress, as minister to England, as president of Harvard College, and as Fillmore's interim secretary of state after Daniel Webster died in 1852. By 1860, however, Everett's reputation rested primarily on his fame as the nation's foremost public orator, who had lent his talents most recently to raising money for the restoration of George Washington's Mount Vernon as a national landmark.

Everett may have personified nationalism, but his inclusion on the Constitutional Union ticket did nothing to enhance the chances that Republicans could be stopped from carrying Massachusetts or any other New England state. Illness had caused Everett to resign his Senate seat on June 7, 1854, but it had also caused him to miss another Senate vote on the Nebraska bill. Free Soilers in the Bay State immediately assailed him as a spokesman for Cotton Whigs who feared antagonizing Southerners, an unfair but wickedly effective charge that still tainted Everett among antislavery men in 1860.

New England Republicans, in fact, contemptuously mocked the Constitutional Union Party from its first stirrings. According to a Maine Republican sheet, an early rally of Massachusetts's Constitutional Union Party held in Boston on April 2 was composed of "Granny-dears" who should have more appropriately met on the preceding day—that is, April Fools' Day.[45] Six months later, when it was finally clear that the Bell men would in fact run their own electoral slate in the Bay State rather than fusing with Democrats against Republicans, the Boston *Daily Advertiser* hooted that Bell's campaign "promises to be not only as brilliant but as hopeless as the Charge of the Light Brigade," which Alfred Lord Tennyson's famous 1854 poem had already made an indelible symbol of futility.[46]

In May, when the Constitutional Union ticket and platform first became known, however, press reaction predictably varied according to the papers' partisan affiliation. The pro-Bell Raleigh *Register* exulted that the nominees were "head and shoulders above any ticket that has been presented to the country since Mr. Clay was nominated in 1844." Because the Democratic Party was "broken to pieces and is now impotent for anything but unmitigated mischief," it added, all who hoped to restore "probity, honesty, and good demeanor" to the national government would vote for Bell and Everett.[47] North Carolina's Fayetteville *Observer*, another Opposition sheet, also called on unionist Democrats to support Bell now that their own party was irreparably split. "If the public mind is wearied of strife and duly alive to the terrible progress we have made towards anarchy and ruin," echoed the *Savannah Republican*, "there are no two men in our broad land, who are better fitted for leaders in a movement for the re-inauguration of the better days of the Republic."[48]

Southern Democratic papers favorable to the bolters at Charleston not only called Bell a traitor who had voted against the South on every congressional measure relating to slavery but also mocked the Constitutional Union Party's say-nothing platform. It failed to vindicate the South's equal rights as the bolters' platform at Charleston had, they cried. Moreover, argued the Democratic *Semi-Weekly Mississippian*, its commitment to the enforcement of the laws pledged the Constitutional Union ticket to enforce all antislavery laws Republicans passed. It was "preposterous in the extreme for any party to attempt to ignore the slavery issue, when no less than six important territorial bills are pending in Congress, and all are aimed at the vital interests of the South, and supported by the Republican party." The issue of slavery's status in the territories "must be met and determined, and it is folly for any party to attempt to evade it."[49]

The Democratic Lexington *Kentucky Statesman* took virtually the same position on the day before the Constitutional Union convention opened. "It is vile nonsense, the merest folly to talk about a third party," it ranted. "It is insulting to the intelligence of the American people to attempt to organize any party which shall ignore the slavery question. That issue must be met and settled." The paper, indeed, provided telling evidence that it was southern Democrats, not their various competitors, who insisted on making slavery the central issue in the 1860 election. "The subject of domestic slavery now overshadows every other issue in American politics, and its consideration cannot be escaped in the pending national canvass. The coming Presidential election will turn upon that question."[50]

The pro-Democratic *New York Herald* sarcastically dismissed Bell as "a hard, dry man of the old school of politicians . . . without any remarkable genius or capacity." He was "an estimable man," wrote Bennett, "but he belongs to the fossil remains of the old Whig strain of political geology. He has no sympathies in common with the present generation and his name will awaken none of the enthusiasm among the young men which is absolutely essential for a successful campaign."[51] This sneer proved to be remarkably prescient. Bell at most would match Fillmore's vote in 1856, Bennett concluded. The real race was between Republicans and Democrats, despite the latter's current division.

The reaction of the Republican press to the outcome at Baltimore varied. Raymond of the *New York Times*, who had tried so hard to persuade Fillmore voters of the Republican Party's acceptability, now groused that the purpose of the Constitutional Union Party "is primarily the defeat of the Republican ticket." He did not believe that Bell would attract a large enough vote in the North to pull it off even though he would run strongly in the South. The Constitutional Union Party had dodged any platform statement whatsoever about slavery, Raymond's paper chided. Thus Bell's "party position does not represent any strong and earnest sentiment of the Northern people."[52]

Raymond had anticipated this reaction in a remarkably insightful (and quotable) editorial he penned in February after a Tennessee Opposition state convention, in which Andrew Jackson Donelson had denounced Buchanan's administration as unspeakably corrupt, had nominated Bell for president. That action, he correctly predicted, meant there would be a "third candidate" in the 1860 race. If Bell was that man, he would run strongly in the South, for in almost all the slave states there existed "a very decided and resolute hostility to the present Administration and to the Democratic party, which it represents." "Sensible" Southerners knew "that the Slavery agitation is due, in a very great degree, to the schemes and projects of the Democratic Party, and especially to the stupidly malevolent policy of the present Administration." They knew as well that "under its present organization" the Democratic Party was "utterly and hopelessly corrupt." Therefore, "if we could have a canvass entirely free from the question of Slavery," Bell as a third-party candidate could sweep the Upper South and border states.

But the 1860 election would not and could not be "free" of the slavery question. Bell would never be nominated by Republicans for he had never taken a clear position on the general question of slavery extension. Republicans were certain to adopt a platform that neither Bell nor his supporters could stomach. Nor could he run successfully as a third-party candidate in the North. "Issues growing out of Slavery dominate the public mind in the Free States." No "successful canvass could be maintained in any of them if these issues were to be discarded." By November other issues might make slavery-related issues "less prominent and absorbing than they threatened at one time to become," but they "will still be sufficiently marked and powerful" to prevent any anti-Democratic party in the South from cooperating with Republicans to "overthrow the party now in possession of Federal power."[53]

Raymond was surely right that Bell as a Constitutional Union candidate could never carry the electoral vote of a single free state. But that was not the point. From the start Bell and his supporters hoped to throw the election into the House, where, they expected, both Republicans and Democrats would prefer Bell to the candidate of the other major party. Thus the issue was whether Bell could draw a sufficiently large vote in the "doubtful" Lower North states to throw them to the Democrats and the final decision to the House of Representatives.

The prospect that Bell's candidacy upon a hollow platform might in fact propel the election into the House of Representatives, where Republicans controlled only 15 of the 17 state delegations they would need to win, infuriated Joseph Medill, editor of the vehemently antislavery, anti-southern *Chicago Press and Tribune*. The Constitutional Union Party's platform, he snarled, was a "stupid absurdity" that "shirk[ed] the responsibility of declaring themselves on the living issues of the day" and marked them with "a degree of cowardice which breeds distrust of the purity of their intentions." The whole Bell ticket was nothing more than "a repetition of the Fillmore swindle of 1856, for the benefit of the mulatto-making Democracy." It insulted Americans' intelligence, Medill declared, "to suppose that any considerable and sufficient number of them can be humbugged, bamboozled [and] swindled" into supporting these self-professed "Union-men only that the Disunion Democracy may be served." Enraged he might be, but Medill in these same editorials estimated that Bell might get 300,000–400,000 votes from "timid souls who would not vote outright for the Democracy whose principles they hate and despise" but might be "persuaded" to do so "indirectly" by supporting Bell.[54] Depending on how those votes were allocated in the North, they might indeed produce the result that so infuriated Medill.

Long the pro-business organ of Massachusetts' so-called Cotton Whigs, the *Boston Daily Advertiser* advocated a different Republican response to Bell's nomination than Medill's angry bellows. Many delegates at the Baltimore convention had in fact "confidently predicted" that they could force the election into the House of Representatives, where they expected Bell to prevail.[55] In a May 15 editorial, the *Advertiser* agreed that this result was likely, especially if Douglas emerged as the Democrats' candidate. To prevent this from happening, the editorial pointed out, Republicans needed to sweep the North's electoral vote. Yet "all of the doubtful states in the North [Pennsylvania, New Jersey, Indiana, and Illinois] are remarkable for the strength of their conservative vote." Those conservatives had gone for Fillmore in 1856, and Bell was very likely to hold the entire Fillmore vote, thus again throwing those states to the Democrats. To prevent that result, "the policy of the republicans is to address themselves to this third party, which thus holds the balance of power." Republican victory utterly depended "upon a proper appeal to conservative elements."[56] It did not take long to see if Republicans heeded this advice from Boston. Their convention opened in Chicago the day after it was printed.

5

REPUBLICANS CHOOSE AN "AVAILABLE" MAN

Republicans hardly needed the Boston *Daily Advertiser* to tell them that they had to carry the so-called doubtful states of the Lower North—Illinois, Indiana, Pennsylvania—to win the presidency in 1860. In 1856 John C. Frémont had taken eleven of sixteen northern states with 115 electoral votes. Since then, the admission to statehood of Minnesota and Oregon had brought the total of electoral votes to 303, meaning it would take 152 to win. At the start of 1860, Republicans expected to add Minnesota's 3 to their column and to lose the 7 from California and Oregon. Even if they managed to carry all of the states Frémont had won, they would still be 34 shy of the necessary total. Pennsylvania alone had 27 electoral votes, Illinois commanded 11, Indiana, 13, and New Jersey, 7.[1] Republicans also knew that the key voters they needed to win in the Lower North had supported Millard Fillmore in 1856 and that they were indeed more conservative, that is, more averse to sectional extremism than the men who had voted for Frémont. They knew, in short, that they needed a candidate who in the argot of the day was "available." This was someone who could appeal to conservatives fearful of disunion should Republicans instead choose a virulently antislavery, anti-southern "radical" but someone who also embodied Northerners' determination that slavery not expand. As an Iowan wrote Abraham Lincoln in February, "We must get a man that while he is reliable is also available."[2]

Here in a nutshell is the traditional explanation of why Republicans in 1860 nominated Lincoln rather than New York's William Henry Seward, the odds-on favorite to take the prize at the start of the year. Lincoln was more conservative than the radical Seward on the slavery issue, so the story goes, or at least was perceived by Republicans to be more conservative, and thus was deemed more "available," more electable in the doubtful states than the New Yorker. This interpretation contains considerable truth. Enough Republicans at the party's national convention were persuaded that Seward could not prevail in the Lower North to scuttle his nomination. As this chapter attempts to demonstrate, however, this conventional wisdom misidentifies the main reasons why Seward lost and Lincoln won the nomination.

At the end of 1859, Republicans' ascension seemed unstoppable because they had achieved popular-vote majorities in low turnout off-year elections in all the Lower North states in 1858 or 1859. At that time as well, a new Constitutional Union Party that might attract Fillmore's 1856 supporters intact was still a pipe dream. Consequently, most Republicans and virtually all people who dreaded a Republican triumph expected Seward to be the Republican nominee. Seward, who would turn fifty-nine in May 1860 while the Republican national convention met, was easily the most prominent and experienced leader in the party. A graduate of Union College and resident of Auburn, New York, he had entered politics as an Antimason in the late 1820s. At that time he began a lifetime alliance with newspaper editor Thurlow Weed, who in the early 1830s would move to Albany, launch the Whig and subsequently Republican *Albany Evening Journal*, and emerge as the leading power broker or boss of first the Whig and then the Republican Party in New York state. Weed never sought public office for himself, but he wrote Seward in 1858 that elevating him to the presidency was "a purpose which for twenty years [has] engrossed my thoughts and controlled my action."[3] The persuasive Weed managed to secure Seward's nomination as the New York Whig Party's very first gubernatorial candidate in 1834. That year Seward lost, but he won the prestigious office in 1838 and again in 1840. In the 1840s he crisscrossed the northern states as a Whig campaigner who stressed Whigs' opposition to slavery extension, and in 1849 the Whig majority in the New York legislature sent him to the United States Senate. There he led northern Whigs' opposition to the territorial provisions of the Compromise of 1850 because they did not guarantee slavery's prohibition from Utah and New Mexico, and again in 1854 he led northern opposition to Stephen Douglas's Kansas-Nebraska bill. As noted in Chapter 1, Seward was a reluctant convert from the Whig to the Republican Party. Once he joined it in late 1855, however, no other Republican matched his eminence.

To most contemporary non-Republicans and to many subsequent historians, the supposed radicalism of Seward's antislavery views was what made him such a controversial, indeed such a dangerous, potential candidate. James Gordon Bennett editorialized in the *New York Herald* on February 1, 1860, for example, that Seward's election as president guaranteed the disruption of the Union and a "war of extermination" between the North and South. Although Seward had indeed stressed his and northern Whigs' opposition to slavery extension since the mid-1840s and while he constantly preached the superiority of free labor over slave labor, his reputation as a militantly anti-southern, antislavery radical was overblown. It rested primarily on two speeches, his so-called Higher Law speech against any compromise in 1850 and his "Irrepressible Conflict" speech of 1858. Both, as he wrote privately on each occasion, had the very specific short-term political goal of firming up his New York allies' antislavery commitment, and neither when closely examined was as sectionally threatening as southern Democrats believed.[4] In the notorious "Higher Law" speech, for example, Seward did not in fact say what many people accused him of saying, namely, that office holders should obey their Christian consciences rather than the U.S. Constitution when formulating policy.

Other aspects of his career, indeed, more accurately suggested his fundamental sectional moderation. Seward never abandoned the bisectional Whig Party to join the exclusively northern and overtly anti-southern Free Soilers as did Charles Sumner or Ohio's Salmon P. Chase, who also yearned for the Republican 1860 presidential nomination. Moreover, much to Free Soilers' annoyance he refused to forsake his alliance with southern Whigs as long as he could after passage of the Nebraska law in 1854. Unlike many other Republican leaders, he befriended Southerners, even southern Democrats, in Congress, including the Mississippian Jefferson Davis, with whom he co-led Senate opposition to the Compromise of 1850. Nor was he ever as abrasively insulting to the South as some other Republican senators—for example, Ohio's Ben Wade, Michigan's Zachariah Chandler, and Sumner of Massachusetts. And unlike those Republican hardliners, Seward would be eager to compromise with Southerners to resolve the secession crisis that followed Lincoln's election.

Perceptions often matter more than reality in motivating historical actors, however, and Seward was most certainly perceived as radical, as the Republican presidential possibility most favored by genuine abolitionists. "Seward Nominated for President by the Abolitionists" blared a sensational—and false—headline in Bennett's *New York Herald* on Christmas Day in 1859. Nonetheless, he was clearly the front-runner for Republicans' nomination at that time. Seward's support concentrated almost entirely in the states Frémont had won, especially the Upper North states. Yet even in these presumably safe Republican bastions competitors appeared. Some Republicans advocated Massachusetts' Nathaniel P. Banks, the first Republican Speaker of the House who was then in his third consecutive term as the Bay State's governor. Ohio's ambitious Salmon Chase, a far more militant antislavery man than Seward who had been sent as a Free Soiler to the U.S. Senate in 1849, had been elected governor as a Republican in 1855 and 1857, and was reelected to the Senate by Republican state legislators at the end of 1859, also thirsted for the nomination. The Ohioan Samuel Galloway assured Lincoln in mid-March that most Ohio Republicans opposed Chase and that "he could not be elected if nominated." According to Galloway, in 1860 Republicans manifestly needed "a candidate of Conservative character." Chase was manifestly not that man.[5]

More important, many Republicans believed that their candidate must come from one of the three most crucial doubtful states. As a result, each of the three advanced candidates of their own whom their friends boomed as more "available" than Seward or anyone else. Illinois had Lincoln, who was widely mentioned as a possible vice presidential nominee but whose most fervent friends dreamed of putting him in the Republican ticket's top spot. Some in Indiana touted Caleb B. Smith, like Lincoln an ex-Whig and former congressman, as a favorite son, but his prospects had disappeared by the time the Republican national convention opened.

Because of Pennsylvania's size and apparent indispensability to a Republican victory, however, Pennsylvania's Republican senator Simon Cameron seemed the biggest threat to Seward's chances. Cameron was an ex-Democrat and former Know Nothing, a well-known champion of protective tariffs, and the most prominent leader in Pennsylvania's polyglot People's Party, which resolutely attempted to downplay the slavery issue. He was also a man with a well-earned reputation for political corruption, whose personal papers are replete with names of state legislators whose votes for the U.S. senatorship that Cameron had most recently won were up for sale. Fillmore had won 18 percent of Pennsylvania's vote in 1856, and Cameron was touted as the only man who could carry the Keystone State precisely because of his Know Nothing background. In contrast, Seward's brave, if politically foolhardy, public opposition to Know Nothings and anti-Catholic bigotry rendered him the least likely of all Republicans to win Pennsylvania. Pennsylvania was deemed so important that even some Chicago Republicans formed Cameron-Lincoln clubs booming the Pennsylvanian for the presidency and their own state's favorite son for second place on his ticket. Iowans also believed that only Cameron could carry Pennsylvania, one of Lincoln's correspondents told him, and they too therefore favored giving Cameron the nomination.[6]

While Seward was never as radical as his reputation implied, contrary to traditional interpretations Lincoln was not regarded by other Republicans as any more conservative and thus more "available" to the Lower North on slavery and sectional issues than Seward. Illinois Republican U.S. senator Lyman Trumbull bluntly made this fact brutally clear to Lincoln in an exceptionally important, if inexplicably little noted, letter from Washington dated April 24, 1860. If the race for the nomination came down to a two-man contest between Seward and Lincoln, Trumbull wrote, Seward would win. When he urged Lincoln's nomination to his fellow Republican congressmen who opposed Seward's nomination, "I am almost always met with the remark, 'if you are going to nominate a man of that stamp, why not take Seward.' There seems to be a disposition in the public mind to associate you together, from the fact, I suppose, that you have both given expression to a similar sentiment in regard to the ultimate extinction of slavery."[7] Another Republican sent the same tidings from Washington. When Lincoln's nomination was urged by Illinois men, "the Seward men say that if he [Lincoln] can be elected, Seward can, they both occupying the same position, and there is some truth in that."[8] In short, it was not only Southerners who perceived the positions of Seward and Lincoln as virtually identical. So did Republican congressmen.

In one respect, in fact, Lincoln was one of the most radical men in the Republican Party. Like others, he repeatedly vowed that neither he nor his party would seek abolition of slavery in the southern states where it already existed. He also demanded that the Fugitive Slave Law of 1850 be obeyed, not flouted as some Republicans insisted. Where he was radical was instead in how he defined the slavery extension issue and justified Republicans' opposition to that extension. Some Republicans condemned slavery expansion because it would prohibit northern farmers and laborers from entering territories where they could not compete with slave labor. Others stressed that the purpose of slavery extension was to increase the political clout of slaveholders, the so-called Slave Power, in the national government; hence, that extension must be blocked to limit the South's political power. Still others warned that the West must not reproduce the hierarchical, economically stagnant, and upward-mobility-crushing society of the South. Instead, the North's free labor, prosperous, and mobility-enhancing society must be fostered in that section. And still others argued that black slaves must be kept out of the territories to preserve those areas exclusively for whites.

Lincoln, in contrast, portrayed the sectional conflict over slavery expansion as fundamentally a moral contest. According to dictionaries, the word *radical* means "from or to the root" of something. Lincoln insisted that *at root* the fundamental problem about slavery extension was the institution of slavery itself. Slavery, he repeatedly declared, was immoral socially, economically, and politically. Unlike Christian ministers or religiously inspired abolitionists, he rarely spoke of slavery as sinful. Rather, his preferred formulation was that slavery was "wrong" or "a wrong." Its extension must be opposed, Lincoln argued, simply because it was wrong, regardless of its deterrent impact on potential northern settlers, societal arrangements in the West, or the sections' relative political power in Washington.

Lincoln, moreover, portrayed American public opinion as divided by the conviction that slavery was, or was not, wrong. Northerners who believed slavery wrong were Republicans; hence, Republicans were committed to stopping slavery's spread. In sharp contrast, northern Democrats, especially Stephen A. Douglas's supporters, did not believe slavery was wrong and did not care one way or the other whether it spread, just so long as local majorities in any territory made the decision. Southerners, finally, believed that slavery was a positive good, and they insisted on its spread precisely because they believed it was good, not primarily to relieve demographic pressure, expand economic opportunities for slaveholders, increase Southerners' political power, or affirm the South's equal rights in the nation.

For Lincoln, then, however accurate or inaccurate his opinions may have been, the right or wrong of slavery was at the root of partisan and sectional differences over slavery expansion. But more than this, Northerners who deemed slavery wrong had an obligation to denounce it as wrong, even though, Lincoln recognized, Southerners resented this constant criticism of an institution they valued as much as they were outraged by Republicans' opposition to slavery expansion and Republicans' insistence that the southern minority submit to rule by the northern majority.

Lincoln held no elective political office for the entire decade of the 1850s, so he could take no action against slavery expansion other than speaking out against it and slavery itself.[9] He did this in scores of speeches to Republican audiences in Illinois, other Midwestern states, Kansas Territory, and, in early 1860, New York and New England. It was the content of those speeches, along with his having gone toe-to-toe with Douglas in 1858, that fueled his rise to regional Republican leadership and made him a credible aspirant for the party's vice presidential or presidential nomination in 1860. Three efforts particularly stand out. One was the "House Divided" speech of June 1858, which made him seem just as radical to southern slaveholders and conservatives fearful for the Union as Seward. The second were the speeches he delivered in his joint debates with Douglas later in that summer of 1858. In late 1859 a publishing company in Columbus, Ohio, persuaded Lincoln that these should be printed as a Republican campaign document, and the booklets appeared in time to be distributed to Republican delegates at the national convention when they gathered in Chicago in mid-May 1860. Especially important in impressing eastern Republicans with Lincoln's "reliability" on the sectionally divisive slavery extension question, however, was a speech he delivered in New York City on February 27, 1860, shorter versions of which he subsequently gave to audiences in Connecticut, Rhode Island, and Massachusetts.

The committee of New York Republicans that invited Lincoln and offered to pay him an honorarium of $200 for his speech originally planned to have Lincoln speak in the famous abolitionist minister Henry Ward Beecher's Plymouth Church between Hicks and Henry Streets in Brooklyn Heights. The spacious Plymouth Church could accommodate almost 3,500 people. Nonetheless as interest in seeing Lincoln grew in February, the organizing committee decided to move the venue out of Brooklyn to the larger Cooper Union in New York City. Lincoln did attend Sunday services at Beecher's church, however, and the pew in which he sat commemorates his attendance.

The carefully prepared speech Lincoln gave in Cooper Union was easily his most important oration since his joint debates with Douglas in 1858.[10] He began by resuming a quarrel with that longtime political bête noire. In Douglas's 1859 *Harper's* article, Douglas had denied that slavery in the territories fell within the constitutional purview of Congress and was instead a domestic issue to be decided by local governments alone. Lincoln set out to prove Douglas wrong. Thus he attempted to demonstrate at length a point he had frequently made since 1854: the Founders—in this case the thirty-nine men who signed the Constitution—opposed slavery's expansion westward, believed Congress had the constitutional authority to bar it from federal territories, and fully anticipated its complete disappearance from the United States in several generations.[11] Lincoln concluded this section of his speech by invoking the formula he said the "fathers" had adopted: Let slavery be "marked as an evil not to be extended, but to be tolerated and protected only because of and so far as its actual presence among us makes that toleration and protection a necessity."

This pledge that Republicans did not seek slavery's abolition in the states where it already existed marked Lincoln's transition into the second section of his address, which was meant to dispel southern misconceptions and fears about Republicans. Southerners charged that Republicans were a sectional party, said Lincoln, but that was because it had no presence in the South. Once it got votes in slave states—as it would in 1860, he promised—Southerners could no longer call it sectional. Moreover, Republicans' commitment to blocking slavery's expansion would not directly harm any southern state. Southerners also claimed that Republicans were revolutionaries while they themselves were "eminently conservative." Yet, Lincoln argued, Republicans espoused the antislavery principles of the Founders while Southerners "spit upon that old policy." Southerners charged that Republicans had made the slavery extension issue more prominent than it had henceforth been, but, insisted Lincoln, it was Southerners and Democrats who did that with the policies they had pursued since 1854. Southerners blamed Republicans for John Brown's raid, but "John Brown was no Republican; and you have failed to implicate a single Republican in his Harper's Ferry enterprise." Far from endorsing slave insurrection, Republican opposition to slavery's extension was "accompanied with a continual protest against any interference with your slaves, or with you about your slaves." The federal government, indeed, had no constitutional right to abolish slavery. Only state governments could do that. To Southerners' insistence that the *Dred Scott* decision held that the Constitution recognized slaves as property that deserved federal protection, Lincoln declared that nowhere in the Constitution were slaves referred to as property. Hence the Supreme Court was wrong. To Southerners' plaints that Republicans would be responsible for destroying the Union should a Republican win the presidential election, Lincoln hooted that this was like a highwayman telling his victim to turn over his money or he would shoot him and then the victim would be a murderer because he defied the demand of the man threatening him.

But it was the last section of this speech that made it something special and brought his audience to their feet with wild applause when he finished. Here Lincoln exhorted Republicans to ignore threats of disunion should Republicans win the White House. The only thing that Republicans could do to satisfy slaveholders, Lincoln declared, was to join Southerners in declaring slavery "right" instead of "wrong." Yet Republicans could not do

Abraham Lincoln in 1859, as he would have looked in photographs during the 1860 campaign. Photograph by S. M. Fassett, courtesy of the Abraham Lincoln Library and Museum, Harrogate, Tennessee.

this, agree to slavery's extension, abide the "don't care" policy of Douglas Democrats, or even stop criticizing slavery as morally wrong. To do so would be "to unsay what Washington said, and to undo what Washington did." Then came the thunderous peroration that Lincoln put in capital letters in the version of his speech meant for publication. We Republicans must not "be slandered from our duty by false accusations against us nor frightened from it by menaces of destruction to the Government," he avowed. Rather,

"LET US HAVE FAITH THAT RIGHT MAKES MIGHT, AND IN THAT FAITH, LET US, TO THE END, DARE TO DO OUR DUTY AS WE UNDERSTAND IT."

This, then, was Lincoln's personal view of what Republicans stood for. They opposed slavery extension because slavery was wrong, and, by implication, everyone who supported Republicans did so because they shared that belief in the wrongfulness of slavery. To repeat, most other Republican spokesmen defined Republicans' mission and sought votes for their party in quite different terms. Many targeted slaveholders and a hostile Slave Power more than the enslavement of African Americans itself. After his election, Lincoln himself ascribed his victory to the fact that voters thought him an honest man, not that they shared his belief about the inherent wrong of slavery. Disgust with corruption, not antislavery sentiment, in short, explained the Republican vote.[12]

Lincoln's Cooper Union address and his New England speeches drew rave reviews from the eastern Republican press, and those reviews reached the Midwest even before Lincoln arrived back home in Springfield, Illinois, on March 14. That very day the *Chicago Press and Tribune*, which had already boomed Lincoln for the top spot on Republicans' ticket, enthused that because of those raves, "We hazard nothing in saying that no man has ever risen so rapidly to political eminence in the United States."[13]

Lincoln's successful foray into the East and the reaction to it in the Midwest undoubtedly increased his belief in the plausibility of his friends' wish to make him the Republican presidential candidate. Students of Lincoln often quote his letter to Lyman Trumbull admitting that "the taste [for the presidential nomination] *is* in my mouth a little."[14] This letter was written on April 29, at least a full month after he had decided to pursue the main prize in earnest. On March 16 he wrote his Kansas friend Mark W. Delahay, a fervent proponent of Lincoln's nomination, that he would loan him the money to pay for his attendance at the Chicago convention so that he could work there on Lincoln's behalf. His letter to Ohio's Samuel Galloway on March 24 constitutes a smoking gun about his intentions. Galloway had written him that while Ohio's state Republican convention had urged its delegation to Chicago to support Salmon Chase for at least one ballot, Chase could never get the nomination and that many Ohio Republicans in any case preferred Lincoln to Chase. In reply, Lincoln spelled out a strategy for winning the laurels. If he had a chance, Lincoln wrote, it was because all northern opponents of the Democrats could vote for him—implying, of course, that this appeal was not true of other aspirants. "My name is new in the field, and I suppose I am not the *first* choice of a very great many. Our policy, then, is to give no offence to others—leave them in a mood to come to us, if they shall be compelled to give up their first love."[15]

Then, in early April, before Lincoln's important exchange of letters with Lyman Trumbull, events occurred that temporarily seemed to threaten both Seward's and Lincoln's chances for the nomination. The results of gubernatorial elections in Connecticut and Rhode Island in April's first week jolted Republicans' confidence about a cakewalk into the White House. They eked out a victory by barely 500 votes in Connecticut, where Frémont had run more than 7,000 votes ahead of Buchanan in 1856.[16] In Rhode Island, where Buchanan had attracted only 33.7 percent of the popular vote in 1856, Democrat William Sprague won the governorship after straight-out antislavery men had defeated former Know Nothings for the Republican gubernatorial nomination in a bitterly divided state convention. New England's spring elections, in sum, appeared to signal a popular backlash against antislavery extremism; they seemed to add Connecticut and Rhode Island to the list of doubtful states. Those results, wrote one of Lincoln's correspondents, "argue strongly against the availability of the Seward movement." If he were nominated "we are doomed to defeat."[17] The Connecticut and Rhode Island results, echoed a Republican from Washington, are "everywhere considered as a protest on the part of these states against the radical tendency of the Republican party."[18]

Significantly, the man to whom suddenly apprehensive Republicans now turned for an alternative to Seward was not Lincoln. Rather, it was Edward Bates of St. Louis, a Whig lawyer who had very publicly supported Fillmore in 1856. Bates was being boomed by Horace Greeley, the most widely read Republican newspaper editor in the country. Greeley had once been a close partner of Seward and Weed in the New York Whig Party, but they had gone through a bitter divorce in the early 1850s. Now he was doing everything he could to block Seward's nomination. Bates, however, had obvious weaknesses as a potential nominee. His free-soil credentials were suspect. More important, his background as a Know Nothing made him anathema to Germans, whose support Republicans considered indispensable. Conversely, according to Lincoln's friend and adviser David Davis, Germans "love[d]" Seward.[19]

An even more far-fetched conservative alternative to Seward—and Lincoln—was John McLean, an associate justice on the Supreme Court. The Ohioan McLean had been a strong contender for the Republican nomination in 1856, but in 1860 he was seventy-five years old. Chicago's Republican mayor "Long John" Wentworth believed that "running McLean at his age is like running a dead man." McLean would, in fact, die in April 1861. But in April 1860, according to Lyman Trumbull, in Washington "this McLean movement is daily gaining strength & even now looks formidable."[20]

Washington Republicans' reluctance to turn to Lincoln when the New England results jeopardized Seward's candidacy helps explain why Lincoln's friends were so disappointed that Stephen Douglas did not win the Democratic nomination in Charleston before the Chicago convention met. What they counted on to establish Lincoln's "availability" was not his alleged conservatism on the slavery extension issue but his residence in Illinois and his identity as a Westerner. That was his sharpest difference from Seward in their eyes. If Douglas were the Democratic nominee, an Iowan wrote Lincoln in December 1859, "The West will not vote for any but a Western Man against a Western Man."[21] Similarly, according to David Davis, Chicago's Wentworth, who deemed both McLean and Bates impossibilities, believed that Lincoln had "excellent" chances for the Republican nomination if Douglas were the Democratic nominee. At Chicago in May, therefore, Republicans working for Lincoln labeled Lincoln the candidate of the West and Seward the candidate of the East.[22]

Aside from his identification as a Westerner in contrast to the New Yorker Seward, Lincoln possessed one other crucial distinction from him. In an 1855 private letter his biographers love to quote, Lincoln had denounced the bigotry of Know Nothings. But he had never criticized the nativists publicly. Thus he might be acceptable to Pennsylvanians if their first choice, Simon Cameron, proved unable to win the nomination. In contrast, as one of Lincoln's friends reported to him with poor spelling and grammar from Chicago two days before the Republican national convention opened there, "The Pennsylvania delegation will not gow [*sic*] for Mr. Seward under no Circumstances."[23] If Seward won the nomination, the Pennsylvanians at Chicago warned, every former Know Nothing in their state would vote for John Bell, allowing Democrats to carry it once again.

Weeks before that convention opened, Lincoln, a fierce political competitor once he plunged into the fray, had responded to other Republicans' panicked reaction to the Connecticut and Rhode Island returns by disparaging—perhaps "knifing" is more accurate—the electoral prospects of other possible Republican candidates in his private correspondence. In the same letter of April 24 in which Lyman Trumbull had predicted that Lincoln would lose a two-way contest for the nomination with Seward, he had reported the boomlets for Bates and McLean in Washington and asked Lincoln how those two and Seward might fare in Illinois in the general election. Lincoln replied on April 29 that neither Bates nor Seward could carry Illinois if Douglas were the Democratic nominee (as the Lincoln men hoped), but that either could if Douglas were not. McLean would actually be the strongest Republican candidate in Illinois and Seward the weakest, he reported. And then he plunged the dagger. "I hear no objection to McLean, except his age; but that objection seems to occur to everyone." Besides, Lincoln added, what about McLean's Supreme Court seat? If he resigned upon accepting the nomination, Buchanan could fill it with a Democrat. If he tried to hold it until after the election, the public outcry could cost Republicans the election.[24]

As the opening of the Chicago Republican convention grew closer, Lincoln continued to rely on pen and paper to advance his cause. On May 1 he wrote an Indianan that he expected to hear of Douglas's nomination at any time now. "This puts the case in the hardest shape for us"—that is, if Republicans nominated anyone but Lincoln.[25] The following day he told Ohio's Richard M. Corwine that the Illinois delegation and perhaps Indiana's would be unanimous for him from the start and that while he was not the first choice of any other delegations, "there is no positive objection" in any of them.[26]

The Illinois Republican state convention in Decatur on May 9 gave Lincoln momentum going into the party's national convention scheduled for Chicago a week later. A tent capable of holding 2,500 persons and called the Wigwam had been erected for what would be the best-attended state convention yet held in Illinois. Thousands of enthusiastic Republicans jammed into the small town, not only filling the tent but surrounding it with an equally large crowd. Lincoln was there at the request of his advisers, and when he was spotted at the back of the tent he was literally passed up to the stage at the front on the shoulders of the packed-in delegates. Once he was there, John Hanks, a cousin of Lincoln's mother, and another man entered the tent carrying two fence rails that Lincoln had supposedly split as a young man with a banner reading "ABRAHAM LINCOLN THE RAIL CANDIDATE FOR PRESIDENT IN 1860."[27] Here was born the sobriquet of Lincoln as the Republican Party's Rail Splitter candidate for president. Far more important in advancing his chances for the nomination, the convention pronounced Lincoln as the state's sole choice for the presidency and committed the delegates to the Chicago convention to support him as a unit. It also gave Lincoln a voice in choosing the four at-large delegates to Chicago, and Lincoln selected them carefully—not simply to put adept workers on the convention floor but also to keep the diverse elements of the heterogeneous, sometimes fractious, Illinois Republican coalition together. Of these, the three most important were Norman Judd, the party's state chairman and an ex-Democrat who had supported Trumbull against Lincoln in the 1855 Senate election; David Davis, a former Whig and Lincoln's unofficial campaign manager; and Gustave Koerner, the most important German American leader in the state.

The Republican national convention had originally been scheduled to meet in mid-June, but in response to protests that this date was too late to organize a successful campaign, the national committee had moved up the date to May 16. During the 1850s Chicago had experienced the most rapid population growth of any city in the United States, and by 1860 it had over 109,000 residents. To host the convention the city's Republicans had erected a large temporary board frame structure also called the Wigwam that could accommodate 10,000 people. As delegates began to arrive in the city in the days before the convention opened, Lincoln and his local friends strove to advance his prospects. On May 12 Lincoln directed his Kansas friend Delahay, who was already in Chicago, to work on the Iowa and Minnesota delegations that were committed to Seward on the first ballot. Copies of the newly published Lincoln-Douglas debates were distributed, and on May 15 the pro-Lincoln *Chicago Press and Tribune* editorialized that Lincoln was indeed a moderate man of the middle and thus the perfect compromise candidate between the Missouri conservative Edward Bates and the New York radical Seward, both of whom it explicitly named.

This carefully contrived editorial averred that Lincoln's "unexceptionable record, his position between the extremes in the party, his spotless character as a citizen and acknowledged ability as a statesman, will, in the approaching canvass, give him an advantage before the people that no other candidate can claim." In short, Lincoln was the most available of all the potential nominees. While Lincoln supported "all the fundamentals of Republicanism," the editorial continued, his "nature has given him that wise conservatism that has made his action and his expressed opinions to conform to the most mature sentiment of the country on the question of slavery." His "avoidance of extremes" was "the natural consequence of an equable nature and mental constitution that is never off its balance."[28]

Eager to confirm this portrait of him as a moderate who differed from Seward, no matter what congressional Republicans believed, on May 17 Lincoln sent the editor of the *Springfield Journal* to Chicago with a brief message for his floor leaders. Lincoln had written this in pencil on the margins of a fragment from the pro-Bates St. Louis *Missouri Democrat* list-

Prominent candidates for the Republican presidential nomination at Chicago, printed in Harper's Weekly *magazine on May 12, 1860. In this group portrait, published four days before the Republican national convention opened in Chicago, William Henry Seward* (center) *is clearly considered the leading candidate for the nomination. In the bottom row are* (from left) *John C. Frémont, the Republicans' 1856 nominee; Abraham Lincoln; John Bell, who had just been nominated by the Constitutional Union Party at Baltimore; and Cassius M. Clay of Kentucky. In the top row are* (from left) *Edward Bates of Missouri and Nathaniel Banks of Massachusetts. Flanking Seward in the middle row are* (from left)*, William Pennington, the Republican Speaker of the House, from New Jersey; Ohio's Salmon P. Chase; Supreme Court Associate Justice John McLean; and Senator Simon Cameron of Pennsylvania.*

ing Seward's more provocative statements about the sectional conflict over slavery extension. "I agree with Seward in his 'Irrepressible Conflict,'" Lincoln said, "but I do not endorse his 'Higher Law' doctrine." The same brief penciled message ordered his floor workers to "*make no contracts that will bind me.*"[29]

Though the Wigwam had been built to accommodate 10,000 delegates and spectators, several reporters estimated that at least 40,000 Republicans descended on Chicago in the days before the convention opened. To the ubiquitous Cincinnati reporter Murat Halstead, who had come to

Chicago by train directly from Baltimore after the Constitutional Union convention adjourned, the hundreds of New Yorkers who had filled at least thirteen train cars and come to twist arms and shout for Seward were easily the most fascinating of this throng. They included suave politicos like Thurlow Weed, intent on charming delegates in one-on-one tête-à-têtes; New York governor Edwin D. Morgan, chairman of the Republican national committee; and *New York Times* editor and owner Henry J. Raymond. More impressive to Halstead, however, were the three-hundred-man uniformed marching band and hundreds upon hundreds of loud-voiced and strong-armed shoulder hitters whose thirst for strong drink amazed him. New Yorkers, he wrote, constituted a "class unknown to Western Republican politicians. They can drink as much whiskey, swear as loud and long, sing as bad songs, and 'get up and howl' as ferociously as any crowd of Democrats you ever heard." They scoffed "at the idea that Seward could not sweep all the Northern States" and had "no particle of doubt of his nomination." Halstead called Seward's backers the "Irrepressibles" in reference to his notorious Rochester speech. Those who denied Seward's electability in the Lower North he labeled "the conservative expediency men."[30]

At least one prominent New Yorker at Chicago was not part of this Sewardite throng; instead, he was loudly and profanely execrated by them. This was Horace Greeley. There as a surrogate delegate from Oregon, who drew crowds wherever he strode, he bad-mouthed Seward even as he talked up the Missourian Bates. One of his charges against Seward, an accusation repeated by many others, was that Seward's partnership with Weed would be fatal because Weed's lackeys in the New York legislature that spring had awarded lucrative street railroad contracts to men in New York City who in turn paid Weed large kickbacks for his help. Nominating Seward, in sum, could cost Republicans the corruption issue they counted on to slay the Democrats. This prospect may have done more than anything else to defeat Seward's nomination. Shortly after the convention, for example, one delegate wrote that "however honest and pure Seward" was personally, Republicans would "have lost much, if not all the capital we have in this campaign in the extravagance and corruption of the Administration, had Seward been our candidate."[31] Lincoln's "Honest Abe" reputation, in short, contributed mightily to his victory over both Cameron and Seward.

Seward's friends nonetheless did everything they could to push the New Yorker over the top. Aside from street demonstrations, songs, and shouts, their leaders approached both the Illinois and Pennsylvania delegations with offers of the second place on Seward's ticket for their respective favorites along with promises of $100,000 in cash to help them carry their respective states. Both delegations spurned the offers, and Lincoln's friends tried to squelch any talk of Lincoln as a vice presidential nominee. Before the convention opened representatives of the Illinois, Indiana, Pennsylvania, New Jersey, and Massachusetts delegations met to hatch stop-Seward strategies, but they could not agree on a single champion since the Pennsylvanians insisted that only Cameron could carry the Keystone State while the Midwesterners insisted they must have a candidate from their own region to compete with Douglas, still the likeliest Democratic nominee. Meanwhile, Henry Lane and Andrew Curtin, respectively, the Republican and People's Party gubernatorial nominees in Indiana and Pennsylvania, told every delegate who would listen that they could not possibly win their state elections in October if Seward were the nominee. October gubernatorial elections in the North had long been considered a bellwether accurately predicting those states' November presidential results, so these warnings also badly damaged Seward's prospects. Lane was especially effective in urging the Vermont and Virginia delegations not to back Seward on the first ballot as they were widely expected to do.

Virginia was not the only slave state, where virtually no Republican Party existed, that sent delegations to Chicago. Kentucky sent 23 men, Maryland 11, Delaware 6, Missouri 18, and even Texas sent 6. None of these delegations were geographically representative of their entire states; rather they came from highly localized pockets where a few men dared to call themselves Republican. Sixteen of the 25 Virginians in Chicago, for example, hailed from counties along the Ohio River that became part of West Virginia; one-third of the 18 Missouri delegates lived in St. Louis.

Except for the Missourians who were committed to Bates, all of these slave state men were expected to support Seward. Thus his representatives on the convention's credentials committee worked successfully to make sure they were admitted even though everyone knew that outside of St. Louis they represented at best a handful of actual voters. How the convention, which purported to represent the entire nation, accounted for the nine slave states with no representation whatsoever at Chicago, provided the first hiccup for the enthusiastic gathering. To increase the number of Republicans in attendance at Chicago, Republicans had given each state floor votes equal to double the number of electoral votes it possessed. Thus New York with 35 electoral votes had 70 voting delegates, Pennsylvania with 27 electoral votes, 54 delegate votes, and so forth.[32] If the convention included the absent slave states in its count of total votes, as anti-Seward men wanted, there would be 606 votes, with 304 as the minimal majority necessary to win the nomination. Sewardites angrily and correctly protested that this figure verged on a two-thirds majority of the 465 voting delegates actually in attendance. That counting absent states to calculate the total required for nomination resembled Caleb Cushing's ruling at Charleston frustrating Douglas escaped no one's attention. Thus the convention's first major decision, a victory for the Seward forces, was to postulate that 233, not 304, delegate votes constituted the majority necessary for nomination.

During the convention's half-day session on May 16 and the first full-day session on May 17, in fact, almost everything seemed to go the Sewardites' way, despite frantic lobbying efforts by the stop-Seward men. George Ashmun of Massachusetts, the convention's permanent chairman, favored Seward, though his few rulings were unbiased. A flap emerged over the platform committee's omission of language from the Declaration of Independence, an intentional omission meant to reassure conservatives but one that infuriated Joshua Giddings, Ohio's venerable former Free Soiler and a foe of Seward's nomination. It was settled when a pro-Seward New Yorker successfully amended the platform with the language Giddings wanted, thus earning his gratitude. With only one or two exceptions the platform in its entirety was wildly applauded and adopted by a nearly unanimous voice vote on May 17, the convention's second day.

Quite unlike Constitutional Union men, who professed such contempt for platforms, Republicans considered their national platform to be absolutely essential to their chances of victory. Aware that whomever they nominated would not campaign personally—taking the stump as a formal nominee simply was not done in that day—Republicans carefully devised a statement that would appeal to as many and offend as few potential constituents as possible. They began by justifying the very existence of their new party. Events since 1856, they declared, had "fully established the propriety and necessity of the organization and perpetuation of the Republican party."[33] It was committed to the principles of the Declaration concerning men's "inalienable rights" and to the preservation of "the Federal Constitution, the Rights of the States, and the Union of the States." The platform held "in abhorrence all schemes of disunion, come from whatever source they may," and boasted that no Republican members of Congress, quite unlike their Democratic counterparts, had ever uttered treasonous threats of disunion. Insisting that the right of every state to maintain "inviolate" and "control its own domestic institutions [i.e., slavery in the South] according to its own judgment exclusively" was essential to the perpetuation of the

Union, it "denounce[d] the lawless invasion by armed force" of any state or territory "as among the gravest of crimes." Here, that is, Republicans denied any connection to John Brown while reminding northern voters of Missouri Ruffians' invasions of Kansas.

After these preliminaries, the platform shifted to the specific reasons men should vote Republican in 1860. A few of these pledged Republican support for federal economic programs that Democrats had thus far stymied: a homestead act, federally subsidized internal improvements, including a railroad to the Pacific Coast, and protective tariffs that would "encourage the development of the industrial interests of the whole country." Even though this last plank carefully eschewed both the adjective *protective* and the noun *tariff* to appease Democrats in the party who had long opposed tariff protection, it ignited thunderous cheers from the Pennsylvanians in the Wigwam. Ex-Democrats there, presumably, sat on their hands.

Other planks merit closer examination. The fifth and sixth planks in this seventeen-plank platform focused on the sins of the Buchanan administration and made it irrefutably clear that Buchanan would be Republicans' chief target, no matter whom Democrats ended up nominating at Baltimore. Whereas foes tried to make the 1860 contest a prospective election, stressing the disaster that might ensue should a Republican win, Republicans strove to make it a retrospective election that emphasized why Democrats must be ousted from power. Buchanan's administration, railed the fifth plank, had exhibited "measureless subserviency to the exactions of a sectional interest"—i.e., the Slave Power—especially in attempting to force the "infamous Lecompton Constitution upon the protesting people of Kansas" and using federal power to protect slavery in the territories. Then the sixth plank, which drew such exuberant and prolonged cheering when it was first read that delegates demanded that it be read again, focused squarely on Democrats' corruption, which Republicans expected to make a centerpiece of their campaign. Americans "justly view with alarm," it contended, the "reckless extravagance" pervading "every department of the federal government . . . the systematic plundering of the public treasury by favored partisans." Along with the recently exposed "frauds and corruptions at the Federal metropolis" [by the Covode Committee], they demonstrated "that an entire change of administration is imperatively demanded."

Planks seven through eleven dealt, finally, with the slavery extension question and where Republicans—and Democrats—stood on it. In ascending order of importance, these demanded immediate statehood for Kansas with its antislavery constitution; condemned southern Democrats' claims that the Constitution "carries slavery into any and all of the territories of the United States"; castigated calls to reopen the African slave trade; blasted the action of federally appointed governors in Kansas and Nebraska vetoing antislavery laws passed by their territorial legislatures as showing the fraudulence of Democrats' popular sovereignty doctrine; and restated, while significantly altering, Republican opposition to slavery's westward expansion.

The second-most controversial section of the entire platform, this eighth plank intentionally refrained from demanding congressional prohibition of slavery from all territories, just as the *New York Times* and others had been recommending for at least half a year because they deemed congressional prohibition no longer necessary. Instead, to the dismay of radicals in the Wigwam, it made such congressional prohibition contingent, not automatic. At the same time, it reemphasized Republicans' opposition to anything resembling a federal slave code. Calling the normal condition of all federal territories "that of freedom," it cited Republicans' "duty, by legislation whenever such legislation is necessary" to maintain that freedom "against all attempts to violate it." Then it flatly "den[ied] the authority of Congress, of a Territorial Legislature, or of any individuals to give legal existence to slavery in any Territory of the United States." Abraham Lincoln's rocklike adherence to this platform plank after his election largely explains why he scuttled an attempted congressional compromise plan to resolve the secession crisis.

Far and away the most controversial plank in the Republican platform, however, had nothing to do with slavery, the South, or even Democrats. Indeed, it was aimed at the Republican Party in Massachusetts. In order to solidify a coalition with Know Nothings, who were especially numerous in the Bay State, it had passed and popularly ratified an amendment to the state constitution barring naturalized immigrants from voting until two years after they gained citizenship. This action infuriated Germans, who at a meeting in Chicago on May 16 had vowed to abandon the Republican Party should it nominate Bates or anyone else like Cameron or Banks who had trucked with Know Nothings. And it was pressure from Germans, especially Carl Schurz, a delegate from Wisconsin, that produced the fourteenth, so-called German plank in the platform. It vowed that the Republican Party opposed "any change in our Naturalization Laws or any State legislation by which the rights of citizenship hitherto accorded to immigrants from foreign lands shall be abridged or impaired." Absolutely nothing in the Republican national platform did as much to jeopardize their chances of carrying all-important Pennsylvania as this calculated slap at Know Nothings.

The Massachusetts delegate and a few others on the platform committee had protested against this plank and warned that including it in their product would offend Know Nothings who were so crucial to the party's chances in the Lower North, especially as the new Constitutional Union Party was now appealing to Fillmore's 1856 supporters. Thus, the convention's apparently overwhelming endorsement of a platform that offended Know Nothings at the behest of Germans like Carl Schurz—there was no roll-call vote so we do not know how Pennsylvanians responded—appeared a distinct victory for Seward, whom Germans adored and Know Nothings despised. So ecstatic were Seward's supporters that, even though it was now past six in the evening, they demanded that the convention move immediately to votes for the nominee. Only Ashmun's ruling that the convention's secretaries lacked the tally sheets necessary to record any votes prevented the Seward men from running away with the trophy.

Still, Seward's supporters left confident of victory the next morning. Weed's inner circle of floor workers would reportedly guzzle over three hundred bottles of champagne that night in the hotel where the New Yorkers were staying as they celebrated Seward's seemingly inevitable victory. Things had gone so well on May 17 for the pro-Seward men that even Greeley telegraphed that night to his *New York Tribune* that Seward would be nominated the following day. The Cincinnati reporter Murat Halstead concurred. "The cheering of the thousands of spectators during the day," he reported that night, "indicated that a very large share of the outside pressure was for Seward. There is something almost irresistible here in the prestige of his fame."[34]

While New Yorkers partied on the night of May 17, Lincoln's friends, captained by the obese but seemingly indefatigable David Davis, worked frantically to prevent a Seward victory on the morrow's first ballot by persuading delegates to abandon Seward. They had already gained a commitment from the Indianans to go for Lincoln on that ballot, probably with a promise that an Indianan would have a spot in Lincoln's cabinet should he win the nomination and election. Davis and others among the Lincoln men in Chicago understood that such commitments had to be made. When Lincoln's order that his friends not make any binding contracts about jobs on his behalf reached Chicago on the morning of May 17, the hard-nosed Davis reportedly snapped: "Lincoln ain't here, and don't know what we have to meet, so we will go ahead, as if we hadn't heard from him, and he must ratify it."[35] Aside from working on the Virginia and some New England delegations, the chief target on the night of May 17 was Pennsylvania. Hard feelings abounded between the New Yorkers and Pennsylvanians in Chicago, and most of the latter were committed to Cameron on the first ballot. The question was what they would do after that vote, for they were realistic enough to know that Cameron had virtually no support outside of Pennsylvania. Evidently with a promise of a cabinet slot for Cameron—certainly Cameron and other Pennsylvanians believed such a commitment had been made—Davis persuaded most of the Pennsylvanians to shift to Lincoln after the first ballot. Weed later wrote Seward that while the Pennsylvanians would never vote for Seward himself, they had broken a promise to stick with Cameron rather than shift their support to anyone else.

Friday, May 18, was decision day for the Republicans. That morning Seward's stalwarts, almost a thousand strong and brimming with confidence, marched behind their band from their hotel to the Wigwam. Once there they discovered the spectator galleries filled with Lincoln's supporters, who had forged admission tickets. Still, enough Sewardites gained admission that a literal shouting match between them and the Lincoln men would be one of the features of that day that men who were there remembered long afterward. William L. Dayton, New Jersey's favorite son who had been Frémont's running mate in 1856, Bates, Chase, Cameron, and McLean were nominated, but interest focused on Lincoln and Seward. Norman Judd nominated Lincoln; Indiana's Caleb B. Smith and Ohio's Columbus Delano seconded him. William M. Evarts of New York nominated Seward, while Wisconsin's Carl Schurz and Michigan's Austin Blair seconded his motion.

After Blair finished, the Sewardites' roar of approval, according to Halstead, "was absolutely frantic, shrill and wild." Men held their ears in pain at the din. "No Commanches, no panthers ever struck a higher note or gave screams with more infernal intensity." From the front stage where reporters sat, all he could see were "thousands of hats—a black, mighty swarm of hats—flying with the velocity of hornets over a mass of human heads." But the Lincoln men topped that spectacular demonstration after Delano finished his seconding speech. "The uproar was beyond description," wrote Halstead. "Imagine all the hogs ever slaughtered in Cincinnati giving their death squeals together." He hadn't thought the "Seward yell" could be surpassed, "but the Lincoln boys were clearly ahead." The Seward delegates from New York, Michigan, and Wisconsin had sat together, and "their faces whitened as the Lincoln *yawp* swelled into a wild hosanna of victory."[36]

Roll-call votes for the nomination proceeded geographically, not alphabetically, starting with northern New England, moving south along the Atlantic coastal states, then into the border states and the Midwest, ending with the two West Coast states and Minnesota. Erosion in Seward's support appeared almost immediately on the first ballot. Seward got 10 of Maine's votes, but Lincoln received 6. New Hampshire gave Seward only a single vote to Lincoln's 7. Then came Vermont's stunner. It gave all 10 of its votes to native son Senator Jacob Collamer, who had not even been formally nominated. Seward garnered 21 of Massachusetts' 25 votes, but he was shut out in Connecticut and Rhode Island, the states whose gubernatorial elections had indicated a revulsion against sectional extremism. In sum, of New England's 81 votes, Seward received only 32 while Lincoln took 19. "So much for the caucusing the night before," concluded Halstead.[37]

New York went solidly for Seward and New Jersey for favorite son Dayton, but in Pennsylvania minor leakage from Cameron toward Lincoln occurred even on the first ballot, indicating the belief that Lincoln was the better stop-Seward hope. The four border slave states together contained 51 votes. Thirty-two of those, including Missouri's entire delegation, went to Bates, while Seward took 8 to Lincoln's 6. Henry Lane's work paid off when Virginia was called. It gave Lincoln 14 votes compared to Seward's 8. All 22 of the Wisconsin and Michigan votes went for Seward, as expected, but they were overmatched by the solid 48 votes Lincoln received from Indiana and Illinois. Lincoln also took 8 of Ohio's 46 votes compared to Chase's 34, indicating the weakness of Chase's chances.

When the roll call ended, Seward led with 173½, trailed by Lincoln with 102, Cameron with 50½, Chase with 49, and Bates with 48. The remaining votes were scattered among Collamer, Dayton, McLean, and Ohio's Ben Wade, while John M. Reed, Charles Sumner, and Frémont each received a single throw-away vote. Rather than winning on the first ballot as the anti-Seward forces had feared, in short, Seward fell 60 votes shy of the necessary majority while Lincoln had done far better than expected.

The second ballot followed immediately. Seward picked up one additional vote in Massachusetts, but Lincoln now garnered 36 of the 82 votes New England men cast on that ballot. New York remained solid for Seward, and four of the New Jersey men switched from Dayton to Seward. The biggest shift on that ballot occurred in Pennsylvania; Lincoln now received 48 of its votes while only one lone delegate clung to Cameron. Lincoln also gained 6 votes in Ohio, 3 in Iowa, and 9 from Delaware, Maryland, and Kentucky. When the ballot had concluded, Seward had climbed to 184½ votes, but Lincoln had soared to 181, a gain of 79 votes. Bates, Cameron, Chase, McLean, and Dayton all declined; the names of Wade, Reed, Collamer, Sumner, and Frémont had disappeared; and the Kentucky abolitionist Cassius M. Clay now surprisingly received 2 votes from Connecticut, where the April election had ostensibly repudiated sectional extremism. Both Seward and Lincoln were 50 votes shy of the necessary majority, but the trend was clear since the nearly one hundred delegates who had not supported either man on that ballot were clearly not Seward's for the taking.

Thus the pro-Lincoln phalanx in the Wigwam buzzed with excitement as the third roll call of the states began. Lincoln gained 5 votes in New England, 4 in New Jersey, 4 more in Pennsylvania, 5 in the border slave states, and 12 in Ohio. Once Ohio had voted, Lincoln's total stood at 173. Illinois and Indiana brought it to 221, and Iowa added 5½ more. Four from Minnesota and 1 from Nebraska Territory pushed him to 231½ as the voting ended. Seward had lost only a single vote since the second ballot, but now the nomination was clearly Lincoln's. Daniel Carrter, chairman of the Ohio delegation, rose to say that four Ohioans were shifting their votes from Chase to Lincoln. This announcement cemented Lincoln's victory, and now the chairs of state after state changed their states' votes to make Lincoln's nomination unanimous. Visibly crestfallen, Evarts, Schurz, and Austin, the men who had nominated Seward, pledged to carry their states for Lincoln in November. Halstead reported the reaction as follows: "The nerves of the thousands, which through the hours of suspense, had been subjected to a terrible tension, relaxed." The throng took "deep breaths of relief" and then "a noise" coursed through the Wigwam "like the rush of a great wind in the van of a storm, and in another breath the storm was there." Thousands cheered "with the energy of insanity."[38]

As the crowd outside the Wigwam reacted to the news of Lincoln's nomination with wild jubilation, the convention recessed for a midday dinner before moving to the nomination of a vice presidential candidate. During the recess the chairs of all the respective state delegations met and offered to let the despondent New Yorkers name anyone they wanted as Lincoln's running mate. Evarts, who though in tears had gallantly been the first to urge making Lincoln's nomination unanimous, declined the offer.

When the convention reassembled, nine men, including two Pennsylvanians, Banks of Massachusetts, and the Texan Sam Houston, whom many conservatives had hoped would be the Constitutional Union presidential candidate, received votes for vice president on the first ballot. No one from New York was in this group. The leaders were Kentucky's Cassius Clay, with 101½ votes, and Maine's Senator Hannibal Hamlin, with 194. Clay received 86 votes on the second ballot, but Hamlin easily prevailed with 367. Hannibal Hamlin was a former Democrat. Thus the party's ticket was headed by an ex-Whig with an ex-Democrat in the second spot, the precise reverse of the political antecedents of the ticket in 1856. Lincoln was fifty-one years old; Hamlin would turn that age in August. Thus the Republican candidates were markedly younger than the aged veterans— many said "fossils"—the Constitutional Union convention had selected a week earlier.

On Saturday, May 19, a small delegation headed by Ashmun, the convention's chairman, and accompanied by *New York Times* editor Henry J. Raymond took the train to Springfield to inform Lincoln officially of his nomination. They met in Lincoln's house for about thirty minutes. Lincoln thanked them, promised to send a formal written acceptance of the nomination in a few days, and said that he was "deeply, and even painfully sensible of the great responsibility" the convention had conferred on him.[39] Dated May 23 and addressed to Ashmun, his brief, formal letter of acceptance stressed his approval of the platform's "declaration of principles and sentiments" and pledged that "it shall be my care not to violate, or disregard it, in any part."[40] This very brief letter would be Lincoln's last statement meant for public consumption about the election or anything else until February 1861 when he traveled from Springfield to Washington for his March 4 inauguration. But time would show that he meant every word of it.

So, why did Seward lose and Lincoln win the Republican Party's presidential nomination at Chicago? Three postmortems suggest some of the reasons. In his last report from the convention to his Cincinnati newspaper, Murat Halstead insisted that the real "fact of the Convention was the defeat of Seward rather than the nomination of Lincoln. It was a triumph of a presumption of availability over pre-eminence in intellect and unrivaled fame—a success of the ruder qualities of manhood and the more homely attributes of popularity over the arts of a consummate politician and the splendor of accomplished statesmanship."[41] This surprisingly bitter summation from Halstead, who had been so objective if not mockingly cynical in his reports from the Democratic and Constitutional Union gatherings, suggests that he was invested emotionally in Seward's nomination. It might be thus translated: the convention preferred a roughhewn Westerner who had the best chance in Illinois and Indiana over the polished, educated, and brilliant statesman from the East. Lincoln's Illinois residence, in sum, explained his availability.

Chagrined and deeply embarrassed by his failure at Chicago, Thurlow

Weed had fled to Davenport, Iowa, where no one knew who he was and from which he wrote his autopsy of the result to Seward on May 20. Pennsylvanians who switched from Cameron to Lincoln on the second ballot rather than sticking with Cameron as they had told him and Ohioans who had promised to go for Seward, not Lincoln, once they abandoned Chase, had both betrayed him, Weed complained. Nathaniel Banks's friends had helped subvert Seward because they needed a Midwestern candidate to advance Banks's hope for the vice presidential nomination. New Hampshire men reneged on pledges to go for Seward on the second ballot, while "Greeley was malignant," misleading "many fair minded men" and turning the Vermont delegation against Seward. Meanwhile, the Blairs—Francis Sr., Francis Jr. (Frank), and Montgomery—were smooth but "perfidious" in turning the Maryland, Virginia, Delaware, and Kentucky delegates "against us." In sum, he concluded, "We were beaten by a combination of all the disappointed, whose diligent assertions (sustained by the delegates from these states) [were] that you would loose [*sic*] New Jersey, Pa.[,] Indiana and Connecticut."[42] Seward's unavailability in the Lower North, in short, was the key. What Weed did not specify because Seward already knew it was that in all four of those states former Know Nothings were simply too critical to Republican success to risk offending them by nominating Seward.

Joshua Giddings, who had stormed out of the convention only to return when the language from the Declaration of Independence was inserted in the platform, and who had lived in the same boardinghouse with Lincoln during Lincoln's single congressional term, had a different explanation. "Your selection was made upon two grounds," Giddings wrote Lincoln on May 19. First, "you are an *honest* man." Second, "you are not in the hands of corrupt and dishonest men."[43] A New York delegate amplified this explanation in a speech at Rochester in June. Seward would have gained the nomination, he told his disappointed fellow New Yorkers, "had not his opponents" alluded "to the corruptions practiced at Albany during the past winter. No man entertained the idea that Mr. Seward was connected with them, but it was charged that his friends were, and it was pretended that if elected the same practices would be transmitted to Washington."[44]

To be sure, other Republicans undoubtedly offered their own explanations for the result at Chicago. What is so noteworthy about these three, however, is the utter absence of any claim that it was Lincoln's supposed moderation contrasted to Seward's supposed radicalism on the slavery issue that produced the outcome. Rather it was Republicans' ability to continue to exploit the corruption issue against Democrats; to have a fighting chance to carry Pennsylvania, something Seward could never have done once his supporters forced the so-called German plank in the platform through the convention; and to compete with Douglas for Illinois and Indiana that explained the outcome. Stephen Douglas, of course, had not yet been officially nominated when Republicans met in Chicago. But, as Republicans expected, he would be when Democrats reconvened in Baltimore in June. Moreover, what Democrats did there seemed likely to increase Republicans' chances of victory in November.

6 DEMOCRATS' NOMINATIONS: ACT II

When the second meeting of the Democratic national convention assembled in Baltimore's Front Street Theater on June 18, the astute newspaperman Murat Halstead reported that "the hostile feeling between the factions of the Democracy was even more embittered than at the time of adjournment at Charleston."[1] Douglas's supporters had brushed aside calls from Democratic papers like the Albany *Argus and Atlas* that Douglas end his candidacy so Democrats could reunite, and they came to Baltimore intent on doing whatever it took to nominate him. Lincoln's surprising selection by the Republicans only increased their determination while providing them leverage with Democrats from the New England and Mid-Atlantic states who had opposed Douglas at Charleston. Just as Lincoln's backers could champion him by arguing that Douglas's likely nomination made it imperative for Republicans to choose a man who could compete with him for Illinois and Indiana, so Douglas's Midwestern supporters could now make the same case for the necessity of picking Douglas to keep those crucial Midwestern states out of the Republican column.

Not all northeastern Democrats succumbed to this argument. Certainly Buchanan's loyalists in Pennsylvania and elsewhere did not. Nonetheless, by early June it appeared that Douglas would have far more support from northern delegates than he had had at Charleston. By the time they reached Baltimore most were determined to deny entry to the reassembled convention by anyone who had bolted at Charleston. In nightly street demonstrations in Baltimore's Monument Square, indeed, they denounced the Charleston seceders and especially Alabama's William Yancey as "disorganizers, bolters, traitors, and disunionists."[2]

Most of the Charleston bolters in fact did present themselves despite attempts in several states to displace them with pro-Douglas men. In Baltimore they were aided, according to a Republican paper, by "the forces of the Administration, from the Cabinet officers down to the clerks in the Departments, all intent on the defeat of Douglas by any means, fair or foul."[3]

At Charleston those delegates who had remained in Institute Hall had "recommended" that the state Democratic parties in the eight southern states whose delegates had bolted fill the "vacancies" with new delegations and send them to the reconvened session in Baltimore on June 18. This call to displace the men who had decamped to Military Hall as their states' official Democratic representatives infuriated them. It increased their determination to stand by their anti-Douglas platform and to represent their states at Richmond on June 11 and, if necessary, at Baltimore a week later. It also increased their willingness to nominate their own candidate if the Douglas men refused to submit to their terms.

A public letter issued from Washington in mid-May by nineteen prominent southern Democratic congressmen reinforced the Charleston bolters' defiant attitude even as it hinted that a separate southern candidate might not be necessary. The signers included both U.S. senators from Arkansas, Georgia, Virginia, and Louisiana as well as Mississippi's Jefferson Davis, who had just concluded a spat in the Senate with Douglas about the relative merits and demerits of popular sovereignty. More important, Davis was also the original author of the "when necessary" language about the congressional enactment of a federal territorial slave code in the platform adopted by the Charleston bolters. The congressmen insisted that there was no time to elect new state conventions before the gatherings assembled in Richmond and Baltimore. In any event, the men who had seceded from Institute Hall remained the official Democratic delegates from their states. Therefore the Democratic executive committees or reassembled conventions should endorse their action at Charleston and send them on to Baltimore in one last attempt to reunite the party. But they should continue to insist on the platform they had adopted in Military Hall, for only it upheld "the equal rights of the States as the very basis of the confederacy."[4] If Democrats could somehow reunite behind some candidate other than Douglas in Baltimore, these congressmen added, the seventeen states that had supported the majority platform, along with ostensibly safe Pennsylvania and New Jersey, possessed enough electoral votes for Democrats to elect him.

Southern Democrats' stress on defending the equal rights of states cannot be overemphasized. It was their shibboleth and their angry retort to Republican demands that the northern majority rule. States, not population, mattered most, southern Democrats insisted. Popular vote majorities or even electoral vote majorities had no right to deny states equal treatment regardless of how small their population might be. Their personal honor and their constituents' rights required southern Democrats to abandon any institution, be it the Democratic Party or the United States government, that treated states unequally.

Despite a consensus about defending state equality, Deep South Democrats' responses to the choices before them between May 3 and June 18 had differed from state to state. Texas, Florida, and Mississippi Democratic state executive committees spurned the call to fill purported vacancies, cheered the actions of their delegates at Charleston, and made no attempt to replace them by reconvening their state conventions. Florida ordered its men to go to Richmond alone; the other two told them to stop off at Richmond but also seek entrance into the Baltimore convention. South Carolina Democrats did hold a new state convention that chose new delegates. They did so, however, because they regarded the original delegation, mostly followers of former Speaker of the House James Orr, as unreliably anti-Douglas. They dispatched the new men to Richmond and Richmond alone. There they could never be tempted to acquiesce to Douglas's nomination should the Baltimore convention make it.

In contrast, Douglas had varying levels of support among Democrats in the other four states whose delegates had walked out in Charleston. In terms of percentages of slaveholders and dependence on plantation production, after all, Arkansas had much in common with the Upper South slave states whose men had remained in Institute Hall. Delegates representing three of Arkansas' four votes had bolted in Charleston, and a district convention attended by fewer than a tenth of the district's Democrats sent three pro-Douglas men to Baltimore to claim one of those votes. In Louisiana, New Orleans editors and Pierre Soulé, a former minister to Spain and bitter factional rival of Senator John Slidell, who had worked relentlessly as an outsider at Charleston to foil Douglas, led the pro-Douglas forces. At a convention attended by men from only twenty of the state's thirty-nine parishes, they sent pro-Douglas men including Soulé to Baltimore, while the officially endorsed state Democratic convention dispatched the Charleston bolters to that destination and Richmond as well. In Alabama, influential Mobile editor John Forsyth and popular former governor John Winston led the pro-Douglas men, thirty-five of whom called for a convention to meet in Selma on June 4 to pick delegates to Baltimore. Barely half of the state's counties were represented at it; still, it sent a full pro-Douglas delegation, including Forsyth, to Baltimore. Meanwhile, the Democrats' state executive committee called for the official state convention to reconvene on June 11; it sent the Yancey-led bolters to both Richmond and Baltimore.

The most important and revealing intraparty fracas occurred among Georgia's Democrats. It was most important because, alone among Deep South delegations at Charleston, almost a third of the Georgia men had refused to abandon Institute Hall and because Georgia was the most populous Deep South state. It was most revealing because the editors of the Macon *Weekly Georgia Telegraph*, who called for Georgia Democrats to ignore the Richmond gathering and send new men to Baltimore, also requested the state's leading Democrats to send the paper their view on what Georgia's Democrats should now do. Almost all called for the previous Democratic state convention, which, it should be recalled, had narrowly rejected demands that a federal slave code plank be included in the party's national platform, to reassemble. After this meeting of the minds, they disagreed sharply. E. A. Nisbet, a former two-term Whig congressman who had prominently supported Buchanan in 1856 and now touted Douglas, deplored the walkout at Charleston and stressed that a slave-code national platform assured defeat for any Democratic candidate in the North. New men, he concluded, must be sent to Baltimore. So did Alexander Stephens, a more prominent former Whig who had converted to the Democratic Party and openly championed Douglas for months, and Hershel V. Johnson, a former Democratic governor and two-time Democratic presidential elector. Democrats, insisted Stephens, must not abandon congressional nonintervention as their rallying cry. On the other side, Democratic congressman James Jackson, treasury secretary Howell Cobb, and E. J. McGehee, one of the bolting Georgia delegates, all defended the walkout and insistence on a slave-code platform because the Cincinnati platform, on which the Douglasites insisted, was given "two interpretations . . . one to suit the North and another to suit the South." "I am an Administration Democrat," declared McGehee, "and opposed to Mr. Douglas' 'unfriendly legislation' doctrines."[5] Most of these men also reiterated an argument frequently made at Charleston and repeated by the southern Democratic congressmen in their public letter. All safely Democratic states supported the majority slave-code platform; only men from states Democrats probably could not carry opposed it. Again, to these Southerners it was the number of states, not the number of people, on each side that mattered.

The old state convention reassembled in Milledgeville, the state capital, on June 4. Over two-thirds of its members voted to send the original delegates who had bolted and insisted on a slave-code platform to both Richmond and then Baltimore. The defeated minority, labeling themselves the National Democratic Party, met the following day and sent a different, pro-Douglas Georgia delegation exclusively to Baltimore—where, everyone knew, Douglas's supporters would control events.

On the convention's first day, pro-Douglas delegates attempted to pass resolutions barring anyone who had gone to Richmond from sitting in the convention and requiring any delegate seated from the South to pledge to support the victorious nominee. Those attempts failed, but North Carolina's William Avery complained that their sponsors were determined to drive Southerners like himself out of the convention. Here Avery identified the tripwire that would blow up the Democratic Party. Ruthless treatment of anti-Douglas men from the Deep South by Douglas's vindictive northern supporters could easily propel the Upper South delegates who had remained in Institute Hall into the arms of the Deep South bolters, most of whom had already determined to nominate their own southern Democratic presidential candidate.

Douglas's nomination—and any possible reunification of the national Democratic Party—now depended on which Southerners were seated in the Front Street Theater. On the morning of the second day a credentials committee composed of men from each of the twenty-five states that had not bolted at Charleston was appointed to decide who should represent Arkansas, Texas, Louisiana, Mississippi, Alabama, and Georgia in the convention.[6] Each state had two representatives and a single vote on that credentials committee. Its members struggled for two full days to reach a consensus, but they failed. Instead, on Thursday, the convention's fourth day, they would deliver both majority and minority reports to the awaiting delegates.

The failure of the credentials committee to agree and the resulting likelihood of a final sectional disruption of the party prompted Douglas—in nearby Washington—to send a letter, dated June 21, to William A. Richardson, his convention floor leader. In it he offered to withdraw his candidacy if, but only if, the convention adopted a platform endorsing congressional nonintervention with slavery in the territories and nominated a man committed to that principle. The union of the nation and of the Democratic Party was more important than his personal advancement, wrote Douglas. Thus Richardson and his other friends should "act with an eye single to the safety and welfare of the country, and without the slightest regard to my individual interests or aggrandizement." The following day he telegraphed the same message to Dean Richmond, chairman of the pivotal New York delegation, whose 35 votes determined the outcome of every roll-call vote on credentials.[7] Both men pocketed the communications without revealing them to the full convention until after it had nominated Douglas.

The credentials committee did not attempt to exclude all the Charleston bolters. With only two dissenters in the case of Mississippi and six in that of Texas, the committee voted to seat their Charleston delegates who had been reendorsed by their state party executive committees. It declared that one of Arkansas' four votes was already represented, and it approved six anti-Douglas men for two of the remaining votes and the three pro-Douglas men for the other vote. It voted 16 to 9 to seat the pro-Douglas delegation from Louisiana; 14 to 11 to seat the anti-Yancey, pro-Douglas delegation from Alabama; and 13 to 10 to admit both sets of claimants from Georgia and give those Georgians half a vote apiece. The majority reported all of these decisions to the convention on its fourth day, Thursday, June 21.

In a scathing, often brilliant report written by Oregon's Isaac Stevens and signed by eight additional committee members, including those from New Jersey, Pennsylvania, California, and all the slave states who had not bolted at Charleston, save those from Missouri and Maryland, a minority (36 percent of the full committee) denounced these decisions. Charleston's bolters had withdrawn from Institute Hall, Stevens contended, but they had not resigned their commissions as officially accredited delegates. They therefore remained the official Democratic delegates from their states. They had been reappointed as delegates to Baltimore by state executive committees or reassembled state conventions that represented majority Democratic opinion in their states, quite unlike the blatantly unrepresentative meetings that had sent pro-Douglas men to Baltimore. The committee had agreed to reseat the Mississippi and Texas bolters. Fairness—that is, equal treatment—thus obligated the convention to admit the bolters from the other states as well. Thus all of Charleston's seceders should be seated, as should Florida's. The majority report, argued Stevens, raised a question "whether the Democratic party in said states shall be ostracized and branded as unworthy of affiliation with the national organization." Should "persons irregularly called, or withdrawing from the regular [state] Convention . . . have the sanction of the National Convention to raise the flag of rebellion against their respective State organizations"? How this convention answered those questions, Stevens grimly warned, would determine "whether there shall be a National Democratic party or not."[8]

The crucial decision came on the morning of Friday, June 22, the convention's fifth day, on a vote to substitute Stevens's minority report for the majority report. Majorities of the delegates from Pennsylvania, New Jersey, and Massachusetts, and all of them from California and Oregon, supported this effort. Nonetheless, three-fifths of the men who voted, including all 35 New Yorkers, opposed it, and it failed. Then the convention voted on the individual recommendations. Louisiana's pro-Douglas dissidents won approval by a vote of 152 to 98. Again New York voted unanimously with the majority, and again 17 of Pennsylvania's 27 delegates and 8 of Massachusetts' 13 voted with the anti-Douglas minority. After this vote, wrote the reporter Halstead, "There was no longer any doubt about the disruption of the Convention."[9] The majority report's recommendations for Arkansas and Alabama were also approved by somewhat similar margins. When Georgia was reached, however, New York's delegation joined the opponents to defeat the recommendations to split that state's vote between rival delegations. According to a *New York Times* reporter, they did so because Virginians warned them they would abandon the convention if the majority's recommendation were accepted.[10] Instead, with New York's solid support, Georgia's bolters at Charleston alone were voted admission.

At this point Benjamin Hallett of Massachusetts denounced the convention's treatment of the eight southern states and predicted that it would drive the remaining southern states out of the convention to join them. Those states, he declared, "will never stay here to the disgrace of their brother States outside."[11] He was right. The convention recessed until 7 p.m., but before it did the chairman of the Virginia delegation warned that at the appropriate time, he had an important announcement to make. "This was the announcement of Virginia that she was about to lead the new secession," reported Halstead.[12]

During the recess the New Yorkers again wavered and offered to the Louisianans still outside the hall to reseat the Charleston delegation rather than the pro-Douglas dissenters. The Louisianans contemptuously rejected this offer, as had the delegates from Texas and Mississippi. They clearly intended to go their own way since the convention refused to treat all southern states equally. The only question was whether other delegates would join them. It was answered when the meeting reconvened on the night of June 22. Once it was clear that the votes on the majority report of the credentials committee were final, 25 of the 30 Virginians, 10 of 12 North Carolina men, and 19 of 24 Tennesseans protesting the unfair treatment of their fellow Southerners withdrew from the hall. Charging that Douglasite "assassins" chortled in an unseemly manner while they "consummated" "the destruction of the Democratic party," California's chairman angrily led his state's delegates out with them. Isaac Stevens, the incisive Oregonian, struck a sadder note. It was, he said, "his most melancholy duty" to take the Oregonians out as well. The convention's majority, he protested, had done "a most grievous wrong and insult . . . to sovereign States." Those states were "the weak parties in this contest, and we have resolved to stand by them and assert their rights."[13] Before the convention adjourned for the night, Delaware's delegation announced that it would remain in the convention hall but refrain from participating in any further proceedings.

The leakage continued on Saturday, June 23, the convention's sixth day. The majority of the Kentuckians withdrew. Then Caleb Cushing resigned as the convention's chairman to cat-calls of relief from the Douglas men, who had not forgiven his anti-Douglas rulings at Charleston. Ohio's David Tod replaced him. Cushing took a seat on the floor with the Massachusetts delegation, but not for long. Led by Ben Butler, most of that delegation soon withdrew from the Front Street Theater and joined the other bolters, as well as the original Charleston seceders who had never entered the convention hall, in the Maryland Institute. At this point, all or at least some of the delegates from a majority of states in the union had abandoned the now undeniably only nominal national convention of the national Democratic Party.

Undeterred, indeed often elated by the walkouts, the remaining delegates in the Front Street Theater rushed to formally nominate Douglas, despite the fact that they represented fewer than two-thirds of the men who had originally convened in Charleston. On the first vote Douglas received 173 of 191 votes cast. The few remaining delegates from slave states cast a total of 37 votes on that ballot. New pro-Douglas delegates admitted from Louisiana, Alabama, and Arkansas accounted for 16 of those few southern votes. James Guthrie of Kentucky came in a distant second with 10 votes, and John C. Breckinridge from the same state was third, with 5. Of the 17 Pennsylvanians who voted, only 10 went for Douglas—presumably the same ten men who had voted to support the majority credentials report. On the second ballot Douglas's total climbed to 181, and the delegates then declared his nomination unanimous even though it was still below the 202 two-thirds majority required by a fully attended convention.

Delegates then fell all over themselves to praise the forty-seven-year-old Douglas as a great statesman, as a native of New England as well as champion of the Midwest, as a loyal Democrat, and as the certain victor in the states they represented. John Cochrane, a New Yorker who had opposed Douglas's nomination, ended the lovefest by declaring: "Patriotism and honesty require that those who have been sent here as delegates are, in strict honor, bound by the actions of this Convention. But above and beyond the obligations of honor there is a volition that will expand from these walls to the whole country, which will resound in huzza upon huzza for Stephen A. Douglas."[14] The convention then recessed so the delegates could eat dinner before reassembling to choose Douglas's running mate.

The delegates' first action upon returning was to appoint a new national executive committee to manage the campaign. To indicate that this rump convention actually represented the entire Democratic Party (which it emphatically did not), it included men from every state in the nation except South Carolina on this executive committee. The most important designee was the New York banker August Belmont, whom the committee would elect as its national chairman.

With this business completed, according to Murat Halstead's report of the proceedings, a Tennessean announced that "the Southern delegates in their Convention have conferred together and have agreed unanimously to nominate for Vice-President of the United States" Senator Benjamin Fitzpatrick of Alabama.[15] The Southerners who had left the Front Street Theater as well as the Charleston bolters who had never entered it officially were meeting simultaneously that Saturday in the Maryland Institute Hall to make their own nominations as the National Democratic Party. Fitzpatrick was emphatically not their pick for vice president, so Halstead's wording here puzzles. In any event, the delegates in the Front Street Theater apparently took the Tennessean to mean that Fitzpatrick's selection for the second spot on the Douglas ticket might offer a way to bring the feuding Democrats back together. So they rushed it through by a vote of 198 to 1. A committee was appointed to go to Washington to notify Douglas and Fitzpatrick of their nominations. Then—and only then in the convention's waning minutes—did it finally take up the matter of a national platform.

In an editorial about the proceedings in Baltimore, the *New York Times* noted on Saturday, June 23, that "nothing has yet been said of a platform at Baltimore, and we are inclined to think that this subject will not be mooted."[16] In Baltimore itself that Saturday night, Ohio's Henry Payne, who had fought so hard against the anti-Douglas forces at both Charleston and Baltimore, declared that "it is generally understood that the platform was adopted at Charleston." Nonetheless, he was willing to let one of the pro-Douglas Louisiana delegates seated by the credentials committee offer an amendment to it.

Here Payne erred, perhaps intentionally. A full platform had in fact not been officially adopted at Charleston. That convention had voted to substitute the minority pro-Douglas platform for the majority anti-Douglas, slave code "when necessary" platform, but then it had never formally adopted that minority platform in its entirety as the 1860 national platform. Instead, it had adopted only the first plank reendorsing the Cincinnati platform, but not the explanatory plank about Supreme Court decisions and territorial legislatures' authority, or the planks regarding a Pacific railroad, protection of naturalized citizens' rights, repeal of personal liberty laws, and the acquisition of Cuba. Instead, pro-Douglas men, having first voted for those additional planks, changed their votes to nays in order to limit the number of Southerners who bolted Institute Hall. Whatever the remaining delegates in Baltimore's Front Street Theater thought, what they had inherited from Charleston was a fragment, not a full national platform. Had Cushing still been in the chair he could probably have told them that.

The amendment that Louisiana's former governor Robert Wickliffe wished to add to the platform simply stipulated that all good citizens should respect whatever the Supreme Court had already or "shall hereafter. . . finally determine" about "the measure of restriction, whatever it may be" that the "Federal Constitution" imposed "on the power of the Territorial Legislature over the subject of domestic relations" "during the existence of Territorial Governments." This amendment, Wickliffe enthused, would win Douglas 40,000 additional votes "in two of the Slave States of this Union."[17] A Virginian protested that this amendment would offset any advantage Fitzpatrick's nomination gave the Douglas ticket in the South. Nonetheless, the delegates adopted it overwhelmingly. The full minority platform substituted at Charleston but never adopted in its entirety there was thus not formally adopted as the national platform. But that full platform, along with Wickliffe's amendment, is what went out from Baltimore to the national press as the National Democratic Party's national platform as adopted at both Charleston and Baltimore.

Its controversial language regarding slavery extension that the southern bolters found so offensive bears repeating here. First, it affirmed its commitment to the Cincinnati platform of 1856, without actually repeating that platform's language concerning popular sovereignty. It then added: "Inasmuch as differences of opinion exist in the Democratic party as to the nature and extent of the Powers of a Territorial Legislature, and as to the powers and duties of Congress, under the Constitution of the United States, over the institution of Slavery within the Territories: Resolved, That the Democratic party will abide by the decisions of the Supreme Court of the United States on the questions of Constitutional law." Then followed the noncontroversial planks pledging to defend naturalized citizens' rights; promising "such Constitutional aid as will insure the construction of a Railroad to the Pacific coast"; favoring the acquisition of Cuba; and condemning northern states' personal liberty laws. Tacked on at the end was now Wickliffe's convoluted amendment that in the context of the full platform seems redundant to the modern eye.[18]

Only after men had been picked to take the news to Douglas and Fitzpatrick and this last-minute fiddling with the platform had ended did Illinois' William A. Richardson read to the convention Douglas's letter of June 21 offering to withdraw his candidacy to save the party and the Union. He called on New York's Richmond to read his telegram of June 22 to that same effect. With these efforts the convention adjourned for the final time.

Douglas orally accepted the nomination as soon as the delegation from Baltimore reached him on Saturday night and then more formally in a letter dated June 27. He did so, he averred, because the platform first adopted at Charleston and readopted at Baltimore reaffirmed the great Democratic doctrine of congressional nonintervention with slavery in the territories. If, in contrast, the power of Congress to make laws about territorial slavery, either to prohibit or to establish it, were admitted, "two hostile sectional parties must be the result; the one inflaming the passions and ambitions of the North and the other of the South;—and each struggling to use the Federal power and authority for the aggrandizement of its own section at the expense of the equal rights of the other."[19] Thus Douglas made clear even in his letter of acceptance that he intended to make war on the platform favored by the southern Democrats who rejected him. What he did not repeat were his oft-chorused assertions about the ability of local residents to prohibit slavery simply by not passing proslavery police regulations.

By June 27, Benjamin Fitzpatrick had declined his nomination in a letter dated June 25 on the grounds that his acceptance would further divide the Democrats in Alabama and the rest of the South. The newly appointed national executive committee had immediately offered the post to Georgia's former governor Herschel V. Johnson. He had accepted with alacrity by telegraph on June 26.[20] So the national ticket would be Stephen A. Douglas and Herschel V. Johnson, aged forty-seven and forty-eight, respectively, and thus slightly younger than the Republican ticket and dramatically younger than John Bell and Edward Everett. The presidential candidate nominated by the bolters in Baltimore's Maryland Institute Hall on Saturday, June 23, would be even younger still.

Those bolters insisted that they, not the pretenders in the Front Street Theater, were the real National Democratic Party convention. They included not simply all, or nearly all, of the delegates the slave states had sent to Baltimore (the South Carolinians remained stranded in Richmond)[21] but also a few men from New York, Vermont, and Minnesota, the entire Oregon and California delegations, twelve Pennsylvanians, and sixteen Massachusetts men including Caleb Cushing, whom this convention now chose as its chairman. Two things struck the observant Murat Halstead about these men. They were harmonious, and they were in a hurry. They were determined to complete their break from the Douglasite Democrats on that Saturday. No one wanted to languish in Baltimore until Monday to finish the job.

The convention unanimously readopted the majority platform reported to the Institute Hall convention at Charleston and adopted by the bolters in that city's Military Hall. To recall, this intentionally anti-Douglas platform stressed that no congressional or territorial legislation could deny citizens their right to slave property in the territories; asserted that the federal government had a duty, when necessary, to protect that right; and contended that only upon attaining statehood would the residents of territories obtain the sovereignty necessary to make their own decisions about slavery. In short, a pox on popular sovereignty!

The convention then moved to the selection of a presidential candidate. To thunderous applause, a Massachusetts man nominated Vice President John C. Breckinridge, and a Pennsylvanian seconded the nomination. An Alabamian nominated Virginia's senator Robert M. T. Hunter, whose name had been mentioned at Charleston; a Tennessean nominated former New York senator Daniel S. Dickinson because he had been so important in securing passage of the Compromise of 1850; and Oregon's Isaac Stevens nominated one of his state's U.S. senators, Joseph Lane, a native of the South and former resident of Indiana. Hunter's name was withdrawn before the voting started. On the first ballot, Breckinridge won 81 of the 105 votes cast, with New York's Dickinson receiving the rest. This total clearly met the two-thirds majority test, and Breckinridge's nomination was made unanimous. Only Lane was nominated for vice president, and he was picked unanimously. Lane, a renowned veteran of the Mexican War who had long served as Oregon's territorial governor before he became its senator, was fifty-nine years old. Breckinridge, though the head of the ticket, was twenty years his junior, at that point the youngest man ever nominated for president of the United States.

So who was John C. Breckinridge, and why did this southern-dominated group of Democratic dissidents nominate him? Unlike many southern Democrats who would support his candidacy, Breckinridge had never threatened secession should a Republican win election as president. Indeed, in a December 1859 speech to the Kentucky legislature Breckinridge had condemned any such talk. "God forbid that such an event should occur," he declared. "God forbid that the step shall ever be taken!"[22] In that same speech he had denied any current necessity for a federal slave code—exactly the position that most southern supporters of John Bell took—but he had, for the first time, agreed one should be passed if it ever proved necessary. Still, he was never as militant in pressing the case for federal intervention as many other southern Democrats. As a lawyer his only slaves were a few house servants, and whether those servants were indeed slaves was a topic of considerable dispute during the subsequent campaign. But he was emphatically not a big slaveholding planter like many Deep South Democratic leaders. Nor was he ever as vindictive or as forthright as most of them in opposing Douglas. Indeed, in 1858 even after Douglas announced his so-called Freeport Doctrine, Breckinridge had endorsed his reelection to the Senate in a public letter, a stance that more deeply froze his icy relationship with President Buchanan. So why did the Douglas-haters in Baltimore, whom Buchanan was openly cheering on, pick him rather than someone else more closely identified with what they stood for?

It's tempting to think that Breckinridge's personal qualities and meteoric political ascent provide the answer. In the 1850s Breckinridge was unquestionably the rising young star of Kentucky's Democratic Party and, indeed, of the party nationally. Described by even political foes as intelligent, honorable, dignified, and "dashing,"[23] he had evident appeal across party lines that was exceedingly rare in that partisanly polarized age. After serving commendably as a major in the Kentucky Rifles during the Mexican War, Breckinridge practiced law in Lexington, the very heart of Whig country, where the Whig Robert Todd—Mary Todd Lincoln's father—and Henry Clay were among his neighbors. He won the House seat from that normally Whig congressional district at the age of thirty in 1851 and again two years later by defeating two Whig titans, first Leslie Combs and then Robert P.

Vice President John C. Breckinridge in 1860, southern Democrats' candidate for president that year. Currier and Ives lithograph, courtesy of the Library of Congress.

Letcher. Nor was the youthful Breckinridge a backbencher once he reached Washington. Rather, he served as Franklin Pierce's main spokesman in the House and was one of only two House Democrats who attended the fateful meeting with Pierce and Douglas in January 1854 in which Pierce signed on to the Kansas-Nebraska bill. He had not sought reelection in 1855, when Democrats lost the district, but his friendship with Pierce made him an obvious choice for the vice presidential nomination in 1856 at the barely constitutional age of thirty-five. Might not such a talented, handsome, and palpably vigorous young man make a perfect candidate to lead the charge against Lincoln and the aged John Bell of the Constitutional Union Party? Perhaps, but the problem with this analysis is that by custom, presidential candidates did not personally campaign in that era—though Stephen Douglas would quickly break with that tradition. In Baltimore that June few, if any, of the men who unanimously chose Breckinridge expected that any voters would ever see or hear him on the stump, quite unlike the voters he had charmed in Lexington's Whiggish Eighth Congressional District. More than likely, that is, his genuine personal attractiveness was not why they chose him.

In Baltimore Breckinridge was reported to have considerable support among Buchanan loyalists in Pennsylvania and New Jersey as well as among the Massachusetts Democrats who had withdrawn from the Front Street Theater. Upon his nomination the Republican *New York Times* immediately charged that he had been chosen specifically and exclusively to draw Democratic voters away from Douglas in the North to prevent Douglas from winning the presidency. By this analysis, undying hatred of Douglas explains what the seceders did in Baltimore. Stopping Douglas, not electing their own man, was their goal. Douglas believed precisely this, and during the subsequent campaign he and his supporters would focus far more of their fire on Breckinridge than on Lincoln or Bell. As the *Times* wrote astutely in this same editorial, printed two days after Douglas and Breckinridge were nominated that Saturday in Baltimore, the Democrats had nominated two candidates "each of whom will aim specially and primarily to defeat of the other."[24] "Douglas and Breckinridge must destroy each other," echoed the *New York Courier and Enquirer*.[25]

Breckinridge was in fact appalled that the Baltimore seceders had selected him because he thought accepting that nomination would finalize the sectional disruption of the Democratic Party and assure Lincoln's election. His initial reaction when he learned of his fate on that Saturday night, therefore, was to reject it, as he instantly told John Beck, one of his friends in the Kentucky delegation at Baltimore. On the morning of Monday, June 25, the same day that the *New York Times* editorial cited above appeared, however, the vice president received a dinner invitation from Mississippi senator Jefferson Davis for 5 p.m. that very day. Caleb Cushing, who had served in Franklin Pierce's cabinet with Davis, and Georgia senator Robert Toombs, who had imperiously demanded that Georgia's delegates desert the proceedings in Charleston's Institute Hall, were also invited. At this repast, according to Breckinridge's biographer, the three men persuaded Breckinridge to accept the nomination with the following argument.[26]

Lincoln was certain to win the election, they maintained, unless the elements now divided among the candidacies of Douglas, Breckinridge, and John Bell united behind a common paladin to defeat him. To effect that merger all three men must be persuaded to withdraw and some other man who could combine their followers be substituted for all three. It is clear from other evidence that the savior whom at least Davis and probably Cushing as well had in mind was their former boss and mutual friend, former president Franklin Pierce, whom Davis vainly and repeatedly begged to return to the fray in order to reunite the Democratic Party and stop Lincoln. For this scheme to work, they argued, it would not do for Breckinridge flatly to reject his nomination; the executive committee appointed at Baltimore would simply name someone else. No, they said, Breckinridge must accept it so that he could withdraw when it was too late for that committee to replace him. How these men could inveigle Bell to withdraw escapes this observer, but Toombs apparently did persuade Benjamin Fitzpatrick that very night to decline his nomination for vice president on the Douglas ticket, which he did the following day.

Following the dinner at Davis's home, he, Toombs, and Breckinridge went to an unoccupied house still under construction for Breckinridge and his large family. Not coincidentally, this edifice on I Street in Washington stood next door to Douglas's own house in the city. Thus, when Breckinridge told a crowd of serenaders in front of that house that he would indeed accept the nomination from Baltimore, his intent may have been to pressure Douglas to withdraw because his chances to win with the Democrats divided behind two candidates were nil. If this was indeed what Breckinridge, Toombs, and Jefferson Davis hoped, they had miscalculated. Breckinridge's acceptance infuriated Douglas, who determined to defeat Breckinridge's election by either the Electoral College or the House of Representatives.

The last act in the long drama of the Democrats' 1860 presidential nomination came a few days later. The South Carolinians still in Richmond and a few Alabama delegates who joined them there on their way home from Baltimore endorsed the Breckinridge-Lane ticket and the platform the bolters had adopted.

Breckinridge accepted this Richmond nomination in a brief, perfunctory note. His letter formally accepting the Baltimore nomination was much longer. Its main theme was southern Democrats' shibboleth: the absolute necessity of preserving the equal rights of all states. Breckinridge praised the platform adopted at Baltimore because, he averred, neither Congress nor a territorial legislature could deny the right of slaveholders to their slave property in federal territories. "These principles flow directly from the absence of sovereignty in the territorial governments and from the equality of the States." The friends "of constitutional equality, do not and never did demand a 'congressional slave code'" for the territories, he declared, but "they assert (fortified by the highest judicial tribunal in the Union) the plain duty of the federal government in all its departments, to secure, when necessary, to the citizens of all the states the enjoyment of their property in the common Territories." It "will be impossible," he concluded, "for a candid mind to discover hostility to the Union, or a taint of sectionalism in the resolutions adopted by the Convention." They simply asserted "the equality" of the States.[27]

As one would expect, newspaper reaction to the breakup in Baltimore varied by party and section. Some Democratic newspapers initially hesitated about which Democratic candidate to support. Others jumped into the race with both feet. "Democratic Principles Triumphant! The People Prevail!" read the headlines of a pro-Douglas Democratic newspaper in New Hampshire. "Proscription, Persecution, Sectionalism, Disunionism, and Ultraism of Every Shade, North and South, Completely Rebuked! DOUGLAS AND JOHNSON! The People's Candidates Nominated."[28] With equal conviction, many southern Democratic papers rejoiced in the nomination of Breckinridge on what, they uniformly boasted, was the only honest Democratic platform as well as the only one that explicitly defended the equal rights of the South. More interesting was the bitter reaction of the *New York Herald*, which celebrated its political independence but had clearly been counting on Democrats to defeat the Republicans in 1860. "We have no regrets" about "the broken down Democracy," editorialized Bennett's paper. "We congratulate the American people that this corrupt and demoralized party of juggling and swindling spoilsmen . . . has at last been broken to pieces from their quarrels over the spoils."[29]

Constitutional Union papers like the Fayetteville *Observer*, *Raleigh Register*, and *Baltimore Clipper* hooted that the Democratic Party had now become sectionalized. Only one national party remained in the 1860 race, they alleged. Hence, all Union-loving men must vote for Bell and Everett in November to defeat the most menacing sectional hydra—the Republican Party. As the Baltimore *Clipper* put it, "Democracy [i.e., the Democratic Party] is dead, and the people look elsewhere for succor against the on-rushing tide of Republican sectionalism."[30]

The Milledgeville, Georgia, *Southern Recorder* made the same point more fully and more emphatically. "The contest is now between Bell and Lincoln," it contended. "The Constitutional Union party is the only national party left in the field to combat the Abolition party. The other factions are merely engaged in a Kilkenny cat fight among themselves." But that fight, it added, would help Bell sweep the South and thus contend with Lincoln. "Douglas and Breckinridge will give Georgia to Bell and Everett." But above and beyond that split, the revelations of the Covode Committee about Democratic corruption under Buchanan "have put the people to thinking. They are beginning to see that turning out one Democrat to put in another, does not remedy the evil complained of. There must be a complete, full, and thorough revolution, if corruption and frauds are to be checked; new men must be put in the place of those now in office."[31] Like the Republicans, that is, Bell's supporters intended to make Buchanan's record a focal point of their campaign.

Predictably, Republican editors from Maine to Minnesota cheered what one headlined as "The Grand Crash at Baltimore."[32] Almost all of them expected that the twin Democratic tickets, precisely because Breckinridge could siphon off Democratic votes from Douglas in northern states, made a Republican victory almost inevitable. "On one side the united National Republican party with unexceptionable candidates and an impregnable platform," boasted a Wisconsin Republican sheet. "On the other, the divided sectionalized Democratic party. . . . Can any sane man doubt the issue of such a contest?"[33] The Democratic rupture, chorused Ohio's *Ripley Bee*, "completely annihilates all hope or fear of the success of either wing in the contest of 1860. Both are doomed to defeat."[34]

New York City's great rival Republican papers, the *Tribune* and the *Times*, reached the same conclusion, but for very different reasons. The Democratic split would make Douglas a far more formidable candidate in the North, argued Horace Greeley's *Tribune*. "Cutting loose from the expiring Administration, they will denounce without measure its corruptions, its imbecility, and its tyranny and endeavor to make capital out of its universal unpopularity." Still, "we can carry every Free State but California, with Delaware to balance her." Hence, Republicans need not worry about who captured the South's electoral votes.[35] Here the *Tribune* stressed its expectation that Buchanan's corruption would be a central, and for Republicans a winning, issue of the campaign. Henry Raymond's *New York Times* also expected Douglas to lose, but it did so because no one believed any longer that it was necessary to elect Douglas to achieve popular sovereignty decisions about territorial slavery. Nine-tenths of American voters now agreed that allowing the residents of territories themselves to decide about slavery expansion was the fairest solution to the slavery extension issue, Raymond's paper contended. That was why the Republican national platform did not demand congressional prohibition of slavery from territories. No matter who won the election, popular sovereignty would prevail, so Douglas now had lost the only thing recommending his election. What he had not lost was his fatal identification as a Democrat.[36]

With the decisions in Baltimore on June 23, four candidates were in the race. Campaigns for them began in earnest in July and continued to election day on Tuesday, November 6. Those campaigns would see a spectacularly successful innovation by Republicans to mobilize young first-time voters, an unprecedented and increasingly desperate personal campaign by Douglas, arguments in Dixie about whether the Kentuckian or Tennessean in the race was the truer true blue Southerner, and frantic efforts to arrange fusion tickets of presidential electors against the Republican menace. Above all, it was an election whose stakes were understood to be unusually high. Its potential outcome evoked both hope and dread among the Americans who experienced it. As the New York Republican state convention had put it in April, they were entering "a campaign fraught with consequences of the most momentous import."[37]

7 VARIEGATED CAMPAIGNS

To make the confusing four-candidate presidential campaign of 1860 more understandable for their readers, some historians portray it as essentially two different races: Abraham Lincoln versus Stephen A. Douglas in the North and John Bell versus John C. Breckinridge in the South.[1] This practice accurately reflects which two candidates garnered the most popular votes in each section on November 6. For several reasons, however, it distorts the five-month campaign that preceded election day.

First, with the glaring exception of Douglas, the candidates themselves did not personally campaign. As was the customary practice in the nineteenth century, they left the job of seeking votes to each party's presidential electors, congressional candidates, outside speakers sent by the parties' national and state executive committees, local activists who distributed printed matter sent by national committees or franked from Washington by congressmen, and newspaper editors. Lincoln remained in Springfield, Illinois, for the duration of the campaign. While correspondents kept him closely abreast of Republican prospects in different northern states, he neither said nor wrote anything for public consumption after accepting Republicans' nomination. He and his secretaries told anyone asking about his stance on particular issues to consult the published accounts of his previous speeches. After Vice President Breckinridge sent his letter of acceptance in June, he gave only a single public address in his hometown of Lexington, Kentucky, in early September. Bell confined his post-acceptance remarks to an interview with a reporter from the *New York Herald* at his Nashville home on August 1. Otherwise, Bell, like Lincoln, urged the curious to consult his previous speeches. To facilitate that research, he had a pamphlet published containing every speech he had given in Congress during his long career there. New York's Washington Hunt, who had presided over the party's national convention, fawningly praised the shrewdness of this dodge. "The manner in which you have disposed of all the appeals . . . to you for new expressions of opinions, vindicates your established reputation for wisdom & sound judgment," he congratulated the candidate. "I have never feared that you w[oul]d give the enemy any advantage by being drawn into needless avowals and discussions."[2]

Second, the intimation that the respective campaigns confined their efforts to a single section, be it the North or the South, is misleading. Republicans did concentrate their efforts almost wholly in the free states, but even they distributed ballots to a few counties in the border slave states, including Virginia. Both the Bell and Breckinridge campaigns sent speakers and held rallies in the North, not just the South. Influencing what happened in the North was, in fact, a central objective of both. Douglas not only gave speeches across the North but made two forays into the South, first into Virginia and North Carolina and then, in October, down the Mississippi and into the Deep South. On election day, Douglas was in Alabama, not Illinois or Washington.

Third, the implication that the campaigns behind Lincoln and Douglas in the North and Bell and Breckinridge in the South focused exclusively on each other in two-man duels etches a far too narrow picture of each campaign's efforts. In Dixie, Bell and Breckinridge men did try to tar the reputation of their foe's champion. But the Bell campaign also fired at the Republicans and at Buchanan's administration as well. Republicans' primary target also was Buchanan's record, not any of Lincoln's three 1860 competitors, although Republican newspapers did, of course, denounce southern Democrats' demand for a federal slave code and mock Constitutional Unionists' attempt to evade the slavery extension issue altogether as "cowardly."[3] Meanwhile, the Breckinridge and Douglas campaigns spent far more time attacking each other than they did either the Republicans or the Constitutional Unionists.

After the Democrats' slugfest at Charleston, Bennett's *New York Herald* warned that the party "has now been split into hostile factions, more bitterly opposed to each other than to the black republicans themselves."[4] After the rival nominations of Douglas and Breckinridge at Baltimore, the astute reporter James E. Harvey had informed Lincoln that "it was desperate at Charleston, but almost demonic at Baltimore, so appalling was the rage, and so earnest & reckless the purpose of the slaughter." Each man's supporters "prefers our triumph to the victory of their rivals," agreed Indiana's Republican congressman Schuyler Colfax. Nor did that mutual dislike diminish over time. An attempted reconciliation of the two factions' campaign leaders in Washington, Harvey wrote in late September, simply "increased hostility, confusion, and acrimony. . . . They are now more bitter against each other than ever & no reconciliation is possible."[5]

As previously noted, the complex four-candidate campaign of 1860 was asymmetrical. The supporters of each man did not emphasize the same things or address the same questions. Republicans did not focus primarily on slavery extension and certainly not on any danger to the Union should they win—although, as will be made clear below, they did attempt to rebut that charge. They defined the election instead primarily as a retrospective referendum on Buchanan's administration, especially its corruption. Both the Bell and Douglas campaigns, in contrast, portrayed the election as a prospective decision about the future because of the grave threat to the Union should either the Republicans or the secessionists gathered behind Breckinridge prevail in November. The top priorities of the Breckinridge effort, in turn, were to ensure Douglas's defeat and to insist on the protection of Southerners' equal rights against a supposedly tyrannical northern majority. With regard to slavery, this second goal entailed not so much a demand for a federal slave code or even slavery's extension as an insistence that Northerners accept without cavil Roger B. Taney's conclusion in the *Dred Scott* decision that the Constitution established a national property right in chattel slaves that the federal government was obliged to protect.

On that insistence, Republicans and Douglas men, on the one hand, and Breckinridge's supporters, on the other, were directly and fundamentally at odds. Douglas Democrats at Baltimore, just like Douglas himself, carped the pro-Breckinridge Athens (Georgia) *Southern Banner*, had refused to recognize the Supreme Court's 1857 decision as dispositive regarding property rights in slaves. Hence, "the question now before the country is, whether slaves are property? And should they not be placed on the same footing as other property?"[6] David Wilmot had given the Republican answer to those queries in a speech at the May national convention. Republicans' mission, he thundered, was "to resist the dogma that slavery exists wherever the constitution extends."[7] To an underappreciated extent, the sectional argument about slavery extension in 1860 had as much to do with Northerners' acceptance or rejection of Taney's *Dred Scott* decision as it did with the potential enactment of a congressional slave code.

However much the four campaigns in 1860 disagreed about what the election's central issues were, they concurred that northern states would determine its outcome. Because free states by themselves possessed enough electoral votes to assure a Lincoln victory, declared a pro-Breckinridge Georgia paper on July 20, "the only point of solution is, can enough [northern] electoral votes be diverted from Lincoln to throw the election into the House? That is the whole story of the canvass." Constitutional Unionists joined Breckinridge men in making this calculation, although they seemed more confident of denying Lincoln northern electoral votes than the Georgia sheet was. In May, several delegates to the Constitutional Union national convention had "confidently predicted" that the House would select the winner. In June, Washington Hunt wrote Bell that they should do "whatever is fair and honorable to carry the election to the House of Representatives." And in his interview with the *Herald*'s reporter on August 1, Bell admitted that he expected to triumph in either the House or the Electoral College. With the stop-Lincoln vote divided among three candidates, Congress appeared the only arena in which the dreaded Republican triumph could be averted. Moreover, if no one marshaled the necessary 17 state votes to win election in the House, as seemed possible, Breckinridge Democrats believed that the heavily Democratic Senate would certainly choose their man, Joseph Lane, as the vice president, who would then serve as the next president.[8]

Unlike some of his northern supporters, Stephen Douglas himself emphatically opposed allowing Congress to determine the winner. "By God Sir," Douglas told a Pennsylvania Republican in October, "the election shall never go into the House." Rather than allow that outcome, "I shall throw it to Lincoln."[9] How Douglas could stop his supporters from voting for him at that late date is unclear, but he steadfastly opposed any fusion electoral tickets with Breckinridge men that might actually cost Lincoln enough northern electoral votes to relegate the decision to Congress.

The prospect of an election by the House appalled Republicans as well. They sought an outright Electoral College majority. To achieve it, they knew, they had to hold the eleven northern states they had won in 1856 and capture Pennsylvania and either Illinois or Indiana. The necessity of attracting the 1856 Fillmore voters in Lower North states had led Republicans to deny Seward their presidential nomination at Chicago. Nonetheless, Republicans realized that a different pool of likely Lincoln voters might also be tapped. These were men who had been too young to vote in 1856 but who had turned twenty-one since that year. Here was a potential cornucopia of new Republican votes. And in the most important innovation of the 1860 election, youthful Republican sympathizers hit upon an ingenious way to recruit them to the Republican cause.

They formed first in Hartford on March 3, 1860. Their goal then was to protect Republican speakers from Democratic hecklers during Connecticut's hotly contested spring gubernatorial election. Soon, however, parading the streets at night became their club's primary activity. Initially they numbered a mere twelve men. By the end of March there were hundreds in and around Hartford. By the fall over a hundred thousand others across the North had enlisted in the organization. Most of the original dozen worked as sales clerks for local textile firms, but one, twenty-three-year-old Henry Sperry, aspired to be a newspaper man. He would become the publicist for the organization who answered the scores of requests for advice from other young men who hoped to produce their own chapters of the club after Connecticut's Republicans eked out a razor-thin victory in the first week of April.

They deliberately affected a military style that demonstrably attracted other young men. They proudly flaunted uniforms consisting of black kepi caps and long, black oil-skin or enameled capes that could deflect spattered drops from the tall, coal-oil-burning torches they bore in nighttime parades. Once marching became their main activity, they practiced the close-order drill prescribed by army manuals used at West Point and ranked leaders as captains, lieutenants, and sergeants. In January, a Connecticut newspaper had described the state's Republicans as wide awake and eager for the impending gubernatorial election. Hence the Hartford men called themselves Wide Awakes.

A *New York Times* reporter enthusiastically described one of their first tightly disciplined marches through Hartford's streets in late March. Both Republicans and Democrats held demonstrations that night. Each had a torch-light procession "accompanied by music, banners, flags and transparencies," and each shot off fireworks. But "the Republicans from their peculiar organization of the Wide Awakes were particularly imposing. The men were drilled in marching [four abreast], and that with their neat uniformly glazed caps and capes, made their regular appearance quite pleasing, while their systematic cheering produced quite a moral effect."[10] It was, indeed, the impact that marching Wide Awakes had on the large crowds that came out for their parades—and not just the growing membership of the organization itself—that brought new voters into the Republican column.

After the April election, when young men from other northern locales

The original twelve Wide Awakes, Hartford, Connecticut, March 1860. Connecticut Quarterly Magazine, *October 1895, p. 322.*

wrote to Hartford for advice about how they could organize their own Wide Awake clubs, Sperry and his friends were happy to oblige. In a form letter Sperry urged them to concentrate their activities in Democrats' urban strongholds: "Wherever the fight is hottest, there is their post of duty, and there the Wide Awakes are found."[11] The Hartford men offered more than advice. With ties to textile manufacturers, they contracted to supply oil-repellent capes for $2 each, and eventually shipped over 20,000 of them to Wide Awakes elsewhere.

Following the advice from Hartford, Wide Awake clubs, usually numbering a hundred men, the size of an army company, took their posts of duty in cities where Democrats concentrated rather than in rural Republican strongholds. By the time of the Republican national convention in mid-May probably a score of such clubs already existed in Chicago (there would be forty-eight by the fall). Their precision marching in a single combined unit so impressed the young Republicans from elsewhere who had flocked to Chicago for the convention that many went home intent on starting their own Wide Awake clubs. Within days of the convention's final adjournment, Wide Awake marchers appeared in Madison, Wisconsin; Bangor, Maine; Columbus and Cleveland, Ohio; Newark, New Jersey; and Brooklyn, New York.

Like Know Nothing lodges half a decade earlier, the Wide Awakes recruited primarily from young day-wage workers, skilled artisans, and middle-class clerks and shopkeepers. Unlike the Know Nothings, Wide Awake clubs were hardly clandestine. They paraded publicly on the streets at night with lanterns burning in order to enlist other young men in, and rouse their enthusiasm for, the Republican cause while simultaneously overawing the Democratic foe with the transparent ardor and seemingly irresistible electoral might of their coordinated columns.

The evidence strongly suggests that older Republican leaders had little to do with launching the movement. Young men without prior political experience took the initiative. But veteran leaders like Seward certainly recognized how Wide Awakes could benefit their party. Young men had slept in 1856 and Republicans had therefore lost, Seward told an assemblage of fifty Wide Awake clubs in Detroit in September. But now, he celebrated, "the young men throughout the land are Wide Awake."[12] The results in November would prove that Wide Awakes had been extraordinarily effective in recruiting young first-time voters into the Republican camp. As one of the original Hartford members proudly reminisced thirty-five years later, "There never was, in this country, a more effective campaign organization than the Wide Awakes."[13]

Street demonstrations and parades by fervent, often rowdy and liquored-up, partisans had been a feature of American politics since at least 1828. What set the Wide Awakes apart were their sober discipline, their close-order drill as they marched, and their carefully affected military mien. Imitation is said to be the most sincere form of flattery, and Republicans' multifold opponents soon organized uniformed marching clubs of their own once they recognized Wide Awakes' effectiveness in attracting youthful men to their ranks. As the *New York Herald* pointed out in a September article about "The Clubs of the Campaign," the purpose of these partisan clubs was "to attract the young men just entering their political careers."[14] Douglas Democrats had the Little Giants and the Chloroformers, whose purpose was to put Wide Awakes back to sleep. Breckinridge Democrats had the Chapultepecs, named after a battle in Mexico where Breckinridge and Joe Lane had fought. In hopes of attracting young blood to their decidedly aged ranks the Constitutional Union men organized the Bell-Everetts, the Minute Men, and, most important, the Bell Ringers, who marched ringing cow bells, dinner bells, fire bells, and any other bells they could find.

In late October all the anti-Lincoln clubs in and around New York City combined for a massive display as they marched along Manhattan's streets.

James Gordon Bennett, who still prayed for Lincoln's defeat, expressed his enthusiasm in huge headlines listed vertically in a single column of his *Herald* like bullets in a modern PowerPoint presentation.[15]

UNION NOW AND FOREVER!
Tremendous Uprising of the People.
Grandest Popular Demonstration Ever Witnessed in New York.
Turn Out of the Conservatives Last Evening.
Seven Miles of Sovereigns in Procession.
37,000 CONSERVATIVES AFOOT.
Over Half a Million of Spectators in the Streets.
The Wide Awakes Completely Squelched.

Despite Bennett's euphoric headlines, the anti-Republican marching clubs were never as numerous or as imposing as the Wide Awakes in the North. In southern cities like Louisville, Nashville, and New Orleans, however, the Bell Ringers caused a sensation. A hostile reporter for the Democratic-leaning *New York Herald* described his reaction to Louisville's Bell Ringers. A new tactic of the Bell men, he carped, was "to supply all the loafers, boys, and negroes they can find with cow bells, dinner bells, tea bells, locomotive bells . . . all being rung together" to make an indescribable "din" that substituted for the normal "yells and shouts" of campaign demonstrations.[16] In the North, in contrast, Republicans often mocked the Bell Ringers. In September one Republican campaigner in New York City jeered that Constitutional Union men answered any question about the campaign by chanting, "Ding-dong, the Constitution, and the Union."[17]

Without question, saving the Union from alleged antislavery extremists in the North and secessionist traitors in the South constituted Bell men's central campaign theme. The main "issue in the coming campaign will be Nationalism against sectionalism," declared a Maryland Bell sheet. Friends of the Union must therefore unite behind Bell and Everett, "the nominees of the only *National* party in existence." In contrast, Republicans "represented the prejudices and radicalism of the anti-slavery sentiment at the North" and appealed to "only one half of the Confederacy" while Breckinridge was "the candidate of the slave-trade revival or disunion wing" of the Democracy.[18] "We must vote against sectionalism in the North and sectionalism in the South," averred a speaker at a Nashville Bell rally.[19] Republicans were a sectional party, chorused Washington Hunt to a pro-Bell crowd in Jersey City, because they excluded "a whole section of the Union" from their national convention and campaigned exclusively in free states, a strategy "calculated to engender strife and heartburning till the enmity between the sections" became "unappeasable and implacable."[20]

Republicans' vicious, hyperbolic, and now supposedly unnecessary antisouthern tirades especially upset Constitutional Union men because those slings manifestly increased white Southerners' propensity toward disunion. A new "Address to the American People" issued on August 1 by the party's national executive committee insisted that the Republican Party no longer possessed a legitimate rationale. Everyone knew that Kansas would become a free state and that slavery could not expand anywhere else within the United States. "What need, then, is there for the further continuance of sectional agitation and for keeping it up by a mischievous sectional organization?" With their ostensible goal already achieved, Republicans now represented nothing but "a combination of ambitious aspirants and greedy office-seekers" who fanned "the fires of sectional hate" by lacerating Southerners with "atrocious and unwarrantable language" while many of their "campaign documents are mere abolition harangues, made up of the foulest and fiercest abuse of the entire South." As a result, "The North is taught to hate the South and the South is taught to hate the North." In both sections, "language is . . . studiously selected for its galling and exasperating qualities." Thus, Lincoln's election "would expose the Union to a peril to which no true patriot should wish it to be exposed."[21]

The Republican Party was founded "upon the sectional indignation of the free states" at the Kansas-Nebraska Act, George T. Curtis accurately told a Constitutional Union rally in Massachusetts, but that anger had perceptibly ebbed since 1858. As a consequence, now "the Republican party is found employing a species of agitation, which at last made them the disseminators of social hatred towards the South that is absolutely inconsistent with the spirit of the Union." Now lacking any useful purpose, Republicans could not win in 1860 "without a direct appeal to sectional passions."[22]

The certain result of that Republican tack, warned Kentucky's aged John J. Crittenden in a rare campaign appearance in September, was that Lincoln's election would be made "a pretext for disunion" in the South.[23] But Crittenden also avowed wherever he spoke that his party would resist any attempt at secession should Lincoln win because "the majority must of necessity rule in all republics."[24] John Bell had said much the same in his interview with the *New York Herald*. Should Lincoln, "a fair, candid, openhearted common sense man," win the election, Bell predicted, the mission of the Constitutional Union Party would be to prevent secession. In that same interview Bell flatly charged that Breckinridge personally, and not just his supporters, sought disunion.[25] Friends of the Union thus had a clear choice between the two men.

Over and over again, Constitutional Union papers and speakers insisted that slavery extension was now a moot issue. "This whole question of Slavery in the Territories as now presented is an abstraction pure and simple, incapable of practical application, and prolific of serious mischief," declared the Washington *National Intelligencer.*[26] "We have not now a single piece of Territory to which slavery would go, if it were invited," Crittenden told a Kentucky audience in August. "Why, then, dispute about a possibility that will probably never arise?" There was no need for either the federal slave code demanded by Breckinridge secessionists or an insulting anti-southern Republican Party whose goals had been achieved. With nothing concrete now to fight over, Republicans and Democrats were simply "the opposing hosts of sectionalism." "Elect a Union man, defeat the republicans, defeat the democrats," Crittenden pleaded to his Nashville audience in September.[27]

Both pro-Douglas and pro-Breckinridge Democrats denounced the Republican menace in strikingly similar language to that of the Bell men, although Democrats proved more eager to tar Republicans as abolitionists. Republicans, declared the pro-Douglas Democratic state convention in New Jersey, "have scattered the terrible seeds of disunion far and wide; and have greatly imperiled the unity, the peace, and the glory of the nation."[28] The "one idea" of the Republicans, insisted Bennett's *New York Herald,* which supported Breckinridge, was "the extirpation of slavery." Hence, a Republican victory meant certain sectional war. Republicans' documents, it insisted, proved that the party's goal was "the abolition of slavery and . . . the destruction of the South." The Republican campaign, declared yet another editorial, was based "on warfare against one section of the country."[29]

Republicans, echoed the Washington *Constitution,* which backed Breckinridge, demanded slavery's "limitation only as a prelude to its destruction. . . . They are bound, if victorious, to push their aggressive policy to its legitimate conclusion; and it were madness in us to doubt what that conclusion is."[30] Similarly, the pro-Douglas Springfield *Daily Illinois Register,* playing on Lincoln's notorious "ultimate extinction" phrase, charged that Lincoln believed that the federal government should "legislate so that slavery must soon be extinguished," and if elected president "he proposes to carry out his policy by freeing the negroes and thus ultimately extinguishing slavery."[31]

Caleb Cushing, who campaigned desperately against Lincoln and for Breckinridge in New York and New England, also charged that Republicans were intent upon abolition as soon as they won the White House. And if they didn't do it then, he told one audience, their party was "a gigantic falsehood, swindle, and fraud." Republicans, he raged in Boston, had "deliberately" made themselves "intensely sectional and therefore odious and dangerous." They had inherited "the religious and political ultraism of the Puritans of New England and the Friends [Quakers] there and in other states." Their "vital spirit" was thus "antislavery fanaticism"; they preached "the gospel of hatred" against the South.[32]

The alleged religious zealotry and intolerance of Republicans became an important subtheme Democrats used to mobilize their voters, many of whom had been targets of Know Nothing bigotry just a few years earlier. New York's Republicans, charged Bennett's *Herald*, were responsible for the recently enacted blue laws forbidding the sale of alcohol on Sundays, most workingmen's only day off. That party, he insisted, had been started by "a pious clique in this country, who have been for the last forty years endeavoring to legalize their peculiar religious views."[33] "The spirit of republicanism," Democratic papers charged, was "to meddle with everything—to meddle with the domestic institutions of other States, and to meddle with family arrangements in their own states—to force their harsh and uncongenial puritan creed down the throats of other men, and compel them to digest it under pains and penalties."[34]

Despite the anti-Republican fears Democrats shared with them, Bell's backers nonetheless contended that Democrats offered lovers of the Union no better alternative than the dangerously sectional and intolerant Republicans. Breckinridge's southern supporters were secessionists to the core, while "few men in all history, have done anything more unwise" than Stephen Douglas's push for the Kansas-Nebraska Act.[35] Besides, neither Douglas nor Breckinridge could possibly win now that the Democracy was split into hostile sectional wings. John Bell was the only "National" alternative in the race. As important, the victory of either Democrat "would continue the abuses and corruptions which have done so much to demoralize our people . . . and against which the unperverted conscience of the whole country so energetically protests."[36]

Fulsome denunciation of Buchanan's alleged corruption infused Bell's campaign just as it did that for Lincoln. After the Democrats' disruption in Baltimore, for example, the pro-Bell *Raleigh Register* gloated: "The friends of honesty and conservatism everywhere will rejoice at the utter destruction of the most villainously corrupt party that ever disgraced any country."[37] "The Augean stable of Democracy needs a thorough cleaning out," declared a Georgia paper a week after Bell's nomination. "The Covode Committee has only exposed the filth in one or two stalls," it continued six weeks later. "The Hercules of Tennessee is the one to turn on the rivers . . . to offer the necessary cleansing."[38] In like vein, Jeremiah Clemens blasted a pro-Breckinridge Democratic editor in Alabama for leading "thousands of true and tried opponents of a corrupt and corrupting Democracy into a position which compels them to become allies of spoilsmen, and forces them to suppress . . . their honest indignation at the frauds, bribing, interference with state elections, speculations, low intrigue, and sordid meanness" of Buchanan's administration. Breckinridge's followers, he added, "have given up everything to the one idea of slavery protection [in the territories] . . . a useless, senseless, and mischievous dogma."[39]

In another public letter Kentucky's Garrett Davis, an important Bell spokesman, rang changes on the same theme. The Covode Committee, he exulted, had exposed "to the scorn of the world the reeking and thorough corruption of the Government under the administration of James Buchanan." Democrats, Davis added, dangerously jeopardized the perpetuity of the Union. He dismissed Stephen Douglas as "a bold, ambitious, talented demagogue without any principles of true statesmanship," but, he insisted, Douglas's southern Democratic enemies were "even worse." They were "open and avowed disunionists . . . hitched on to the Southern car of disunion." Nor was there any reason for anyone in the North to support Lincoln. The slavery extension issue had long been settled. For years it "has merely been kept in motion as a political football for contending demagogues and partisans. It is high time," he desperately contended, "for it to be ignored in national politics, and for the Presidency to be taken upon other more appropriate and more important issues."[40]

As they had at their May national convention, Constitutional Unionists often tried metaphorically to sweep the slavery question under a rug, to deny its urgency, indeed its very legitimacy as a campaign issue. On September 8, for example, the *Raleigh Register* reprinted the round-robin letter of 1851 as a compelling endorsement of the Bell-Everett ticket. What possible relevance did this dated and little-known document have to the 1860 race, one might reasonably ask. After all, it was a pledge of commitment to the Compromise of 1850 as a final settlement of the slavery question, a transparently mistaken and anachronistic hope by 1860. Several possible answers can be suggested. For one thing, the sainted Henry Clay, the

"Great Compromiser" who had repeatedly saved the Union, led the list of forty-four Whigs and Democrats who had signed that circular, and Constitutional Unionists certainly viewed Bell and Everett as carrying on Clay's unionist tradition. More important, the round-robin pledged its signers never again to support anyone for federal office who dared to speak another word about slavery in the public arena. In short, its intent had been to extinguish the slavery issue once and for all, to expunge it from American politics forever. However hopelessly unrealistic that aim strikes us today, given what we know happened after 1851, that is precisely what the Constitutional Union campaign hoped to do in 1860.

Bell's backers deployed these themes across the nation, but they developed unique variations in the slave states. There Bell men had their best chance of actually carrying electoral votes. There Breckinridge Democrats, not Republicans, constituted their principal enemy while they viewed Douglas's southern Democratic backers as potential allies. And there Breckinridge Democrats fired regionally oriented criticisms at Bell that his supporters had to rebut. In Dixie, both the Bell and Douglas campaigns blasted Breckinridge's supporters as secessionists while Breckinridge men portrayed themselves as the only reliable defenders of the South's "equality" or "equal rights" in the Union. Thus, one paper referred to Breckinridge's supporters as "the Equal Rights Democratic Party."[41]

This stress on defending the minority South's political equality with the northern majority, so different from Crittenden's acknowledgment that in republics political minorities must submit to majority rule, suffused the rhetoric of the Breckinridge campaign. Even James Buchanan in remarks endorsing Breckinridge over Douglas to a crowd outside the White House rehearsed the theme. Southerners could never abandon their insistence on equality, he declared, "without self-degradation. Never! Never without an acknowledgement that they are inferior in this respect to their sister States."[42] Treasury secretary Howell Cobb sounded the same note in a public letter to his fellow Georgians endorsing Breckinridge. The presidential election, he averred, "involves the future of the South. It is a question of right, justice, and equality on the one hand, and wrong and degradation on the other."[43] Republicans aimed "to degrade the southern states from their position of equality in the Union," a Mississippi Democratic sheet declared even before Breckinridge was formally nominated.[44] Southerners, chorused a South Carolina sheet, must resist "the inferiority to which Republican rule would sink the South. We advocate resistance . . . because we see such abasement in a Union so administered."[45] Even a Tennessee paper warned that Lincoln's election would force Southerners to secede "to save themselves from [the] degradation and dishonor" inherent in surrendering to Republicans' "insolent, tyrannical, and insulting demands and purposes."[46]

Breckinridge could defend southern equality and Bell could not, charged pro-Breckinridge speakers and editors. At Baltimore in May the Constitutional Union convention had adopted a meaningless "milk-and-cider" platform while the platform endorsed by the anti-Douglas convention in that city six weeks later was a principled defense of southern rights that explicitly rested on Southerners' constitutional property rights in slaves as adumbrated in the *Dred Scott* decision.[47] The very attempt to "organize any party which shall ignore the slavery question" insulted "the intelligence of the American people," declared the Democratic paper in Breckinridge's hometown. "That issue must be met and settled."[48] In the South, Breckinridge men taunted, they were the only ones openly and honestly to make defense of slave property a priority, unlike Bell supporters with their vapid slogans about the Constitution and the Union. "The subject of domestic slavery now overshadows every other issue in American politics, and its consideration cannot be escaped in the pending national canvass," averred that Kentucky sheet.[49]

This attack on the emptiness of the Constitutional Union Party's platform by Breckinridge's southern champions forced Bell's proponents in Dixie to double down on the criticism of all party platforms they had voiced in Baltimore. Thus Crittenden boasted to a Kentucky audience: "We want no platform to captivate or ensnare men . . . no subtle discriminations, no dubious resolutions, no *ad captandium* phrases, no creeds proclaimed to bind the hearts and blind the judgments of men."[50] Party platforms, carped a Georgia Bell sheet, expressed "the veriest clap-trap, so worded and explained as to suit every section and every interest, no matter how they may clash with avowed principles of any section, their object being to please all sides and all men, regardless of their future bearing upon the interests of the country." John Bell and Edward Everett had no need for such flummery. Instead, they stood upright upon the Constitution "and offer as an interpretation of the Constitution, their past lives in the councils of the nation."[51]

What most sharply distinguished the 1860 campaign in the South from that in the North, in fact, was how much the former focused on the two candidates, Bell and Breckinridge, rather than on the opposing parties that backed them. To be sure, Breckinridge's supporters constantly attacked Douglas for his refusal to accept the finality of the Supreme Court's ruling in 1857 that property rights in slaves must be protected in the territories.

But only Bell had a chance of taking southern electoral votes away from Breckinridge. Hence they concentrated their fire on him.

Bell's congressional career as presented in the pamphlet of his speeches became the basis for a prolonged shouting match between his friends and foes about whether Bell had been a consistent defender of slaveholders' interests or their betrayer.[52] While in Congress, Breckinridge men spat, Bell had opposed the gag rule in the 1830s, Texas annexation in the mid-1840s, the Kansas-Nebraska bill in 1854, and the admission of Kansas as a slave state in 1858 while he had supported the abolition of the slave trade in the District of Columbia and Congress's robbery of lands Texas claimed as her own in 1850. He had always betrayed the South, they blared.

No, no, no, retorted pro-Bell papers. All of those stances, and particularly Bell's farsighted opposition to the Nebraska measure and its outcome, had aimed at preventing the growth of dangerous antislavery sentiment in the North that had now culminated in the rising Republican storm. That storm in fact was directly attributable to Democrats' colossally foolish Nebraska Act and attempt to bring Kansas in as a slave state under the patently unfair and undemocratic Lecompton constitution.

Besides, Bell papers trumpeted, Breckinridge was hardly a reliable champion of the South or slavery. Democrats themselves should put no faith in Breckinridge, railed a North Carolina Bell paper, because, it reported accurately, in his acceptance letter Breckinridge had not supported the demand for a congressional slave code in the platform on which he was running. He had, in fact, flatly denied that that platform demanded a federal slave code.[53] In speeches as a vice presidential candidate in 1856, Constitutional Unionists maintained, Breckinridge had endorsed the "squatter sovereignty" interpretation of popular sovereignty that his 1860 nominators claimed to find so outrageous—namely, that during the pre-statehood stage of territories their legislatures could indeed bar slavery from them. Moreover, while John Bell, a large slaveholder himself, clearly shared the interests of slaveholders, Breckinridge owned no slaves. Indeed, he did not even own any real estate in Lexington or any taxable assets in the South. Instead, they charged, he rented housing and hired free blacks as servants when he returned to Lexington. "Is John C. Breckinridge a Slaveholder?" headlined a Charleston, South Carolina, paper that questioned his reliability.[54] How could such a rootless man champion the South? To cement their case, Bell papers printed a statement from Thomas Watts, a well-known proslavery Southern Rights Whig leader from Alabama, attesting that Bell's previous speeches about slavery extension proved him to be staunchly proslavery and pro-Southern while Breckinridge was an "eleventh-hour convert" to the Southern Rights cause.[55] Even the *New York Herald*'s Bennett, who ended up supporting Breckinridge because he believed Breckinridge was the only Democrat candidate who could garner electoral votes, initially called him "a mere adventurer" after his nomination whereas Bell "represents the respectable and wealthy classes, identified with the great slaveholding interests in the South."[56]

Nonsense, responded Breckinridge's friends. He had never endorsed squatter sovereignty in 1856, as both Bell men and Douglas's allies alleged. Moreover, while Breckinridge was not a large slaveholder, his house servants were indeed slaves, not hired free blacks. And while Bell nominally possessed far more slaves than Breckinridge, the Kentuckian's supporters insisted, they were legally owned by Bell's wife, not by Bell himself. Breckinridge, not the subversive Bell, was the South's true tribune. To which Bell men repeatedly retorted, Breckinridge was a mere figurehead for secessionists who would destroy the Union whereas Bell would protect the South's rights within the Union.

This school-yard back-and-forth continued up to election day in Dixie. On October 10, a North Carolina Bell sheet mocked "the puny efforts of the envenomed [Breckinridge] partisans who day after day and week after week reiterate the false and slanderous charge that John Bell is unsound on the slavery question." A pro-Breckinridge Mississippi editor responded two weeks later, "If we intend to eat our own words, give up our rights and equality, and admit that Mississippi is inferior to Massachusetts, then we can vote for John Bell."[57]

As noted, Douglas's supporters in the South joined in the assault on Breckinridge as complicit in disunion schemes. Nonetheless, Douglas himself led the attack on Breckinridge and the Democrats who had bolted the party at Charleston and Baltimore. In early July he sent two letters to lieutenants that spelled out the themes of the campaign he intended to run. His friends must show the Breckinridge men no quarter, and certainly they must not fuse with them behind common slates of presidential electors. "Any Compromise with the Secessionists would be ruinous," he told one. "An amalgamation tickett [*sic*] with the bolters would disgust the people & give every Northern State to Lincoln." "We must make war boldly against the Northern abolitionists [i.e., Republicans] and the Southern Disunionists, and give no quarter to either," he urged another. "We should treat the Bell & Everett men friendly and cultivate good relations with them, for they are Union men. . . . We can have no partnership with the Bolters."[58]

Douglas had two main priorities for his campaign. First, he sought to rally voters in defense of the Union against the threats he perceived to it. Second, he wanted to reunite and regain control of the national Democratic Party, which he thought Southerners had intentionally wrecked at Charleston and Baltimore in order to sabotage his chances of winning the White House. To accomplish these goals he quickly decided that he must personally campaign in as many places as possible. He would first go northward from New York City, where he had helped install his national campaign committee, into New England. He would then follow up that campaign swing with forays into Maryland, Virginia, and North Carolina.

Personal electioneering by presidential candidates simply was not done. Any such overt display of ambition was considered gross, if not disqualifying. To justify his initial travels, therefore, Douglas announced that he was visiting his aged mother in upstate New York, attending his new, second wife's younger brother's graduation from Harvard College in Cambridge, and paying homage to his father's gravesite in Vermont. This tissue-thin cover story fooled no one. His foes criticized his unprecedented campaigning from the outset. The reporter Harvey, who was in Saratoga Springs when Douglas made five speeches there, told Lincoln that "Douglas has become a peripatetic champion of himself & his cause, but is hardly verdant enough to expect any practical result from these unseemly exhibitions." Republican papers, a national committeeman told Lincoln, mocked Douglas's supposed search for his "anxious mother's pantry," and "hold up your quiet and dignified retirement in contrast."[59]

Douglas spoke at Albany and Saratoga, New York, and in every New England state except Maine by the time he finished the tour at Newport, Rhode Island, in late July. Those speeches iterated several themes: the superiority of his version of popular sovereignty over the schemes of northern Republicans and southern Breckinridge men for congressional interference with slavery in the territories; the dangerous sectional extremism in both North and South that must be resisted to preserve the Union; the infamy of the Southerners who had split the party in order, Douglas charged, to assure his loss to Lincoln; and the absolute reprehensibility of any truck between his supporters and the Buchanan administration toadies who were backing Breckinridge in the North. Astute newspaper correspondents noted that he in fact said very little negative about Lincoln but was relentlessly critical of Breckinridge as an apostate from Democratic orthodoxy and a secessionist sympathizer. As one reporter wrote in late July, "He cares nothing about his own personal success and comparatively little for the success of the

Democratic party as it stands at present. *But he intends to crush out utterly and forever the Disunion Party*, if it is in his power to do so."[60]

After recuperating from the rigors of his New England swing for a week at Newport, Douglas headed south. The need to help his first wife's brothers dispose of their mother's property in North Carolina now provided his excuse. On August 25 he arrived in Norfolk, Virginia. There the most renowned exchange of his entire campaign took place. Midway through his speech stressing his determination to save the Union, he was handed a slip of paper containing two questions from a Breckinridge supporter in the crowd. The first asked if southern states would be justified in seceding from the Union should Lincoln win the election. "To this I emphatically answer No," Douglas thundered. The second asked if he would advise forcible federal resistance to a southern state's secession after Lincoln was inaugurated. "No!" groaned the Virginia crowd. "Yes," avowed Douglas. The president had a constitutional duty to enforce all the laws, and he would do everything he could to aid the government in upholding its laws against any resistance. Whoever the next president was, Douglas elaborated, he should treat any attempt at secession exactly as Andrew Jackson had treated South Carolina's Nullifiers in the winter of 1832–1833. He hoped, Douglas concluded, that these same questions would be put to Breckinridge to elicit *his* views on secession.[61]

Southern Breckinridge men reacted to Douglas's "Norfolk Doctrine" with outrage, but he maintained his defiant antisecessionist stance for the rest of this foray into South Atlantic states. Lincoln's election would be "a great public calamity," he maintained at Petersburg, Virginia, but it would not justify secession. "There is no evil, and can be none, for which disunion is a legitimate remedy." In Raleigh, North Carolina, on August 30, he declared: "I would hang every man higher than Haman who would attempt to resist by force the execution of any provision of the Constitution." Returning north, he told a Richmond audience that his version of popular sovereignty, absolute noninterference for or against slavery in territories by the federal government, was the only way that "the perpetuity of the Union can be ensured." Not every Breckinridge man was a disunionist, he admitted in Baltimore, but every disunionist was a Breckinridge man. The only reason he had taken the stump that summer, he averred, was to save the Union from the secessionist plot of those Breckinridge supporters. "I am not seeking the Presidency," he baldly contended. "My object is to preserve this Union by pointing out, what, in my opinion, is the only way in which it can be saved."[62]

Rebutting Douglas's calculated slurs against his campaign and differentiating himself from the Little Giant were Breckinridge's primary objectives in his single speech of the campaign on September 5. Henry Clay's son James had offered him the use of Clay's Ashland estate near Lexington for this effort, and between 10,000 and 15,000 people attended it. He had never endorsed Douglas's version of popular sovereignty in 1856 or at any other time, Breckinridge insisted. Thus Douglas's charge that he had opportunistically abandoned it for the 1860 campaign was false. In any event, the Supreme Court had settled that question by declaring that territorial legislatures could not bar slavery. He fully accepted and endorsed that decision. Douglas did not. Nor had he ever uttered anything hinting of secessionist sentiment. Douglas's attempt to pin that label on him was not simply spurious. It was outrageous.

The most striking aspect of Breckinridge's speech was its omissions. At Norfolk, Douglas had challenged him to address the same questions about secession that he, Douglas, had so forthrightly answered. But the Kentuckian said nothing about them other than to deny that he sought disunion. Moreover, he said much about Douglas but nothing significant about either Lincoln or John Bell. Lincoln was hardly a threat to carry Kentucky, but Bell clearly was. Indeed, he would carry it. That Breckinridge said nothing to deter Kentuckians from backing Bell seems strange in hindsight. But Breckinridge had been fatalistic about his actual chances of winning from the moment he accepted the Baltimore nomination, so perhaps he had already written off his home state as a lost cause.

In any event, Breckinridge and Bell men understood that the election would be decided in the North, not in the slave states. Democrats loyal to Buchanan intended to run separate Breckinridge electoral tickets in most northern states to take votes away from Douglas, whom Buchanan so hated. Republicans expected those tickets to vaporize Douglas's chances in the North. For the most part, however, that hope proved delusive. Whatever Buchanan's vengeful wishes, Democrats in most free states ultimately put a priority on trying to defeat Lincoln, not Douglas. Breckinridge Democrats in northern states were in fact far more eager to construct fusion Democratic electoral tickets than were Douglas's friends. Within weeks of the Democrats' split-up at Baltimore, for example, Pennsylvania's pro-Buchanan Democratic state executive committee constructed a ticket composed of both Douglas and Breckinridge electors with the understanding that they would support whoever had the better chance to deny Lincoln an Electoral College majority. When Douglas protested this arrangement, his friends created an electoral slate composed exclusively of Douglas electors, but Pennsylvania's Democratic voters in November heavily preferred the joint ticket. After several false starts, by November New York and New Jersey Democrats also managed to cobble together fusion electoral tickets that also included Constitutional Unionists. Rhode Island Democrats also eschewed a separate slate of Breckinridge electors while Breckinridge tickets received such a minuscule vote in Iowa, Vermont, Michigan, and Minnesota that they could not have been distributed very broadly.

Illinois, the home state of Lincoln and Douglas, provides an especially interesting case of Democratic wavering about which one of those two men to oppose. According to Lincoln's correspondents, Buchanan directly ordered Ike Cook, his anti-Douglas postmaster in Chicago, to arrange a Breckinridge electoral ticket to eradicate Douglas's chances of carrying Illinois. Cook did so. But then Cook and his lieutenants decided that Lincoln could be stopped only if Douglas took the electoral votes of key northern states like Illinois. So convinced, Cook withdrew the electoral slate he had formed at Buchanan's order. Another separate Breckinridge slate was created, perhaps in response to new orders from the White House. The anti-Douglas Danites, however, apparently made little effort to distribute ballots for it very widely in the state. In November it received only 2,300 votes compared to the 160,000 for the straight Douglas ticket.

While Republicans hoped that Breckinridge might siphon off potential Douglas voters in the North, they initially feared far more what separate Bell electoral tickets might do to their own vote. They especially worried about losing votes to Bell and thus the states' electoral votes to Douglas in Pennsylvania and Indiana, states absolutely critical for Republicans to amass an electoral-vote majority. Constitutional Union men, in turn, disagreed with each other about what was the better strategy for damaging Lincoln—running separate electoral slates to subtract from Republican totals or foregoing a separate ticket and adding their votes to Douglas's column. A few, like Indiana's foremost Constitutional Union leader Richard W. Thompson, who complained that "impracticables" on the party's national committee insisted on running separate Bell tickets in every state, opposed doing anything that might help Democrats.[63]

From Republicans' perspective, the main problem in Pennsylvania was the potential size of the vote for a Bell electoral ticket. In 1856 John C. Frémont had garnered only 32 percent of Pennsylvania's popular vote while Fillmore's 82,000 votes had constituted 18 percent of the statewide total. After 1856 Pennsylvania's Republicans had worked mightily to court those

American Party voters. They shared down-ticket nominations with Know Nothings; they incorporated anti-Catholic planks into state and local platforms; they downplayed the slavery issue and stressed the need for higher tariff rates after the Panic of 1857, a stance popular with the ex-Whigs who had composed the great majority of Fillmore's voters; and they had carefully shunned the very name "Republican" with its radical anti-southern connotations and instead adopted less threatening labels like "Union Party" or "People's Party" for their coalitions.

By 1858 these tactics had helped the polyglot anti-Democratic elements in Pennsylvania construct a statewide majority. To preserve that majority in 1860, Pennsylvanians at the Chicago convention had fought tooth and nail against nominating Seward, who was anathema to Know Nothings. They had succeeded in stopping Seward only to have the convention adopt the notorious "German plank" in the national platform, a pro-immigrant, overtly anti–Know Nothing concession to Carl Schurz. That plank implicitly criticized Massachusetts Republicans for delaying the right of naturalized immigrants to vote in the Bay State. It was gall and wormwood to the tens of thousands of Pennsylvania nativists, nervous Republicans warned from Washington.[64] "I wish our German friends could have been satisfied without such a resolution," Senator Lyman Trumbull moaned. It could cost Lincoln both Pennsylvania and New Jersey. Pennsylvania's Americans, whose vote "*we must have*," absolutely detested Schurz's handiwork, echoed Illinois congressman Elihu Washburne.[65]

Fortunately for Lincoln's chances in the Keystone State, the Republican national platform also included a plank advocating "an adjustment" of "duties upon imports" so as "to encourage the development of the industrial interests of the whole country." This weak language was far too vague for some People's Party adherents. They begged Lincoln to send copies of anything he had previously said about tariffs so they could distribute them. Still, Pennsylvanians could spin the ambiguous plank as endorsing protective tariffs even though it never used the words "protective" or "tariff." Interest in raising tariff rates was especially strong in central and eastern Pennsylvania, precisely the areas of the state where Fillmore voters had been most numerous. The tariff would be "the overshadowing question" in those regions, where "the *Conservative* element predominates," the People's Party state chairman wrote Lincoln. Republican congressman Thaddeus Stevens, an ironmaster himself who lived near Lancaster in southeastern Pennsylvania, was hardly a "Conservative." But he concurred that the tariff "was the all absorbing question here in Pennsylvania."[66] Thus People's

Party spokesmen played up Republicans' purported support for higher tariff rates to offset Pennsylvania Americans' detestation of the "German plank." By the late summer they were also deploying prominent Know Nothings like Isaac Hazlehurst, Pennsylvania's American gubernatorial candidate in 1857, and Daniel Ullmann, New York's Know Nothing gubernatorial candidate in 1854, to campaign for Lincoln and People's Party candidates.

All of the worries about a potentially catastrophic movement of Fillmore voters to Bell in Pennsylvania were expressed in the days following Lincoln's nomination but before Democrats' final blow-up at Baltimore in the third week of June. Because Buchanan's machine in Pennsylvania was expected to go all out for Breckinridge, thus denying the state to Douglas, Republicans' warnings of potential disaster quickly changed to predictions of Lincoln's inevitable triumph there. "I think you may begin to block out the inaugural & perhaps to look abroad [i.e., in other states] for future associates at the green [Cabinet] table," Harvey wrote Lincoln a week after Democrats' explosion at Baltimore.[67] Two days later, on June 27, a Chicago ally assured Lincoln that he should be considering "the quality and cut of your inaugural suit."[68] Soon, however, new anxieties about Pennsylvania would emerge.

Lincoln kept an especially close watch on neighboring Indiana, the other state where the Constitutional Union threat caused Republicans particular concern. He had campaigned there in 1859, personally knew many of its Republican leaders, and had received its support on every ballot at the Chicago convention. During his single term in Congress in the 1840s, moreover, Lincoln had befriended Indiana's Richard W. Thompson, then a fellow Whig congressman and now that state's man on the Constitutional Union national executive committee. At the urging of Schuyler Colfax, another ex-Whig but also, like Thompson, a former Know Nothing, Lincoln wrote Thompson soon after accepting the Republican nomination to find out if the Bell men intended to run a separate electoral ticket in the Hoosier state. For the remainder of the campaign, Thompson and other Indianans kept Lincoln well informed about developments there.

In early 1860 Crittenden had been warned that Know Nothings in Indiana would never support a third party if it would help Democrats carry the state as Fillmore had done in 1856. Thompson was of like mind. Ousting Democrats from the White House was his top priority. He hoped Lincoln would be elected, but as the foremost Constitutional Union man in the state, he told Lincoln, he could not campaign openly for him. Instead, he initially sought to persuade Indiana's Constitutional Union men not to run a separate Bell electoral ticket. Over considerable resistance, he had almost succeeded when influential Bell leaders from Kentucky, who hoped to throw the election into the House, came into Indiana and demanded that the Indianans not run their own ticket but instead throw their support to Douglas so that he might carry the state. Infuriated by this outside interference, the Indiana Bell men did precisely what Thompson most feared. They created a Bell electoral slate and named Thompson himself one of the two state at-large electors on it.

Thompson could hardly refuse the honor, but instead of campaigning enthusiastically for Bell, he devoted most of his canvass in the state to reassuring his fellow conservative ex-Whigs that Lincoln was just as moderate on the slavery extension issue as they were. Indeed, Thompson iterated and reiterated, he and Lincoln had voted precisely the same way on roll calls in the House when they jointly served in the Twenty-Seventh Congress. He also promised both Northerners and Southerners on the Constitutional Union national committee that should Lincoln win, he would choose cabinet members from both sections and run "a Conservative and national administration, which, the Slavery question out of the way, would bring about the restoration of Whiggery."[69]

Thompson, however, could not control what all the former Fillmore supporters in Indiana did. Many feared that a Lincoln victory meant disunion despite Thompson's assurances about Lincoln's Whig background. It soon became clear to such men that the best chance of frustrating Lincoln was not in November, when the anti-Lincoln vote would be divided three ways, but in October's gubernatorial election. Then there would be only two candidates, not four: the Republicans' Henry Lane and Democrats' Thomas Hendricks. Both wings of the Democracy would support Hendricks. The question was what the estimated 5,000–10,000 former Fillmore voters who had not yet joined the Republicans would do in October, for as one Hoosier told Carl Schurz, most of his state's "Bell men" were "malignant fellows who will do all the mischief they can."[70] Why this mattered so much was that, as Schuyler Colfax warned Lincoln, "The October vote at the State Election will probably decide our Pres[identia]l vote."[71] And that election, Chicago Republican newspaper editor Joseph Medill had learned, "will be a close squeeze . . . with the chances against us."[72]

Pittsburgh's influential Republican editor Russell Errett used quite similar language about Pennsylvania's crucial October gubernatorial election. "Everything in Pennsylvania depends upon the result of the first election," he warned fellow editor Medill. "If we elect our Governor, all will be well in

November. If not, the November Contest will be doubtful, with the chances against us."[73] That was because both Douglas and Breckinridge Democrats would vote for Henry D. Foster, the Democratic gubernatorial candidate, who opposed the People's Party's Andrew Curtin. To boot, the 9,000 Bell men in and around Philadelphia were likely to vote for Foster as well. They saw it as the best way to deny Lincoln the state's electoral votes in November. Worse still for Republicans, their problems in Pennsylvania did not end there.

No state had caused the Republican Party more trouble in 1856 than Pennsylvania, and the same was true in 1860. Manifold difficulties confronted Lincoln's supporters in the October contest. Andrew Curtin, according to the astute newsman Harvey and others, was an exceptionally weak candidate. He lacked "discretion and high moral principle. But there he is," wrote Harvey, "and we must make the most of him." Curtin, Harvey repeated in September, "is a drag upon us in many respects & in many localities." He mistakenly believed Bell men were on his side. He offended voters wherever he spoke. And, a Philadelphian warned, Curtin was guilty of some unspecified "moral turpitude" in Philadelphia that "we are studiously keeping . . . secret."[74]

Curtin, however, was not the People's Party's only problem. Its top leadership was bitterly split. Senator Simon Cameron, the People's Party's highest elected official, despised both Curtin and Curtin's ally Alexander K. McClure, chairman of the People's state committee. Cameron and his friends accused McClure of ineptitude and dishonesty. He had infuriated the party's biggest potential donors in Philadelphia by seeking outside funding from New York City, of which Philadelphians were deeply jealous. McClure was also suspected of stealing some of the campaign cash he did raise. Thus, the Philadelphia money men refused to give any funds to McClure's committee. Cameron tried to form a rival state committee, much to the annoyance of McClure, who curried Lincoln's favor by boasting that he had thoroughly organized every county in the state for the crucial October election. Neutrals begged Lincoln and his advisers to send savvy politicos like Leonard Swett and David Davis from Illinois to Pennsylvania to straighten things out. After visiting there, Davis urged the national committee to send as much money as possible to Indiana and Pennsylvania to help carry the crucial October elections.

Aside from nervousness about Indiana and Pennsylvania, however, Republicans expressed confidence about carrying most other northern states. They had several advantages in 1860, and not just because their opposition was divided. Edwin D. Morgan and his fellow members of the Republican national committee raised more money for campaign expenses than any of the three campaigns opposing Lincoln.[75] As noted earlier in this chapter, Republican Wide Awake clubs also proved unrivaled in attracting first-time voters to their candidate. Nonetheless, Republicans' confidence also rested on what they believed was the superiority of the message they presented to the electorate.

So, what was that message? What did Republicans in 1860 tell people about why they should vote for them? Did the Republican campaign in fact focus on the escalating sectional conflict over slavery and slavery extension, as the standard accounts of this election have so long held? To understand what Republicans said, one must remember that they were running against fellow Northerners, not directly against the southern Democrats whom they attacked as an aggressive and arrogant Slave Power. As a Cincinnati Republican paper succinctly put it in an October editorial, "The Republican party has been produced by the irrationally arrogant demands of the politicians of the South, and systematic aggressions by [their] use of the Federal power. Its mission is to check those aggressions."[76] In 1860, however, the bitter attacks on Douglas, who *was* Lincoln's chief competitor for northern electoral votes, by Breckinridge Democrats made it impossible to label Douglas a lackey of the Slave Power, especially since by 1860 Republicans themselves admitted that his popular sovereignty formula could in fact stop slavery extension.

Attacking southern Democrats' demands concerning slavery's protection and extension, in sum, did not and could not suffice in 1860 as the way to compete with the Douglas campaign for Northerners' votes. Nevertheless, Republicans still had to make clear what their future course of action toward the South might be in order to deflect three potentially crippling charges lodged against them by their political foes. All were related in one way or another to what Republicans thought and intended to do about African American slavery.

Since the Republican Party's birth in mid-decade, Democrats had race-baited against them to exploit the northern electorate's pervasive anti-black sentiment. Democrats labeled them "Black Republicans" because they supposedly advocated blacks' social and political equality with whites. Republicans' antislavery program, ranted Bennett's *New York Herald*, "aims to establish a new social policy in this country—the policy of an equalization of the white and black races."[77] Republicans, chorused the pro-Douglas Springfield *Daily Illinois Register*, sought "a gradual mingling of the races in the political control of the government," while Democrats insisted that "this nation is a nation of white men, in which negroes have no voice whatever in the regulation of its political affairs" and that "Negroes . . . are the inferior race, and must remain so, politically, forever."[78] From their party's birth, in turn, most Republicans had strenuously denied that they sought equal rights for, let alone social equality with, blacks. Moreover, as was shown in Chapter 1, those denials were often expressed in contemptuously racist language.

Nonetheless, in some northern state legislatures, Republicans had in fact been distinctively more favorable than Democrats to eliminating legal discrimination against free blacks. In 1860 itself, New York's Republican legislators had allowed a referendum on a state constitutional amendment regarding blacks' rights to be scheduled for the very day of the presidential election. That revision would remove the existing property qualifications on black suffrage that severely limited how many black men could vote. Republican newspapers intentionally ignored that impending referendum so as not to identify it as a Republican measure. It is likely, moreover, that the ballots Republicans printed for voters to cast took no position on the amendment, whereas all New York Democratic ballots that year had votes against its adoption printed on them.[79]

In November, the amendment lost by 140,000 votes even as Lincoln racked up a 50,000-vote majority. That differential is significant. Despite the now well-documented racism of northern whites, including many Republican supporters, Democratic race-baiting had failed to deter a majority of people from voting Republican, although it may well have stopped even more of them from doing so. Republican voters were not deterred by Democratic accusations for two likely reasons. Their own racist feelings may have helped them believe the defensive protests from most Republican politicians, including Abraham Lincoln, that they did not seek or wish social and political equality for the North's free blacks. Second, they thought that the 1860 decision involved other things of greater and more immediate importance.

Far more threatening to Republicans that year, in fact, were the related Democratic charges that Republicans' real goal, no matter what they said, was the abolition, and not just the geographical restriction, of slavery and that precisely because abolition was their true goal, a Republican victory in 1860 would make southern secession inevitable. Southern Democrats had been threatening to secede in the event of a Republican triumph since the party first emerged in the mid-1850s. Those threats had escalated in number and ferocity since John Brown's raid on Harper's Ferry in October 1859. More than anything else, Republicans well knew, those threats could deter the crucial Fillmore voters in Lower North states like Indiana and Pennsylvania from supporting Lincoln's election.

To defuse those threats, Republicans insisted in every platform they issued, virtually every editorial they wrote, and every speech they gave that they in fact had no intention whatsoever of interfering with slavery in the states where it already existed. Republicans proudly trumpeted their desire to destroy the Slave Power's control of the national government by ousting Democrats from power. But they denied that they sought to destroy the institution of slavery in the states where it existed in 1860. Therefore, Republicans explained, white Southerners had no need to secede in order to protect their slave property from nonexistent schemes for federally imposed abolition.

As the historian Daniel W. Crofts has demonstrated beyond cavil in his important recent book, Republicans did not just make that pledge for public consumption in order to win elections while concealing their true goal. They were in fact dumbfounded by the charge that they sought abolition *within* the slave states by federal action because, as they wrote each other in letter after letter privately, they personally had no intention of doing that and knew of no other Republican officeholders who did. Contrary to what some historians have recently contended, the vast majority of Republicans were not committed to slavery's abolition at the time of Lincoln's election.[80]

What about ultimate objectives, rather than proximate goals? In 1855 Republican senator Henry Wilson of Massachusetts, an ex–Free Soiler and radical antislavery man like his Bay State Republican Senate colleague Charles Sumner, bluntly told a Michigan Republican convention: "Let it be distinctly understood that our [Republican] objective is the emancipation of the bondsmen in America."[81] Wasn't he then revealing his party's true goals, no matter their frequent denials of any such intention?

The use of the word *emancipation* rather than *abolition* here is all-important. It referred to the voluntary freeing of slaves by individual owners or by state constitutional amendments in slave states that would supposedly be induced, or coerced, by stopping the territorial expansion of slavery. Without fresh lands, many Republicans argued and some Southerners apparently believed, slavery would eventually become uneconomical. Once it did, Southerners themselves would move to get rid of the financial burden slavery entailed. After all, hadn't Lincoln himself asserted that stopping the spread of slavery would put it on the road to "ultimate extinction"? Wasn't that long-term prospect, even without the danger of immediate coercive federal abolition, enough to explain southern vows to secede should Lincoln win?

Some Southerners said exactly that. Georgia's Robert Toombs, for example, compared the prospect of slavery contained within the fifteen current slave states to a tarantula hemmed in by a ring of fire and stinging itself to death. Fear of a long-term erosion of white Southerners' commitment to slavery should Republicans dictate federal policy did not depend on the accuracy of that fear. Nonetheless, was it justified? Would stopping slavery's expansion in fact render the institution economically infeasible and cause Southern slaveholders themselves voluntarily to abandon it? No one can say for sure. But slavery was a remarkably versatile form of labor that did not necessarily depend on fresh lands for plantation production to survive. There is very little evidence that slaveholders feared that long-term economic strangulation of slavery was the biggest menace Republicans posed. And Lincoln, who was intransigently opposed to slavery's expansion, apparently did not believe that restriction would engender emancipation. In 1855 he complained to a Kentucky judge that "experience" since enactment of the Missouri Compromise in 1820 "has demonstrated, I think, that there is no peaceful extinction of slavery in prospect for us." Kentucky's failure to heed Henry Clay's pleas for his state to adopt gradual emancipation in the 1840s "together with a thousand other signs extinguishes that hope utterly." The "spirit" of the Revolution that caused northern states to pass gradual *post-nati* abolition plans in the eighteenth century had evaporated. "So far as peaceful, voluntary emancipation is concerned," Lincoln despaired, "the condition of the negro slave in America . . . is now fixed, and hopeless of change for better." Russia's czar would surrender his crown and free the serfs "sooner than will our American masters voluntarily give up their slaves."[82]

Lincoln's pessimism may well explain why his controversial reference to slavery's "ultimate extinction" in the "House Divided" speech of 1858 was worded so convolutedly. A famously honest man, Lincoln did *not* promise that blocking slavery's extension would eventually bring about its demise. Rather, he said that "arrest[ing] the further spread of" slavery could "place it where the public mind shall rest in the belief that it is in the course of ultimate extinction."[83] That phrasing suggests that his goal was to give Northerners who deeply disliked slavery a sense of doing at least something to undermine the institution, in addition to smiting the Slave Power, when they voted Republican even if their efforts produced no immediate result.

Lincoln's now-famous prediction that slavery might survive for another hundred years into the 1950s, well beyond the life expectancy of anyone old enough to vote in 1860, may have had the same goal.

The crucial point is that Republicans did not aim for abolition in addition to stopping slavery's spread. They not only emphatically denied this charge against them but also found it simply unbelievable because they knew it was not true. As the modern-day historian Crofts brilliantly suggests, precisely because they found Southerners' accusations of their own abolitionist intentions unfounded and unbelievable, they never believed Southerners' threats that they would secede rather than abide the election of a "Black Republican" president. As a Connecticut Republican sheet bluntly asserted ten days before the election, Southerners' threat to secede should Lincoln win "is an empty sham."[84] By 1860, in sum, the United States suffered from twin delusions that would shortly bring about a bloodbath. Southern Democrats refused to believe Republicans' protests that their real goal, no matter what they said, was not abolition of Southerners' property rights in slaves, and Republicans refused to believe, indeed found unbelievable, Southerners' threats to break up the Union rather than accept a Republican president.[85]

As pointed out in a previous chapter, Republicans reacted to southern Democrats' talk of secession in various ways. They denied that the threats were serious or that they represented majority opinion in the South. They called them unwarranted since Republicans posed no direct threat to slaveholders and other white Southerners. Or, like Russell Errett, the Pittsburgh Republican editor, they urged Northerners to defy the attempt of slaveholders to frighten them away from voting Republican. According to Errett, northern men should vote for Lincoln if only to prove that the United States was still a republic where the majority did in fact rule.

Aside from trying to blunt the connected charges that they were abolitionists whose victory guaranteed disunion, Republicans talked about slavery and slavery expansion in a variety of often contradictory ways in 1860. The national platform adopted in Chicago ostensibly spelled out the party's official line on the extension issue. Its eighth plank declared:

> That the normal condition of all the territory of the United States is that of freedom. That as our Republican fathers, when they had abolished Slavery in all our national territory, ordained that "no person should be deprived of life, liberty, or property, without due process of law," it becomes our duty, by legislation, whenever such legislation is necessary, to

maintain this provision of the Constitution against all attempts to violate it; and we deny the authority of Congress, of a territorial legislature, or of any individuals, to give legal existence to Slavery in any Territory of the United States.

This plank seems clear and straightforward. Republicans would resist any attempt to enact a federal slave code for the territories, but they would not insist on congressional prohibition unless it became necessary, presumably, that is, unless some future territorial legislature attempted to legalize slavery. The modern observer will note that like Lincoln, the plank identifies the Republicans' stance on slavery expansion with that of the revered Founders. He or she can also applaud the cleverness of the Republicans in resting their case on the same Fifth Amendment that Taney had used to rule congressional prohibition unconstitutional in the *Dred Scott* decision.

What this plank asserted, however, was not completely accurate. When the Founders wrote the Constitution and adopted the Bill of Rights, they had not abolished slavery south of the Ohio River, although that vast area had not yet been formally organized into federal territories. Since 1850, moreover, some slaves had legally existed in New Mexico Territory in compliance with the territorial law enacted as part of the Compromise of 1850. And after Lincoln's election Massachusetts Republican congressman Charles Francis Adams, among others, proposed admitting New Mexico as a slave state as a concession to the South.

Nor did Republicans agree with each other on what they and their supporters thought about the institution of slavery and its role as an issue in the 1860 campaign. In April, John Sherman, the one-time Republican candidate for House Speaker, declared to a party rally in New York's Cooper Union: "The Republican party affirms that Slavery is a social, moral, and political evil, and it is the right and duty of Congress and the people to prevent its extension into free territory."[86] This affirmation suggests that Republicans considered their opposition to slavery and its extension a critically important facet of their electoral appeal. A month later, however, Henry Raymond editorialized in his Republican *New York Times* that "We do not believe that the conflict [between North and South, Republicans and Democrats] is between Slavery and Freedom." Rather, "we regard the struggle as one for political power, and Slavery as playing merely a secondary role on either side."[87]

As was noted earlier, Abraham Lincoln repeatedly asserted in his speeches and correspondence that Northerners who supported the Republican Party did so because they shared his conviction that the institution of slavery was a moral "wrong" whose extension must be prohibited. Yet Horace Greeley, Henry J. Raymond's great Republican editorial rival in New York City, admitted privately that "I *know* the country is not Anti-Slavery. It will only swallow a little Anti-Slavery in a great deal of sweetening."[88]

Republicans campaigning for Lincoln in the North did denounce southern plans to impose slavery on territories with a congressional slave code, and they vowed to end the Slave Power's control of the federal government. Had Douglas been the nominee of a unified Democratic Party so that he could be implicated as an ally of southern Democrats, such appeals may have sufficed. In 1860, however, they had lost their most vivid examples of Slave Power aggressions against Northerners' rights, and Douglas was palpably the target, not the ally, of the Slave Power. So Republicans did need to add "a great deal of sweetening" to their attempts to mobilize northern voters against the man who was now the target of southern Democrats' attacks.

Indiana's Schuyler Colfax proudly wrote Lincoln upon Congress' adjournment in late June that congressional Republicans had generated a package of issues mostly unrelated to sectional strife over slavery extension that "are all good we think & calculated to help us with the popular vote." The Republican congressional campaign committee would remain in Washington over the summer to frank tens of thousands of printed versions of Republicans' speeches stressing the importance of those issues. "With Kansas [statehood] rejected [by Senate Democrats], Homestead vetoed, Corruption exposed, & Democracy divided & discordant," Colfax exulted, "it seems as if there ought to be no such word as fail."[89]

During the campaign a Minnesota resident told Lincoln that Republicans' support for the homestead bill that Buchanan had vetoed was their biggest selling point in his state. As noted above, many Pennsylvanians thought Republican support for a tariff increase that Democrats had squelched during the first session of the Thirty-Sixth Congress was their winning issue in the Keystone State. Massachusetts and New Jersey Republicans also proudly contrasted their party's support for a protective tariff with Democrats' record of opposition to it. But if northern Democrats had had access to the list Colfax sent Lincoln, the issue they would have picked out as by far the most damaging to their chances and the most helpful to Lincoln's was the reference to the Covode Committee's exposure of Democratic corruption.

The *New York World*, which would become the most important Demo-

"Our National Bird as It Appeared When Handed to James Buchanan, March 4, 1857, and the Identical Bird as It Appeared in A.D. 1861." This before-and-after 1860 Republican cartoon by Michael Woolf wonderfully illustrates Republicans' attempt to make the 1860 campaign a retrospective referendum on Buchanan's administration.

cratic newspaper in the United States during Reconstruction, wrote in July that the anticorruption plank was by far "the strongest practical point" in the Republican national platform. "The great document of this canvass will not be the Kansas Committee report, but the Covode Committee report; and the great watchword will not be antagonism to slavery, but '*honest* Abe Lincoln.'"[90] Republicans, echoed Ohio's Democratic *Newark Advocate,* had made the claim that they were the only honest party in the race by far their "main" campaign appeal. But that claim was false, the paper proclaimed. The well-known corruption of Republican state legislators in New York and Pennsylvania belied it.[91]

Citing another story from the *New York World* as evidence of how much disgust at Democrats' corruption helped Republicans, a North Carolina Bell paper editorialized in October that "thousands of intelligent" Northerners supported Republicans not because "they care a broken tobacco-pipe for the negro question, but because they see no other way to honest management at Washington."[92] Granted, that paper's primary objective in saying this was most likely to reduce North Carolinians' fear of Lincoln's likely victory. What matters here is that it accepted the New York paper's explanation of northern voters' motivation.

Republicans themselves, of course, also acknowledged the centrality and the potency of highlighting and promising to end Democratic corruption as the weapon with which they could carry the necessary northern votes to put Lincoln in the White House. Lincoln's most important duty once he was elected, Ohio's antislavery lion Joshua Giddings wrote him a month after his nomination, would be to undertake "the reformation of our government."[93] The New York Republican state central committee circulated a broadside in October declaring that Americans were "weary of misrule."[94] Democrats' "corruptions are countless and undeniable," declared a Connecticut Republican sheet on October 25.[95] The Republican Party's primary "mission," chimed the Republican *Milwaukee Daily Sentinel* three days before the election, "is to restore to the public mind the belief that there can be honesty in politics."[96]

Without the advantage that modern polling and especially exit polling gives analysts of contemporary elections about which issues most motivated voters to choose one party or another, it is impossible for the historian to say whether Republicans' free-soil commitments, anti–Slave Power diatribes, or denunciations of Democrats' corruption primarily caused men to vote Republican in 1860. One thing, however, is clear. The threat of slavery extension into western territories was far more urgent and the extent of Democratic corruption far less publicized in 1856 than in 1860, yet in 1856 almost 400,000 Northerners had supported Millard Fillmore rather than John C. Frémont. In 1860 the great majority of those Fillmore men would migrate to the Republican column, and many observers attributed their conversion to disgust with the Buchanan administration's venality.

That movement of Fillmore voters had become clear by the time the Milwaukee paper printed the editorial quoted above. By then its editor and almost all Republicans thought Lincoln's victory a certainty. By early November so did Douglas and his followers, the Breckinridge men, and the Constitutional Unionists, who had failed to get much traction outside of the Upper South. The reason for this consensus opinion was what had happened in state elections in the second week of October. As southern Democratic newspapers had predicted since the early spring of 1860, the election's outcome was determined in the North, not the South.

8

AMERICA VOTES

As was the case in all nineteenth-century presidential election years, partisan activists in 1860 closely examined results from statewide gubernatorial elections held before November for clues about how individual states might go in the presidential contest. Thus, as shown earlier, the April results from Connecticut and Rhode Island jolted Republicans' confidence that they could win with Seward as their nominee. Conversely, the September statewide results from Maine and Vermont, where Republicans rolled up 14.4 and 46 percentage point margins, left no doubt that Lincoln would garner those New England electoral votes.

Only three slave states scheduled either gubernatorial or congressional elections prior to November in 1860. Florida's October gubernatorial contest confirmed what everyone already knew. Breckinridge's electors would carry it in a rout. August elections for governor in North Carolina and Missouri, in contrast, were closely watched for clues about the fall. North Carolina's contest was expected to indicate whether John Bell or John Breckinridge would capture it. In 1859 Democrats' opponents, having renamed themselves the Whig Party, had captured four of North Carolina's eight House seats. Thus, the 1860 governor's race between incumbent Democratic governor John Ellis and Whig John Pool was expected to be close. Democrats there, as in almost all slave states, adopted the Breckinridge men's line in 1860. Protecting Southerners' property rights in slaves and white Southerners' equal rights in the nation from the purported Republican threat to them, they chanted for months before the August election, was the only issue that mattered. All North Carolina voters therefore must rally behind the Democrats' banner even in a gubernatorial election with no in-state Republican opponent. Poppycock! replied the many newspapers supporting Pool and Bell. Harping on the outside Republican threat, they insisted, was "a *decoy* cry" meant to distract voters' attention from "the *true issue.*" That was "the *corruptions of the Democratic party—the profligacy* of the Administration, the wasteful extravagance of the party!" The greatest threat to the equal rights of North Carolinians in 1860, they insisted, came not from the Republicans but from the Democrat-controlled state government's refusal to tax slave property at the same rate as other forms of property.[1] However valid this Whig argument may have been, it proved insufficient to generate a victory. The Democrat Ellis had won in 1858 by 16,000 votes; Pool reduced that margin to 6,000, the closest any Whig had been to winning since 1854. Still, it was a Democratic majority, and unless Stephen Douglas could garner a significant fraction of Ellis's 59,400 votes, Breckinridge seemed the likely victor in November.

Missouri's gubernatorial and congressional contests on August 6, in contrast, augured the four-way split as well as the huge jump in voter turnout that would characterize its vote in November. In the gubernatorial contest, rival Douglas and Breckinridge Democrats ran against a Constitutional Union candidate. The winning Democrat attracted 17,000 more votes than the victorious Buchanan had won in 1856 while the second-place Constitutional Union candidate, with 42 percent of the vote, outpaced Fillmore's 1856 total by 18,000 votes. In the congressional elections the same day, Democrats won five of the seven districts, a Constitutional Union candidate carried one, and in the St. Louis district the Republican Frank Blair, son of the old Jacksonian editor Francis P. Blair and brother of Montgomery Blair, who would serve in Lincoln's cabinet, won by a plurality of 44 percent in a three-way race.

What happened in North Carolina and Missouri had no bearing on Republicans' chances of electing Lincoln. The pre-presidential contests of most concern to them took place on October 9 in all-important Indiana, with the governorship and eleven House seats at stake, Ohio with twenty-one congressional seats up for grabs, and Pennsylvania with control of the statehouse and twenty-five House seats to be determined. Since Republicans' strong victory in Ohio's 1859 gubernatorial election, the Buckeye state seemed safely Republican. Thus, Republicans' wins in thirteen of twenty-one congressional districts and a statewide race for supreme court justice only confirmed their confidence about November. The crucial doubtful states of Indiana and Pennsylvania were another matter. Lincoln and other

Republican leaders had been focused on their gubernatorial contests for months. Lincoln's supporters in both had warned that a loss in October would probably mean defeat in November. In both states, moreover, all Democrats and many Bell men as well were expected to support the Democratic candidates, Thomas Hendricks in Indiana and Henry D. Foster in Pennsylvania.

Nonetheless, in Indiana the Republican Henry S. Lane outpolled Hendricks 136,725 to 126,968, the first time in twenty years that a non-Democrat had won Indiana's governorship. Republican gains had been enormous since 1856. In defeat, Hendricks garnered 8,000 more votes than the victorious Buchanan had in 1856 while Lane's total surpassed the combined 1856 vote for Frémont and Fillmore by 20,000. Lincoln's Indiana correspondents had rejoiced about a heavy swing of Protestant Germans from the Democratic to the Republican column prior to October, yet the most sophisticated statistical analysis of voter movement between 1856 and Indiana's October election found virtually no Democratic conversions to the Republican camp. Instead, young men mobilized by Wide Awakes and almost all former Fillmore men, who were determined to crush the hated Democrats, contributed to the Republican surge.[2]

As impressive as Republican gains in Indiana were, they paled next to the stunning performance of Pennsylvania's People's Party. James Buchanan's home state, Pennsylvania had been a normally reliable Democratic fiefdom. Of fifteen statewide races for governor or president since 1835, non-Democratic candidates had prevailed only four times—by 550 votes out of 287,800 cast in the presidential election of 1840, by 300 votes out of 336,000 cast for governor in 1848, by 12,700 out of 369,400 cast in November that year, and by 37,000 votes for governor in 1854 when the Whig victor had Know Nothing support. In no election prior to 1860, moreover, had any non-Democrat surpassed the Whig James Pollock's total of 203,000 votes for governor in 1854. Yet, in 1860, when Democrat Henry D. Foster garnered 230,259 votes, just 650 shy of Buchanan's winning majority in 1856, he earned only 46.7 percent of the total. Meanwhile, the supposedly flawed People's candidate Andrew D. Curtin amassed an astonishing 262,403 (53.3 percent). Estimates indicate that almost one-seventh of Buchanan's 1856 supporters, concentrated primarily in coal-mining and iron-making counties still suffering from the 1857 depression, as well as almost all of Fillmore's 1856 Pennsylvania supporters largely account for this unprecedented surge by the People's Party.[3]

Predictably, Republicans' smashing October victories spurred boasts of

Lincoln's certain triumph in November. Within two days of October 9, the Republican national committee issued a new address to the electorate congratulating Republican voters on Lincoln's imminent elevation to the White House and urging them now to concentrate on carrying as many congressional districts as possible in November.[4] "The doubts and fears of the Republicans of the nation are dispelled," rejoiced the *Chicago Press and Tribune* on the day after the elections. Republican "labor is rewarded by the prospect of a triumph which will be both splendid and enduring."[5] Democratic politicians in Washington, gloated the *New York Times* Washington correspondent, "were never before so thoroughly overwhelmed with a sense of ruin," especially as the fatal "blow comes from the old Keystone State."[6] Adopting a metaphor Democrats had used earlier in the year, the *Times* editor predicted even bigger Republican margins in November. "It is utter folly," he wrote, "to expect that a tide, which has thus been rolling in and rising higher and higher during the last year or two, is to stop in mid-ocean and flow back before it strikes the shore."[7] The Ohio, Pennsylvania, and Indiana returns, chorused the Republican *Milwaukee Sentinel* on October 12, "only render more certain the decisive triumph of the Republican cause in those States." "He who says this result does not foretell the issue of November is either fool or knave," echoed the Cleveland *Herald*. "The same causes that controlled the October elections in the three States will control the election in all the Free States in November." The victories, it added, represented a spontaneous and "mighty upheaving of the people . . . against the power of a wicked administration with millions of money at command, united with a still more greedy array of political rascals seeking to secure the official plunder."[8] Those state elections, in sum, had been a punishing referendum on Buchanan's record and eight years of Democratic misrule.

Democrats were as dismayed as Republicans were delighted by the results. A Mississippi editor reverted to the metaphor of a terrible gathering storm to express his thoughts. "If the Black Republicans, in November, follow up the victory which they have just won in these States," he groaned, "there is but too much reason to fear that the storm which is now threatened, will end in the wintry and tempestuous night of a Black Republican triumph, in the election of Lincoln." Southerners, he added, had counted on Indiana and Pennsylvania to stem the Republican tide. Now, their only hope was that New York, with its 35 electoral votes, without which Lincoln could not win an Electoral College majority, might do it. "Will she save the Republic?" he prayed.[9] The October defeats, in fact, caused the chairman of

Douglas's campaign in New York state finally to relent and join in a hastily constructed and frantically distributed fusion electoral ticket with Bell and Breckinridge men that might marshal enough votes to prevent a Lincoln triumph.

Other southern Democratic sheets admitted that the October contests had squelched any hope, that Lincoln's election was certain, and that secession was now Southerners' only option. Thus William Lowndes Yancey's organ in Montgomery, Alabama, told voters that after November's election, they must choose between "submission to the rule of a party whose avowed purpose is the abolition, not the restriction, of slavery, and a glorious career of uninterrupted prosperity as a separate nationality." An Atlanta paper chimed, "It is the solemn determination of the eight cotton states to secede immediately on his [Lincoln's] election."[10]

No one in 1860 took those southern threats more seriously than Stephen Douglas. By October he was in the Midwest vowing to audience after audience that "We, in the Northwest, cannot permit this Union to be dissolved."[11] In Cedar Rapids, Iowa, when telegrams brought news of the October state results, he immediately told those traveling with him that "Mr. Lincoln is the next President." Hence, "we must try to save the Union. I will go South."[12] After passing back through Illinois, Douglas headed into the Deep South via Memphis, Nashville, and Chattanooga, Tennessee, in an effort to prevent secession in response to Lincoln's now inevitable victory.

This mission constituted the most heroic, if futile, chapter of Douglas's political life. In Georgia, Alexander Stephens introduced him with great praise to an enthusiastic crowd in Atlanta and accompanied him to Macon, where Douglas's running mate, Herschel Johnson, joined him for speech-making. From Georgia, Douglas then headed to Montgomery and Mobile in Alabama. The Breckinridge press in the South heaped invective upon him, mocking his "bloated visage" induced by his notorious heavy drinking and his "pinchbeck principles," but Douglas was undeterred.[13]

As he had in Virginia and North Carolina, he told his Deep South audiences that disunion was no remedy for the South's concerns and that he would wholeheartedly support efforts by the federal government to resist any state's secession. In Montgomery, with Yancey himself listening, he declared, "It is the duty of every good citizen to frustrate the scheme" to break up the Union. "If Lincoln is elected, he must be inaugurated. . . . I hold that the election of any man on earth by the American people, according to the Constitution, is no justification for breaking up this government." All good Union men, he concluded, should "rally around the principle of non-intervention, and we will crush out Northern abolitionism and Southern disunion."[14]

On the night of November 5, election eve, he gave the last speech of his campaign in Mobile, where he had been greeted by former governor John A. Winston, one of the newly chosen pro-Douglas delegates to the Democrats' June Baltimore convention. Again, he vowed to help the federal government put down secession, but to a question whether he would accept a seat in Lincoln's cabinet, he angrily barked that he would never "accept office under Mr. Lincoln or Mr. Breckinridge or any other sectional candidate who advocates the doctrine of Congressional intervention." The local Bell paper praised this valedictory effort as "a triumphant vindication of his consistency since 1850."[15]

Douglas spent the following night in the newspaper office of John Forsyth, who had steadfastly supported his candidacy throughout 1860 and who had helped organize the pro-Douglas, anti-Yancey delegation Alabama sent to Baltimore after the Democrats' smash-up at Charleston. Telegraphic returns that night were only partial, but they established that Lincoln was sweeping virtually the entire North. What bothered Douglas most about these preliminary results, however, was how little support he appeared to be garnering in the South.

In Springfield, Illinois, Douglas's long-time rival Lincoln, after having been mobbed by his excited fellow townsmen when he went out to vote that afternoon, read telegraphic reports of the returns on election night in the local Western Union office. By midnight it was evident that he had carried the Midwestern states and Pennsylvania, but no news about New York had yet arrived when he and his jubilant fellow Republicans went across the street for a midnight supper prepared by the town's Republican ladies. Lincoln had barely sat down when news arrived that his electors had also triumphed in New York.[16] In the dining hall and in the streets, Lincoln's townsmen exploded with cheers.

The final results showed that Lincoln had swept all but three of the free states' electoral votes for a winning total of 180, which was 28 more than the majority he needed. Those 3 New Jersey votes went to Douglas, while Lincoln with only 48 percent of that state's popular vote captured its other 4. This outcome was attributable to the peculiar way New Jersey allotted its electoral votes.[17] But it was emblematic. While Lincoln had a clear majority of electoral votes, he garnered only 39.9 percent of the nation's popular votes. He won because his popular support was concentrated in the North. Of his total of almost 1.9 million popular votes, only some 26,000 came

Table 8.1 The Popular Vote for President in 1856 and 1860

	Free States	Slave States	Total	Electoral Vote
		1856		
Frémont	1,339,341	1,194	1,340,535	114
Buchanan	1,226,105	606,850	1,832,955	174
Fillmore	395,246	466,485	871,731	8
		1860		
Lincoln	1,839,205	26,388	1,865,593	180
Anti-Lincoln Vote	1,572,637	1,248,520	2,821,157	
Fusion	580,426	15,420	595,846	
Douglas	815,857	163,568	979,425	12
Breckinridge	99,381	570,091	669,472	72
Bell	76,973	499,441	576,414	39

Source: William E. Gienapp, "Who Voted for Lincoln?" in John L. Thomas (ed.), *Abraham Lincoln and the American Political Tradition* (Amherst: University of Massachusetts Press, 1986), p. 77. Gienapp's table mistakenly credits Fillmore with 10,000 more northern votes in 1856 than he won. He gives the correct total, which I've used here, in his magnificent *The Origins of the Republican Party*.

from slave states. Douglas ran second in the popular vote but last in the electoral count, with only 12—Missouri's 9 and those 3 from New Jersey.

Fusion tickets in New York, New Jersey, and Pennsylvania render it impossible to determine precisely how many popular votes Douglas actually received in 1860. It is clear from Table 8.1, however, that his disappointment about his poor southern showing was merited. The great majority of his popular votes did come from the North, even though the only state whose electoral vote he captured was the nominal slave state of Missouri.

Douglas's biographer states that his total vote in 1860 was 1,365,976 and that 88 percent of his votes came from free states, but it is not clear how he estimated that total.[18] According to the figures from Walter Dean Burnham's *Presidential Ballots, 1836–1892* that I use in Table 3, Appendix A, in turn, Douglas's total was 1,005,456, of which only 163,096 came from slave states. What is clear is that Missouri was the only slave state where his share of the total popular vote exceeded 20 percent and that he failed to achieve even 10 percent in Arkansas, Delaware, Florida, Maryland, Mississippi, North Carolina, Tennessee, Texas, and Virginia.

One reason for Douglas's poor showing in the region, apparently, is that Dixie was overwhelmingly rural. Outside of Maryland Douglas tended to run far better in the South's cities than its rural areas. To give just a few examples, Douglas garnered 35.5 percent of Louisville's vote, but only 16 percent of rural Kentucky's. He won 17 percent of Richmond's vote and 34 percent of Petersburg's, but only 9 percent in Virginia's rural counties. He won 28 percent of New Orleans' large vote, besting Breckinridge there, but he polled a dismal 11 percent in rural parishes. Finally, he won a striking 44 percent of the vote in Memphis, Tennessee's most populous city, while failing to achieve even 7 percent in rural counties.[19]

This urban/rural split in Douglas's vote undoubtedly reflects his weakness among slaveholders. By no means did all rural counties in the South have large or even substantial proportions of slaves and slaveholders, but cities had demonstrably fewer than the staple crop growing areas of the South, no matter whether that staple was hemp, tobacco, cotton, rice, or sugar. A statistical analysis of the 1860 returns in the Deep South states of Louisiana, Mississippi, and Alabama, indeed, suggests that Douglas was weakest in the counties and Louisiana parishes where slaveholders were most numerous and the growth of the slave population during the 1850s had been most rapid. In those states, the heaviest slaveholding areas had traditionally been Whig, not Democratic, and in 1860 they again voted predominantly for John Bell while low-slaveholding upcountry rural counties formed the backbone of Breckinridge's support.[20]

Conversely, the traditional pattern of partisan support by slaveholding and nonslaveholding areas in Virginia and North Carolina had always been precisely the reverse. Slaveholders heavily supported Democrats, and non- and low-slaveholding areas preferred their opponents. The very best research we have shows that this pattern held in 1860. According to the historian Daniel W. Crofts's regression estimates, in Virginia 58 percent of the slaveholders who voted in November preferred Breckinridge, compared to 42 percent for Bell. Nonslaveholders in the Old Dominion divided their votes more narrowly, 47 percent for Bell and 53 percent for Breckinridge and Douglas. In North Carolina, voting slaveholders preferred Breckinridge to Bell by a 2-to-1 margin while 53 percent of the nonslaveholders preferred Bell to 47 percent for Breckinridge and Douglas. Tennessee, which Bell won narrowly, in contrast, emulated the Deep South's pattern. Voting slaveholders preferred Bell by a 57 to 43 percent margin while nonslaveholders favored Breckinridge and, clearly, Douglas by 55 to 45 percent.[21]

Outside of Baltimore, the nation's fourth-largest city in 1860, and Savannah, Georgia, in fact, Breckinridge ran far more poorly in urban than in rural areas. Still, he swept to decisive majorities in Alabama, Arkansas, Florida, Mississippi, and Texas while carrying Delaware, Georgia, Louisiana, and Maryland by pluralities and eking out a majority of 50.2 percent in North Carolina. Bell captured Kentucky, Tennessee, and Virginia by pluralities. Some of these outcomes were exceptionally close. Breckinridge's margin over Bell in Maryland, for example, was only 522 votes out of some 92,000 cast; Bell nipped Breckinridge by only 166 votes, about 1 percent of the total vote, in Virginia; and Douglas prevailed over Bell by a mere 140 votes out of over 165,000 cast votes in Missouri.

If there was a distinct rural/urban split in voting patterns in the slave states, there was also a notable regional pattern in Dixie as a whole. With the exception of Arkansas, Louisiana, and Georgia, Breckinridge ran far more strongly in the Deep South than the Upper South slave states. He led Bell by 23 percentage points in Alabama, 26 in Florida, 20 in Mississippi, and 51 in Texas. The first three of those would be the first to secede following the lead of South Carolina, where the legislature unanimously cast its electoral votes for Breckinridge. Conversely, of the seven Deep South States that initially seceded in response to Lincoln's election, secessionists met their staunchest resistance in Georgia and Louisiana, where Breckinridge had failed to secure an outright majority. Both Bell men and Douglasites in the South had staunchly opposed secession throughout the 1860 campaign. Thus, it is telling that their combined share of the popular vote was 51.2 percent in Georgia, 55.1 percent in Louisiana, 64.4 percent in Kentucky, 51.6 percent in Maryland, 70.7 percent in Missouri, 49.6 percent in North Carolina, 55.5 percent in Tennessee, and 54.3 percent in Virginia. Adding in Lincoln's share of the vote produces anti-Breckinridge majorities of 54.5 percent in Delaware, 54.3 percent in Maryland, 81 percent in Missouri, and 55.5 percent in Virginia.

One other aspect of the South's returns merits comment. Most voters in 1860 understood that much rode on the election's outcome, even though they defined that "much" in very different ways depending on their party and their section. As a result of that understanding and of some very thorough canvassing by party workers to get voters to the polls, the proportion of the eligible electorate who voted in 1860 nationally was 81.2 percent, slightly higher than the massive outpouring of voters in the famous "Log Cabin–Hard Cider" campaign of 1840 and second only, in all of American history, to 1876's 81.8 percent turnout rate.[22] A Philadelphia Republican paper had commented on "the immense issue at stake" in the election a day after it occurred,[23] and without question the highest turnout rates in individual states occurred in the North: 94.2 percent in Iowa, 95.5 percent in New York, and a barely believable 97.8 percent in lightly populated Oregon. Yet, turnout was also lower in ten of sixteen free states than it had been in 1856.[24] Instead, it was a surge of voters to the polls in slave states that accounts for the jump in the national turnout rate from 78.9 percent in 1856 to 81.2 percent in 1860. Of fifteen slave states, only Kentucky and Tennessee, two of the three states Bell carried, experienced a small drop in the rate of participation. Everywhere else it was up—and often significantly: 7.7 points in Alabama, 19 in Arkansas, 11.2 in Mississippi, 14.4 in Missouri, and 9.3 in Texas. (See Table 4, Appendix A.)

Which candidates benefited most from this surge in the South varied from state to state. In Alabama, Arkansas, Florida, and especially Texas, which had been roiled throughout the summer of 1860 by rumors of rebellious slaves poisoning wells and torching masters' houses, Breckinridge clearly benefited most from the leap in participation. In Missouri, in contrast, it was evidently Douglas and Bell, and in Virginia, where Douglas and Breckinridge simply split the vote Buchanan had garnered in 1856, Bell attracted the lion's share of additional post-1856 voters.

If the pattern of which candidate benefited most from a larger turnout in 1860 varied from state to state in Dixie, the verdict in free states was unambiguous. Republicans profited most from the surge. In the North Lincoln attracted 500,000 more voters than Frémont had, and the size of the anti-Lincoln vote in that section was almost identical to the combined anti-Frémont vote in 1856. Because Fillmore voters moved massively into the Republican column between 1856 and 1860 and Bell received slightly less than a fifth of Fillmore's total, obviously Democrats also added voters to their column since 1856. Moreover, Republicans actually lost votes between 1856 and 1860 in Maine, Massachusetts, and Vermont, where turnout rates also dropped, and only held their own in other New England states. Elsewhere, however, Republicans' gains were large, especially if measured as a percentage of their 1856 vote itself: 18,000 (90%) in California, 75,000 (78%) in Illinois, 44,600 (47%) in Indiana, 26,500 (60%) in Iowa, 30,000 (107%) in New Jersey, 86,600 (31%) in New York, 47,000 (25%) in Ohio, and 120,500 (82%) in all-important Pennsylvania. As a result of these gains, Lincoln's share of the North's popular vote burgeoned to 53.9 percent, compared to Frémont's 45.2 percent.

To view this performance in another way, in 1856 Republicans had won 77 percent and Fillmore, 23 percent of the North's anti-Democratic vote. In 1860 Republicans won 96 percent and Bell only 4 percent of anti-Democrats who voted. That is, Lincoln prevailed in 1860, while Frémont had lost in 1856, because the number of northern voters determined to smite the Democrats had soared and Republicans had consolidated the vast majority of them behind their own banner.

As in the October state elections, Republican gains in November, according to William Gienapp's definitive statistical analysis, came primarily from Fillmore's 1856 supporters and men who had either abstained in 1856 or been too young to vote that year. Conversions from those latter two groups outpaced Democratic additions from them by a 2-to-1 margin in Maine and New York, an 11-to-9 margin in Indiana, and a 3-to-2 margin in Illinois. But in those states as well as in Ohio and Pennsylvania, Douglas also did well among previous nonvoters. Measuring this voter movement in a different way indicates more starkly how important it was to Lincoln's victory outside New England. Roughly one-third of Lincoln's total in New York, two-fifths of it in Pennsylvania, one-fifth of it in Ohio, one-third of it in Indiana, one-half of it in Illinois, and two-fifths of it in Iowa came from men who had voted for Millard Fillmore in 1856 or not voted at all that year.

In a few states, these additions were crucial. Lincoln carried the two West Coast states with only a small plurality of a vote total divided four ways, and even then, Douglas was only 644 votes shy of taking California from him while Breckinridge trailed him by a minuscule 264 votes in Oregon. Democratic divisions in those two states obviously benefited Lincoln, but he would have still won in the Electoral College without their combined 7 electoral votes. It's the closeness of the vote elsewhere that merits attention. Despite his huge gains in Illinois, Lincoln obtained a bare majority of 50.7 percent, and his 12,000-vote edge over Douglas represented only 3.6 percent of the total the two men received. Lincoln's margin over Douglas was twice as large in Indiana, but only because Breckinridge electors attracted six times as many Hoosier votes as they did in Illinois. Significantly, in fact, Lincoln's 51.1 percent of Indiana's popular vote was a slightly smaller proportion than Henry Lane had won in October. Conversely, in Pennsylvania, the most important Lower North state, Lincoln ran 6,000 votes ahead of Curtin and rang up an impressive 56.2 percent of the vote compared to Curtin's 53.3 percent. Yet the main reason that Lincoln ran so far ahead of Curtin in proportionate terms is that Henry D. Foster, the Democrats' gubernatorial candidate, garnered 22,000 more votes in October than all of Lincoln's opponents in November and approximately 45,000 more than the two Democratic electoral tickets combined in November.

Defeatism among Democrats caused by the October result offers the best explanation for this plunge in Democratic turnout between October and November. But it also explains what happened in certain New England states, as the data in Table 4 of Appendix A indicate. Total turnout in Maine was almost 10 points lower in November 1860 than in November 1856, largely because both Republicans and Democrats knew, after September's gubernatorial election, that Democrats' chances of stopping Lincoln there were hopeless. The same pattern prevailed in Vermont, Massachusetts, New Hampshire, and, to a lesser extent, Connecticut because Republicans knew they could not lose and Democrats knew they could not win in November.

Democrats' likely defeatism in a number of northern states helps cast fresh light on one of the oldest questions concerning the 1860 election. Namely, did the division between the candidacies of Douglas and Breckinridge contribute to Lincoln's sweep of the North? As very good historians have argued, only in Oregon and California did Democrats' divisions allow Lincoln to win with small pluralities, and he would still have won in the Electoral College without those two states' electoral votes. Elsewhere in the free states, except New Jersey, Lincoln won with a popular vote majority—so that even if all his competitors combined as they did in New York, he would still have won the election with, say, 170 electoral votes.

This assertion is surely true of the votes that were cast. But what about potential Democratic voters who stayed home because they believed their party's division made their chances of victory hopeless? The estimated rates of voter participation in Iowa and New York suggest that very few, if any, Democrats failed to go to the polls in November. But the case in other states is not so clear. Apparently one-fifth of the potential electorate failed to vote in Illinois. Had Douglas been Democrats' only candidate there and received all the Democratic votes cast, and had 10,000 more men voted for him, Lincoln would have lost Illinois. In Indiana, where one-tenth of potential voters apparently abstained, 12,000 more voters for a single Douglas candidacy would have cost Lincoln those 13 electoral votes as well. Combined with the 7 electoral votes Lincoln won from the West Coast only because Democrats ran two candidates, the 24 from Indiana and Illinois equaled 31, and without those electoral votes Lincoln's total would have been only 149, which was 3 less than the necessary majority of 152. With slightly fewer than 23,000 more votes for Douglas (or Breckinridge in Oregon) in those four states, the equivalent of 0.7 percent of the total northern vote cast, Lincoln could have been denied victory in the Electoral College. Thus, the Democratic split may have had a far more telling impact on the result than it is currently fashionable to believe.

As had been the case since the emergence of the Republican Party, it ran more strongly in certain rural areas than cities. This pattern was true of most New England states, New York, New Jersey, Pennsylvania, Ohio, Michigan, and Wisconsin. Nonetheless, there were exceptions. Cities that had been strongly Whig, like Pittsburgh and its neighbor Allegheny City—which gave Lincoln his largest majorities of any northern cities—Cleveland, and, understandably, Chicago gave Lincoln large votes, whereas he ran poorly in traditional Democratic strongholds like New York, Brooklyn, Albany, Jersey City, New Haven, Milwaukee, and Cincinnati. Rural counties, moreover, had sharply split along partisan lines. Counties with high proportions of families who had moved from the South in Ohio, Indiana, and Illinois were heavily Democratic whereas rural counties in New York and the Midwest where New England Yankees predominated went strongly Republican. Similarly, while most farmers apparently supported Lincoln, those with the smallest, least-productive farms did not. The extant evidence also suggests that skilled artisans were far more likely than unskilled day laborers to vote Republican. Irish Catholics strongly supported Democrats, as did Catholic Germans. The non-Catholic "Pennsylvania Dutch" and German Lutherans in Ohio went predominantly Republican. Quakers everywhere were strongly Republican, but other Protestant denominations, including Baptists, Methodists, and Presbyterians, divided their vote depending upon their local social context.

There is significant evidence that where Presbyterians lived close to Catholics (whom they usually despised), as in Pittsburgh, Cleveland, and Cincinnati, they went heavily Republican precisely because they correctly identified Catholics as Democrats. Republican newspapers openly played on their prejudice, predicting that because Douglas's new wife was Catholic and the nation's leading Catholic prelate Archbishop John Hughes supported him, Douglas would be a pawn in the Pope's hand should he win election. In 1858 Pittsburgh's leading Republican newspaper had actually italicized the names of all Catholics on the Democratic local ticket and bluntly asked Protestants how they could possibly vote for such a party. In 1860 the same paper openly called on Protestants to support the People's Party to retaliate against Catholic priests who were publicly attacking its gubernatorial candidate Andrew Curtin, a former Know Nothing.[25]

Lincoln himself was no anti-Catholic bigot, but many who voted for him were. Visceral anti-Catholic sentiment as the primary reason some Protestants voted against the Democratic Party hardly subsided with the disappearance of the Know Nothing Party as an independent electoral force after 1856. That motivation flourished for the rest of the decade, indeed for the remainder of the nineteenth century in many places.

Some contemporary Republicans and Democrats pointed to Lincoln's personal reputation as the reason many Northerners voted for him. According to a few, Lincoln's image as a self-educated "rail splitter" who had worked his way up from humble beginnings explained much of the support he won from men who viewed him as both someone like themselves and a model for their own aspirations. Others recognized, correctly, that his identity as a Western man was probably critical to his defeating Douglas in Indiana and Illinois. In 1860, however, both Democrats and Republicans, like Lincoln himself, pointed more often to Lincoln's reputation as "Honest Abe," who would cleanse the Augean stables Democrats had built in Washington, as the reason he triumphed. Lincoln's victory, enthused an Indianan the day after the election, "enables us [Republicans] to turn out the Goths and Vandals who have so long had possession of the government."[26] Chorused Carl Schurz from Wisconsin, Lincoln now had a chance to undertake "the greatest mission that ever befell the lot of mortal man: the restoration of the original principles of the model Republic of the world."[27] We "got Lincoln nominated on the *idea* of his honesty," wrote *Chicago Tribune* editor Joseph Medill in a private letter the following January, "and elected him by endorsing him as 'honest Abe.'"[28]

What made Lincoln's reputed honesty salient as a motivating factor, of course, was not his personal virtue alone but its contrast with the reputed dishonesty and corruption of the Buchanan administration. Republican victory in 1860 was not a rousing endorsement of the still little-known and as yet unmartyred Abraham Lincoln. It was instead an emphatically punishing referendum on office-holding Democrats, an insistent demand to throw those rascals out and purify the public place.

Testimony that anti-Democratic hostility primarily motivated Republican voters abounds. "Large numbers of true men, from all parties, joined our standard because of the corruptions of the national administration," New York's Republican congressman Francis Spinner told Salmon Chase. Iowa's Republican senator James Grimes agreed that "[our] triumph was achieved more because of Lincoln[']s reputed honesty & the known corruptions" of Democrats than because of "the negro question." Anger at Democratic corruption also trumped the fears of conservative former Whigs and Democrats that a Lincoln victory meant disunion. A friend of Crittenden explained after the election why he and other former Fillmore men in Connecticut did not support Bell as Crittenden had hoped. "Multitudes of us voted the republican ticket because we wanted *honesty* to displace corruption." "I voted for Mr. Lincoln," the political economist David A. Wells told

Tennessee's Andrew Johnson, "not because I hated slavery, or thought it a sin, or wished in any way to do my neighbor a wrong—but because I was disgusted with the present Administration & wished for a change."[29]

New York banker August Belmont, chairman of the Douglas Democrats' national committee, reached the same conclusion in a November letter to John Forsyth, the Mobile, Alabama, editor who had worked so faithfully for Douglas throughout 1860. Belmont had hoped that Fillmore's many New York supporters would back the fusion electoral ticket against Lincoln but was disappointed. "The country at large had become disgusted with the misrule of Mr. Buchanan, and the corruption which disgraced his Administration. The Democratic party was made answerable for his misdeeds, and a change was ardently desired by thousands of conservative men out of politics." "We owe the election of Lincoln only to the misrule of the present Administration," Belmont repeated in another letter to Forsyth a month later.[30] James Gordon Bennett, who had prayed for Lincoln's defeat during the campaign, agreed in a *Herald* editorial on November 8. Conservative New Yorkers had voted for Lincoln rather than the fusion ticket, he asserted, because "they believe that his administration will restore the peace to the country, North and South, which the reckless and treacherous leaders of the democracy so rudely destroyed."[31]

For most Republican voters, indeed, Democratic "misrule" included more than pervasive corruption. Many celebrated their victory as a revolution that at long last had toppled the arrogant and insulting Slave Power from control of the government. Lincoln's triumph was "a revolution occasioned by the *permanent conviction of the American people*," exulted one Republican sheet. "No pro-slavery party can ever again be successful in the United States. It had its day. For it there is no revival."[32] Lincoln's election guarantees "the repression of the blighting curse of slavery," echoed the *Boston Advertiser* the day after the election. "The great object of my wishes & labors for nineteen years is accomplished in the overthrow of the Slave Power," a jubilant Salmon P. Chase told Lincoln.[33] On that same day incoming Massachusetts Republican congressman Charles Francis Adams wrote in his diary: "There is now scarcely a shadow of a doubt that the great revolution has actually taken place, and that the country has thrown off the domination of the slaveholders." The New Yorker Seward, who would be Chase's great rival in Lincoln's cabinet, put the same thought in the past tense a few days after Lincoln's inauguration when he remarked that "the battle for freedom had been fought and won."[34] Still the nation's best-known Republican leader, Seward obviously did not believe that federally imposed abolition on the South was on his party's future agenda. For him, the sectional conflict over slavery should have ended with Lincoln's victory.

Republican editors in the North fully recognized that many Southerners misunderstood what the results of a new Republican administration might be for them. Thus, the *Chicago Tribune*, the *New York Times*, and the *Boston Advertiser*, to name just three, stressed that Republicans had failed to win control of either the House or the Senate and consequently could enact no legislation harmful to the South. Most Republican papers as well eschewed lengthy attempts to explain or crow about the Republican victory and instead published multiple reports from the South stressing widespread hostility to secession outside of South Carolina.

Moderate Republican papers also downplayed the role that antislavery or anti-southern sentiment played in motivating Republican voters. The immediate postelection analysis in the Philadelphia *North American and United States Gazette*, for example, flatly denied that "slavery was the dominating idea of [the] Presidential contest." It instead attributed the result to a litany of the Buchanan administration's misdeeds. Republicans' triumph "was rendered inevitable by the crimes and follies of the party which is now doomed and defeated," it began. Echoing an argument also advanced by the equally moderate *New York Times*, it contended that Republicans' opposition to slavery extension had in fact contributed only modestly to the Republican showing. "No such issue was practically asserted," at least in eastern Pennsylvania, "because the complexion of all the present territories is settled, and the declaration of the Chicago Convention against the extension of slavery, and the power of Congress over the territories, can only be applied when the . . . contingency [of new territorial acquisitions] should arise." Instead, "the great idea settled by this election, and which, perhaps, operated as much as any on the public mind, was the purpose to change the administration of public affairs at Washington, and to purge and purify the whole political machinery of the government." The public was infuriated by "examples of corruption and profligacy . . . encouraged and favored by" the purported "guardians of the public treasury." People "saw power and patronage employed to establish a sectional domination, and the influence of our government openly enlisted in Kansas to force slavery upon an outraged and unwilling people." They witnessed "our material interests neglected and injured, the press subsidized, elections controlled by money extorted from Federal office-holders, unworthy partisans rewarded by jobs and contracts . . . defalcations common and countenanced . . . and abuses defying opinion everywhere." Because the electorate remembered all of these sins, they "determined they should be punished and the democracy expelled from power. This general purpose operated more than any other upon the election."[35]

In his immediate excitement caused by the early returns, Henry Raymond gloated in a *New York Times* headline that the huge Republican vote represented "The North Rising in Indignation at the Menaces of the South." But he also gave a fuller prediction of what Lincoln's victory portended in an accompanying editorial that put Republicans' anti–Slave Power mission in a broader, less sectionalized context. "The policy of extending slavery, and increasing its political power, will now be checked. The Slave interest will no longer impose its claims and its laws upon the federal Government. The Constitution will no longer be regarded as a mere instrument for fortifying and increasing Slavery." "But above all," he added, "we shall have established at Washington a rule of honesty and patriotism, in place of the corruption, imbecility, and intrigue which have controlled our public councils for the last few years."[36]

The *Boston Advertiser*, long a favored sheet of Boston's business community, portrayed the consequences of Lincoln's victory in even less sectionally threatening terms. Lincoln's triumph, it hymned the day after the election, guaranteed "a return to the policy of the founders of the government, involving equal and exact justice to the people in every part of the nation." It meant "an honest and economical administration of the government, the development and protection" of the nation's "industrial resources," an end to slavery extension, and thus "the removal of the discussion of agitating [sectional] questions." "All these things," it concluded in one of the most profoundly wrongheaded predictions in newspaper history, "promise for the people of the United States under the administration of Abraham Lincoln, a career of peace and prosperity unexampled in the history of the world."[37]

On the day after that Boston paper issued its rosy prediction, a prosecession Charleston sheet tersely refused to comment on the result. "It is time for action, not words," it growled.[38] The four most important federal officials in that city had already acted on the very day the Boston paper had waxed so optimistically. Upon learning the result, the U.S. marshal, the federal customs collector, the U.S. attorney, and Andrew McGrath, the judge of the U.S. District Court, dramatically resigned their commissions in protest against serving in a federal government that a hated Black Republican was elected to lead. On November 9 the leading Democratic newspaper in Mississippi's state capital reported a "remarkable unanimity" among its residents "in favor of immediate withdrawal from the Northern States and the establishment of a Southern Confederacy" rather than submitting to "the election of Lincoln and the prospective installation" in the federal government "of his sectional party."[39] Thus began the movement for secession in the Deep South that Lincoln's triumph instantly triggered, and, make no mistake about it, Republican victory was the indispensable ammunition men who had long but unsuccessfully sought disunion needed to consummate their goal at long last.

Southern secession following Lincoln's victory is the topic of other books, not this one. Nonetheless, the story of the 1860 election would be incomplete without a brief examination of how different interpretations of its meaning shaped different responses to the secession movement in the South and North.

Southern proponents of secession, for example, refused to credit Lincoln's election to a repudiation of Buchanan and his minions. For them, people who backed Lincoln shared Republicans' hatred of white Southerners. Lincoln was supported, protested the Jackson *Semi-Weekly Mississippian*, "upon the one idea of hostility to the Southern States." That was why those states must secede.[40] True, they admitted, Republicans had minuscule support within the South itself and less than two-fifths of the nationwide vote. But they had won a majority of the North's vote, and that majority, as secessionists saw it, was permanent. They agreed with those Republicans who boasted that a proslavery Democratic Party could never again win control of the national government.

Lincoln's win, in sum, meant to secessionists that a permanent majority of Northerners were dedicated to the subjugation of the South. His northern vote represented "huge mountainous waves . . . beating down on the South with resistless force." To remain in the Union was to submit meekly to inevitable northern tyranny. Southerners, argued the *New Orleans Bee*, could trust neither "the conservatism of the North" nor "the strength of party to neutralize Black Republican hatred." The South must not remain "in the Union upon sufferance; the mere vassal and thrall of a party which aims at her ruin and degradation. . . . Such a state of practical servitude and submission where all sense of equality would be lost . . . would necessarily become perfectly intolerable."[41]

Nor did it matter that Republicans in fact would not control either house of Congress or be able to pass any overtly antislavery legislation as Republican papers instantly pointed out. For secession's proponents, control of the executive branch by an almost exclusively northern and overtly anti-southern party alone assured a humiliating southern enslavement to northern tyranny that no honorable southern white man could possibly abide. "Talk of negro slavery," proclaimed Virginia's George Fitzhugh, "it is not half so humiliating and disgraceful as the slavery of the South to the North." Virginia's most determined secessionist, Edmund Ruffin, agreed. "A Northern sectional party, and majority, directing the action of the federal government," he wrote in 1860, "need not exercise any unconstitutional power, or commit any 'overt' act of usurpation, to produce the most complete subjection and political bondage, degradation, and ruin of the South."[42]

In contrast, secession's opponents in Dixie denied that Lincoln's majorities in northern states were evidence of permanent sectional hostility to white Southerners or of the inevitable imposition of political enslavement upon them. They instead attributed Lincoln's election to two temporary causes that were bound to disappear after 1860: the Democrats' inability to unite behind a single presidential candidate that year and the universal revulsion at the pervasive corruption of Buchanan's administration. That administration's "unparalleled corruption, apart from the Slavery question, had arrayed against it the undoubted majority of the American people," editorialized an antisecession Virginia paper. "The Republican vote was made up in very large proportion, not of sympathizers with MR. SEWARD, but the enemies of MR. BUCHANAN."[43] Even before the election, a pro-Douglas and antisecession North Carolina paper insisted that "it would be a nice piece of folly to dissolve the great and glorious Union simply because" Democrats' intraparty quarrels had "permitted a minority to gain a *temporary ascendancy*."[44]

It was the tenuous and ephemeral, rather than the permanent, nature of Lincoln's 1860 northern majorities that impressed southern antisecessionists. All Southerners had to do, they contended, was wait for Lincoln's administration to self-destruct and his temporary majority support to melt away. As Tennessee's Andrew Johnson, the South's most prominent antisecession Democrat, declared in a Senate speech on December 19, 1860, "In four years from this day, Lincoln and his administration will be turned out, the worst-defeated and broken-down party that ever came into power. It is an inevitable result from the combination of elements that now exists."[45]

Disagreements about the robustness or fragility of the majorities Lincoln had amassed in northern states also influenced the division among Republicans over how they should react to the secessionist rage that erupted across the Deep South after November 6. Confident of Republican control of the North and sensitive to the seriousness of the secession sentiment in the Deep South, Republican editors like Thurlow Weed in Albany, Henry Raymond in New York City, and John D. Defrees in Indianapolis, among many others, called on Lincoln to bolster antisecessionist forces in the South by issuing public statements that Republicans intended no harm to slaveholders and no tyranny over white Southerners generally. Some even urged immediate concessions on the slavery extension issue because they believed that territorial settlers themselves, without any federal action that Southerners regarded as discriminatory, could prevent it.

Hardliners with whom Lincoln sided during the secession crisis rejected such advice on the grounds that any retreat from Republicans' platform commitments and any conciliation of the South would be cowardly, unnecessary, destructive of what Republicans had achieved with their victory, and, equally important, certain to destroy the Republican Party by instantly turning former Free Soilers and other antislavery extremists against it. On November 15 the *Chicago Tribune*, a paper Lincoln read regularly, reprinted an editorial it credited to the *Cincinnati Gazette* entitled "An Inaugural Asked for in Advance." What is so striking about this piece is that it denounced any pre-inaugural statement from Lincoln about his intentions regarding the South in precisely the same language that Lincoln was using in his private responses to Weed, Raymond, Truman Smith, and others about why he refused to make any conciliatory comments prior to his inauguration. One wonders, indeed, if Lincoln had ghost-written this piece for his friend Joseph Medill to print, for he had often salted papers with his own unidentified editorial views during his career.

To give but one example, on November 10 Lincoln wrote Truman Smith that he would not issue any statement to reassure Southerners. He could not, he explained, say anything he had not already said that was "in print and open for the inspection of all." To repeat himself for those who refused to believe what he had already said "would be wanting in self-respect, and would have the appearance of sycophancy and timidity, which would excite the contempt of good men, and encourage bad ones to clamor the more loudly."[46]

Compare that with the editorial the *Chicago Tribune* ran five days later. Any pre-inaugural concessions to Southerners' fears, it huffed, would be "unmanly and dishonest." Lincoln had already put his "opinions" "on record in every possible form," and "no decently informed man" could "be ignorant" of them. Demands that Lincoln speak out before his inauguration was "to ask the Republican party, through Mr. Lincoln, to apologize for what they have done! It is to undo its great work of November 6th." Lincoln was "not the man" to do it, the editorial concluded, "nor are Republicans."[47]

Lincoln, of course, famously told congressional Republicans the same thing in December and January about acquiescing to any plan that would allow slavery extension into any existing or future federal territory. Any such concession, he contended, would betray the Republican platform commitment, force Republicans to redo the work they had accomplished in 1860 all over again, and quite possibly drive extreme antislavery men away from the party. Throughout his period as president-elect, in sum, Lincoln sided with his party's hardliners, who pooh-poohed the seriousness of the secessionist threat and resolutely opposed any hint of softening the position against slavery extension the party had taken in its 1860 platform.

On November 15, the very day that the *Chicago Tribune* reprinted the editorial denouncing any pre-inaugural concession to the South, Michigan's Republican senator Zachariah Chandler penned an especially militant version of that hardliner stance to his Illinois Republican senate colleague Lyman Trumbull. "I trust Mr. Lincoln's nerves are not disturbed by this disunion howl," he began. "Let them howl. . . . I would rather see every traitor in South Carolina hanged & Charleston burned, than to see one line from Mr. Lincoln to appease them, in advance of his inaugural."[48] Chandler closed this defiant epistle with a blood-curdling postscript that he labeled "Confidential." With regard to what he had called "a set of prating, bragging, bullying cowards" in South Carolina, "Individually, I do want a little shooting or hanging done before this matter is ended if we have a decent excuse for it."

Other Republicans had a far more astute appreciation of the seriousness of the secessionist threat. They argued that the party could benefit, rather than suffer, from making concessions by forming a winning political alliance with the southern opponents of secession who were pleading for evidence that Republicans would not subject white Southerners either to abolition or to degrading political subjugation. Of these Republican conciliators, none scandalized hardliners more than Thurlow Weed, the Albany editor, Seward partner, and long-time behind-the-scenes manager (a.k.a. "Boss") of New York's Whig and then Republican parties. In editorials in his *Albany Evening Journal* on November 19 and 24 he called on northern states to repeal their personal liberty laws that Southerners found so offensive. On November 24, in flat violation of the Chicago platform's pledge never to allow slavery to spread to a single square foot of American territory, he called for the restoration of the Missouri Compromise line westward to the California border in order to secure to the South "all territory, adapted by soil and climate [of which, Weed realized, there was none], to 'its peculiar institution.'" "A Victorious Party can afford to be tolerant," he explained in a November 30 editorial, "not as our friends assume, in the abandonment or abasement of its principles or character, but in efforts to correct and disabuse the minds of those who misunderstand both." Southern secessionists were "in earnest. There is imminent danger of a dissolution of the Union." That danger could "only be averted by such moderation and forbearance as will draw out and strengthen and combine the Union sentiment of the whole country." Republicans, he added in a December 17 editorial, could safely count on the residents of the territories themselves to prevent slavery extension, especially as the men they appointed as territorial governors would not, like Buchanan's minions, veto laws banning slavery passed by territorial legislatures. This was the position Raymond's *New York Times* had taken for over a year.[49]

On December 10 Weed wrote Preston King, a former Free Soiler and now one of New York's two Republican U.S. senators, that King and other Republicans grossly underestimated how real the threat of disunion was. "Let us [Republicans] set ourselves right in the judgment of the world," he urged. "The continued blindness of Democracy and the continued madness of slavery enabled us to elect Lincoln. That success ends our mission, so far as Kansas and the encroachment of slavery into free territories are concerned." With Lincoln appointing territorial governors, slavery could not expand into any existing territory. "The fight is over. Practically, the issues of the late campaign are obsolete." Because the "normal proclivities of the American people are Democratic, . . . we, the party in power, need to have our wits about us, and a stronger issue than that which has just given us success." Thus, Republicans must unite with antisecessionists in the South in a new coalition dedicated to saving the Union. That union was why Republicans must make concessions on the slavery extension issue. "My dear old friend, the sooner you put on your thinking cap and impress your colleagues with a sense of our dangers, the more you will rejoice for the rest of your life."[50]

King and the majority of congressional Republicans, like Lincoln himself, ignored this advice and the pleas from southern Unionists and moderate Republicans to throw the South a bone. In his inaugural address Lincoln would offer what he considered significant concessions, but they proved to be too little and far too late, for by the date of his inauguration on March 4,

1861, seven Deep South states had already formed the Confederate States of America and had no intention of scrapping it. The result would be far more shooting, very little hanging, and much, much more bloodshed than the blustering Zachariah Chandler had called for in his letter of November 15. It was that terrible war that made the presidential election of 1860 by far the most consequential such contest in all of American history.

APPENDIX A

ELECTION RETURNS

Table 1. Popular and Electoral Votes by State in 1856

	Frémont	Buchanan	Fillmore
North			
California (4)	20,695 (18.8%)	**53,368 (48.4%)**	36,210 (32.8%)
Connecticut (6)	**43,077 (53.4%)**	35,028 (43.4%)	2,615 (3.2%)
Illinois (11)	96,158 (40.2%)	**105,526 (44.1%)**	37,595 (15.7%)
Indiana (13)	94,378 (40.1%)	**118,673 (50.4%)**	22,405 (9.5%)
Iowa (4)	**43,954 (49.1%)**	36,170 (40.4%)	9,380 (10.5%)
Maine (8)	**67,129 (61.3%)**	39,080 (35.7%)	3,325 (3.0%)
Massachusetts (13)	**108,190 (64.8%)**	39,240 (23.5%)	19,626 (11.7%)
Michigan (5)	**71,766 (57.2%)**	52,138 (41.5%)	1,660 (1.3%)
New Hampshire (5)	**37,473 (53.7%)**	31,892 (45.7%)	410 (0.6%)
New Jersey (7)	28,339 (28.4%)	**47,446 (47.5%)**	24,114 (24.1%)
New York (35)	**276,007 (46.3%)**	195,878 (32.8%)	124,809 (20.9%)
Ohio (23)	**187,497 (48.5%)**	170,874 (44.2%)	28,121 (7.3%)
Pennsylvania (27)	147,510 (32%)	**230,700 (50.1%)**	82,176 (17.9%)
Rhode Island (4)	**11,467 (57.8%)**	6,680 (33.7%)	1,675 (8.5%)
Vermont (5)	**39,561 (78.1%)**	10,569 (20.9%)	545 (1.1%)
Wisconsin (5)	**66,090 (55.3%)**	52,843 (44.2%)	580 (0.5%)
Total North	1,339,341 (45.2%)	1,226,105 (41.4%)	395,246 (13.4%)
Electoral Votes	115	66	0
Border Slave States			
Delaware (3)	308 (0.2%)	**8,004 (55.2%)**	6,175 (44.6%)
Kentucky (12)	314 (0.02%)	**74,642 (52.4%)**	67,416 (47.6%)
Maryland (8)	281 (0.03%)	39,115 (45.0%)	**47,460 (55%)**
Missouri (9)	0	**58,164 (54.5%)**	48,669 (45.5%)
Remaining Slave States			
Alabama (9)	0	**46,739 (62.1%)**	28,552 (37.9%)
Arkansas (4)	0	**21,910 (67%)**	10,787 (33%)
Florida (3)	0	**6,358 (56.8%)**	4,833 (43.2%)
Georgia (10)	0	**56,581 (57.1%)**	42,439 (42.9%)

(continued on the next page)

Table 1. (*continued*)

	Frémont	Buchanan	Fillmore
Remaining Slave States			
Louisiana (6)	0	**22,164 (51.7%)**	20,709 (48.3%)
Mississippi (7)	0	**35,446 (59.4%)**	24,195 (40.6%)
North Carolina (10)	0	**48,246 (56.7%)**	36,886 (43.3%)
South Carolina (8)*			
Tennessee (12)	0	**73,636 (52.7%)**	66,728 (47.3%)
Texas (4)	0	**31,169 (66.6%)**	15,639 (33.4%)
Virginia (15)	291	**89,706 (59.9%)**	60,310 (40.1%)
Total South	1,196 (0.1%)	606,850 (56.0%)	476,485 (43.9%)
Electoral Votes	0	112	8

*No popular vote; Buchanan received the electoral votes.

Note: The number of electoral votes each state cast is included in parentheses after the name of the state. The candidate who won each state's electoral vote is indicated by boldface type.

Table 2. Comparison of Votes in Presidential Election of 1856 with Aggregate Popular Vote by State in 1858–1859 Congressional Elections in the North

	1856		1858–1859	
	Republicans	Democrats	Republicans	Democrats
California	20,695 (18.8%)	53,368 (48.4%)	43,484 (43%)	57,508 (57%)
Connecticut	43,077 (53.4%)	35,028 (43.4%)	39,731 (51.1%)	38,071 (48.9%)
Illinois	96,158 (40.2%)	105,526 (44.1%)	125,668 (49.9%)	126,291 (50.1%)
Indiana	94,378 (40.1%)	118,673 (50.4%)	111,748 (51.6%)	104,637 (48.4%)
Iowa	43,954 (49.1%)	36,170 (40.4%)	49,032 (51.8%)	45,693 (48.2%)
Maine	67,179 (61.3%)	39,080 (35.7%)	60,584 (53.7%)	52,115 (46.3%)
Massachusetts	108,190 (64.8%)	39,240 (23.5%)	70,154 (60.5%)	38,912 (33.6%)
Michigan	71,766 (57.2%)	52,138 (41.5%)	65,789 (54.2%)	55,613 (45.8%)
New Hampshire	37,473 (53.7%)	31,892 (45.7%)	35,844 (52.1%)	32,949 (47.9%)
New Jersey	28,339 (28.4%)	47,446 (47.5%)	41,218 (47.7%)	41,500 (48%)
New York	276,007 (46.3%)	195,878 (32.8%)	286,268 (53.5%)	228,716 (42.8%)
Ohio	187,487 (48.5%)	170,874 (44.2%)	184,062 (53.6%)	159,464 (46.4%)
Pennsylvania	147,510 (32%)	230,700 (50.1%)	197,595 (53.4%)	172,096 (46.6%)
Rhode Island	11,467 (57.8%)	6,680 (33.7%)	9,398 (74.2%)	3,257 (25.8%)
Vermont	39,561 (78.1%)	10,569 (20.9%)	28,589 (71%)	11,667 (29%)
Wisconsin	66,090 (55.3%)	52,843 (44.2%)	61,356 (52.6%)	55,243 (47.4%)
Minnesota			21,360 (55%)	17,666 (45%)
Oregon			5,630 (49.9%)	5,646 (50.1%)

Note: The aggregate popular votes in the 1858–1859 congressional elections were calculated from the returns listed in Michael J. Dubin, *United States Congressional Elections, 1788–1997: The Official Results* (Jefferson, N.C.: McFarland, 1998). In those districts where pro- and anti-Lecompton Democrats ran along with a Republican candidate, I counted both Democrats in the Democratic column. In those where only an anti-Lecompton Democrat opposed a pro-Lecompton Democrat and no Republican ran, I counted the anti-Lecompton Democratic vote in the Republican column. In all cases where the two parties' proportion of the vote failed to equal 100 percent, American Party candidates received the balance of the vote. Of the northern congressional elections recorded for 1858 and 1859, California, Connecticut, Minnesota, New Hampshire, Oregon, and Rhode Island voted in the latter year.

Table 3. Electoral and Popular Votes for President in 1860

	Lincoln	Douglas	Breckinridge	Fusion	Bell
North					
California (4)	38,667 (32.3%)	38,024 (31.7%)	34,048 (28.4%)		9,137 (7.6%)
Connecticut (6)	43,488 (54.0%)	17,464 (21.7%)	16,174 (20.1%)		3,331 (4.2%)
Illinois (11)	172,171 (50.7%)	160,205 (47.2%)	2,331 (0.7%)		4,947 (1.4%)
Indiana (13)	139,033 (51.1%)	115,549 (42.5%)	12,295 (4.5%)		5,225 (1.9%)
Iowa (4)	70,406 (54.9%)	55,050 (42.9%)	1,046 (0.8%)		1,763 (1.4%)
Maine (8)	62,811 (62.2%)	29,973 (29.7%)	6,368 (6.3%)		2,046 (3.8%)
Massachusetts (13)	106,533 (63.0%)	34,372 (20.3%)	5,939 (3.5%)		22,331 (13.2%)
Michigan (5)	88,450 (57.2%)	64,889 (42%)	805 (0.5%)		415 (0.3%)
Minnesota (3)	22,070 (63.4%)	11,937 (34.3%)	744 (2.1%)		53 (0.2%)
New Hampshire (5)	37,519 (56.9%)	25,887 (39.2%)	2,125 (3.2%)		412 (0.6%)
New Jersey (7)	58,234 (48.1%)			62,801 (51.9%)	
New York (35)	362,646 (53.6%)			314,282 (46.4%)	
Ohio (23)	231,709 (52.3%)	187,421 (42.3%)	11,406 (2.6%)		12,330 (2.8%)
Oregon (3)	5,270 (37.9%)	3,447 (24.8%)	5,006 (36%)		183 (1.3%)
Pennsylvania (27)	268,036 (56.2%)	16,765 (3.5%)	178,871 (37.5%)		12,770 (2.8%)
Rhode Island (4)	12,244 (61.4%)	7,707 (38.6%)			
Vermont (5)	33,808 (75.7%)	8,649 (19.4%)	218 (0.5%)		1,969 (4.4%)
Wisconsin (5)	86,110 (56.6%)	65,021 (42.7%)	889 (0.6%)		151 (0.1%)
Total North	**1,839,205 (53.9%)**	**842,360 (24.7%)**	**278,365 (8.1%)**	**377,083 (11.0%)**	**77,056 (2.3%)**

NORTH 3,413,969 Total Popular Votes

Slave States					
Alabama (9)	0	13,678 (14.9%)	48,669 (54.0%)		27,835 (31.1%)
Arkansas (4)	0	5,307 (9.9%)	28,732 (53.1%)		20,063 (37.0%)
Delaware (3)	3,822 (23.7%)	1,066 (6.6%)	7,339 (45.5%)		3,888 (24.2%)
Florida (3)	0	222 (1.7%)	8,157 (62.2%)		4,736 (36.1%)
Georgia (10)	0	11,627 (8.9%)	52,172 (48.8%)		43,069 (40.3%)
Kentucky (12)	1,365 (0.3%)	25,141 (17.2%)	53,146 (36.3%)		66,068 (45.2%)
Louisiana (6)	0	7,625 (15.1%)	22,681 (44.9%)		20,194 (40.0%)
Maryland (8)	2,294 (2.7%)	5,966 (6.5%)	42,282 (45.7%)		41,760 (45.1%)
Mississippi (7)	0	3,636 (5.2%)	40,464 (58.3%)		25,335 (36.5%)
Missouri (9)	17,020 (10.3%)	58,502 (35.4%)	31,427 (19.0%)		58,362 (35.3%)
North Carolina (10)	0	2,700 (3.2%)	48,530 (50.2%)		44,882 (46.4%)
South Carolina (8)*					
Tennessee (12)	0	11,410 (7.9%)	64,406 (44.5%)		68,768 (47.6%)
Texas (4)	0	18 (0.1%)	47,561 (75.5%)		15,402 (24.4%)
Virginia (15)	1,887 (1.2%)	16,198 (9.7%)	74,325 (44.5%)		74,491 (44.6%)
Total Slave States	**26,388 (2.1%)**	**163,096 (12.8%)**	**569,891 (44.7%)**		**514,853 (40.4%)**

SLAVE STATES 1,274,228 Total Popular Vote

UNITED STATES	**4,688,197 Total Popular Votes**				
Candidates	1,865,593 (39.8%)	1,005,456 (21.4%)	848,156 (18.1%)	377,083 (8.0%)	591,909 (12.6%)
Electoral Votes	180	12	72	39	

*No popular vote; legislature chose Breckinridge electors.

Note: Returns are taken from Walter Dean Burnham, *Presidential Ballots, 1836–1892* (Baltimore: Johns Hopkins University Press, 1955). The Breckinridge total for Pennsylvania is for the joint Douglas-Breckinridge electoral slate arranged by the Democratic state executive committee. The number of each state's electoral votes is included in parentheses after the name of the state.

Table 4. State-by-State Comparisons of Party Votes and Turnout Rates in 1856 and 1860 Elections

1856			1860		
			North		
California	Republican	20,695 (18.8%)	California	Republican	38,667 (32.3%)
(81.8%)	Democrat	58,368 (48.4%)	**(71.2%)**	Democrats	
				Douglas	38,024 (31.7%)
				Breckinridge	34,048 (28.4%)
	American	36,210 (32.8%)		Const. Union	9,137 (7.6%)
Connecticut	Republican	43,077 (53.4%)	Connecticut	Republican	43,488 (54.0%)
(81.3%)	Democrat	35,028 (43.4%)	**(73.3%)**	Democrats	
				Douglas	17,464 (21.7%)
				Breckinridge	16,174 (20.1%)
	American	2,615 (3.2%)		Const. Union	3,331 (4.2%)
Illinois	Republican	96,158 (40.2%)	Illinois	Republican	172,171 (50.7%)
(72.4%)	Democrat	105,526 (44.1%)	**(80.3%)**	Democrats	
				Douglas	160,205 (47.2%)
				Breckinridge	2,331 (0.7%)
	American	37,595 (15.7%)		Const. Union	4,947 (1.4%)
Indiana	Republican	94,378 (40.1%)	Indiana	Republican	139,033 (51.1%)
(88.3%)	Democrat	118,673 (50.4%)	**(89.4%)**	Democrats	
				Douglas	115,549 (42.5%)
				Breckinridge	12,295 (4.5%)
	American	22,405 (9.5%)		Const. Union	5,225 (1.9%)
Iowa	Republican	43,954 (49.1%)	Iowa	Republican	70,406 (54.9%)
(87.0%)	Democrat	36,170 (40.4%)	**(94.2%)**	Democrats	
				Douglas	55,050 (42.9%)
				Breckinridge	1,046 (0.8%)
	American	9,380 (10.5%)		Const. Union	1,763 (1.4%)
Maine	Republican	67,179 (61.3%)	Maine	Republican	62,811 (62.2%)
(78.1%)	Democrat	39,080 (35.7%)	**(68.9%)**	Democrats	
				Douglas	29,973 (29.7%)
				Breckinridge	6,368 (6.3%)
	American	3,325 (3%)		Const. Union	2,046 (3.8%)
Massachusetts	Republican	108,190 (64.8%)	Massachusetts	Republican	106,533 (63.0%)
(69.8%)	Democrat	39,240 (23.5%)	**(65.8%)**	Democrats	
				Douglas	34,372 (20.3%)
				Breckinridge	5,939 (3.5%)
	American	19,626 (11.7%)		Const. Union	22,331 (13.2%)
Michigan	Republican	71,766 (57.1%)	Michigan	Republican	88,450 (57.2%)
(81.1%)	Democrat	52,138 (41.4%)	**(80.0%)**	Democrats	
				Douglas	64,889 (42.0%)
				Breckinridge	805 (0.5%)
	American	1,660 (1.4%)		Const. Union	415 (0.3%)

1856			1860		
New Hampshire	Republican	37,473 (53.7%)	New Hampshire	Republican	37,519 (56.9%)
(87.9%)	Democrat	31,892 (45.7%)	**(80.7%)**	Democrats	
				Douglas	25,887 (39.2%)
				Breckinridge	2,125 (3.2%)
	American	410 (0.6%)		Const. Union	412 (0.7%)
New Jersey	Republican	28,339 (28.4%)	New Jersey	Republican	58,234 (48.1%)
(83.1%)	Democrat	47,446 (47.5%)	**(89.4%)**	Fusion	62,801 (51.9%)
	American	24,114 (24.1%)			
New York	Republican	276,007 (46.2%)	New York	Republican	362,646 (53.6%)
(89.9%)	Democrat	195,878 (32.8%)	**(95.5%)**	Fusion	314,282 (46.4%)
	American	124,809 (21%)			
Ohio	Republican	187,497 (48.5%)	Ohio	Republican	231,709 (52.3%)
(82.3%)	Democrat	170,874 (44.2%)	**(88.3%)**	Democrats	
				Douglas	187,421 (42.3%)
				Breckinridge	11,406 (2.6%)
	American	28,121 (7.3%)		Const. Union	12,330 (2.8%)
Pennsylvania	Republican	147,530 (32%)	Pennsylvania	Republican	268,036 (56.2%)
(80.85%)	Democrat	230,700 (50.1%)	**(78.4%)**	Democrats	
				Douglas	16,765 (3.5%)
				Breckinridge	178,871 (37.5%)
	American	82,176 (17.9%)		Const. Union	12,770 (2.8%)
Rhode Island	Republican	11,467 (57.8%)	Rhode Island	Republican	12,244 (61.4%)
(62.9%)	Democrat	6,680 (33.7%)	**(59.4%)**	Democrat	7,707 (38.6%)
	American	1,675 (8.5%)			
Vermont	Republican	39,561 (78%)	Vermont	Republican	33,808 (75.7%)
(72.5%)	Democrat	10,569 (20.8%)	**(63%)**	Democrats	
				Douglas	8,649 (19.4%)
				Breckinridge	218 (0.5%)
	American	545 (1.2%)		Const. Union	1,969 (4.4%)
Wisconsin	Republican	66,090 (55.3%)	Wisconsin	Republican	86,110 (56.6%)
(80.8%)	Democrat	52,843 (44.2%)	**(79%)**	Democrats	
				Douglas	65,021 (42.7%)
				Breckinridge	889 (0.6%)
	American	580 (0.5%)		Const. Union	151 (0.1%)
		Slave States			
Alabama	Democrat	45,739 (62.1%)	Alabama	Democrats	
(71%)			**(78.7%)**	Douglas	13,678 (14.9%)
				Breckinridge	48,669 (54.0%)
	American	28,552 (37.9%)		Const. Union	27,835 (31.1%)
Arkansas	Democrat	21,910 (67.1%)	Arkansas	Democrats	
(60.2%)			**(79.5%)**	Douglas	5,457 (9.9%)
				Breckinridge	28,732 (53.1%)
	American	10,732 (32.9%)		Const. Union	20,063 (37.0%)

(continued on the next page)

Table 4. (*continued*)

1856			1860		
			Slave States		
Delaware	Republican	310 (2.1%)	Delaware	Republican	3,822 (23.7%)
(78.5%)	Democrat	8,004 (54.8%)	**(79.5%)**	Democrats	
				Douglas	1,066 (6.6%)
				Breckinridge	7,339 (45.5%)
	American	6,284 (43.1%)		Const. Union	3,888 (24.2%)
Florida	Democrat	6,402 (56.6%)	Florida	Democrats	
(77.6%)			**(79.5%)**	Douglas	222 (1.7%)
				Breckinridge	52,172 (48.8%)
	American	4,900 (43.4%)		Const. Union	4,736 (36.1%)
Georgia	Democrat	56,618 (57.1%)	Georgia	Democrats	
(82.8%)			**(85.1%)**	Douglas	11,627 (8.9%)
				Breckinridge	52,172 (48.8%)
	American	42,478 (42.9%)		Const. Union	43,069 (40.3%)
Kentucky	Republican		Kentucky	Republican	1,365 (0.3%)
(76.7%)	Democrat	69,509 (52.3%)	**(74.1%)**	Democrats	
				Douglas	25,641 (17.2%)
				Breckinridge	53,146 (36.3%)
	American	63,401 (47.7%)		Const. Union	66,068 (45.2%)
Louisiana	Democrat	22,164 (51.7%)	Louisiana	Democrats	
(53.6%)			**(58.6%)**	Douglas	7,625 (15.1%)
				Breckinridge	22,681 (44.9%)
	American	20,709 (48.3%)		Const. Union	20,194 (40%)
Maryland	Republican	281 (0.1%)	Maryland	Republican	2,294 (2.7%)
(80%)	Democrat	39,115 (45%)	**(81.1%)**	Democrats	
				Douglas	5,966 (6.5%)
				Breckinridge	42,282 (45.7%)
	American	47,762 (54.9%)		Const. Union	41,760 (45.1%)
Mississippi	Democrat	34,457 (58.7%)	Mississippi	Democrats	
(78.3%)			**(89.5%)**	Douglas	3,636 (5.2%)
				Breckinridge	40,464 (58.3%)
	American	24,191 (41.3%)		Const. Union	25,335 (36.5%)
Missouri	Republican		Missouri	Republican	17,020 (10.3%)
(54.7%)	Democrat	57,964 (54.4%)	**(69.1%)**	Democrats	
				Douglas	58,502 (35.4%)
				Breckinridge	31,427 (19.0%)
	American	48,528 (45.6%)		Const. Union	58,362 (35.3%)
North Carolina	Democrat	48,246 (56.7%)	North Carolina	Democrats	
(66.7%)			**(70.9%)**	Douglas	2,700 (3.2%)
				Breckinridge	48,530 (50.2%)
	American	36,886 (43.3%)		Const. Union	44,882 (46.4%)

	1856			1860		
Tennessee	Democrat	73,638 (52.7%)	Tennessee	Democrats		
(82.9%)			**(80.9%)**		Douglas	11,410 (7.9%)
					Breckinridge	64,406 (44.5%)
	American	66,128 (47.3%)		Const. Union		68,768 (47.6%)
Texas	Democrat	31,955 (66.6%)	Texas	Democrats		
(58.1%)			**(67.4%)**		Douglas	18 (0.1%)
					Breckinridge	47,561 (75.5%)
	American	16,010 (33.4%)		Const. Union		15,402 (24.4%)
Virginia	Republican		Virginia	Republican		1,887 (1.2%)
(67.8%)	Democrat	90,083 (60%)	**(71.5%)**	Democrats		
					Douglas	16,198 (9.7%)
					Breckinridge	74,325 (44.5%)
	American	60,150 (40%)		Const. Union		74,491 (44.6%)

Note: Numbers in bold represent the turnout rate for each state.

APPENDIX B

THE PARTIES' 1860 NATIONAL PLATFORMS

NATIONAL DEMOCRATIC (DOUGLAS) PLATFORM

1. *Resolved,* That we, the Democracy of the Union, in Convention assembled, hereby declare our affirmance of the resolutions unanimously adopted and declared as a platform of principles by the Democratic Convention in Cincinnati, in the year 1856, believing that Democratic principles are unchangeable in their nature, when applied to the same subject matters; and we recommend, as the only further resolutions, the following:

Inasmuch as differences of opinion exist in the Democratic party as to the nature and extent of the powers of a Territorial Legislature, and as to the powers and duties of Congress, under the Constitution of the United States, over the institution of Slavery within the Territories:

2. *Resolved,* That the Democratic party will abide by the decisions of the Supreme Court of the United States on the questions of Constitutional law.

3. *Resolved,* That it is the duty of the United States to afford ample and complete protection to all its citizens, whether at home or abroad, and whether native or foreign.

4. *Resolved,* That one of the necessities of the age, in a military, commercial, and postal point of view, is speedy communication between the Atlantic and Pacific States; and the Democratic party pledge such Constitutional Government aid as will insure the construction of a Railroad to the Pacific coast, at the earliest practicable period.

5. *Resolved,* That the Democratic party are in favor of the acquisition of the island of Cuba, on such terms as shall be honorable to ourselves and just to Spain.

6. *Resolved,* That the enactments of State Legislatures to defeat the faithful execution of the Fugitive Slave Law, are hostile in character, subversive of the Constitution, and revolutionary in their effect.

7. *Resolved,* That it is in accordance with the true interpretation of the Cincinnati Platform, that, during the existence of the territorial Govern-

ments, the measure of restriction, whatever it may be, imposed by the Federal Constitution on the power of the Territorial Legislature over the subject of domestic relations, as the same has been, or shall hereafter be, finally determined by the Supreme Court of the United States, shall be respected by all good citizens, and enforced with promptness and fidelity by every branch of the General Government.

NATIONAL DEMOCRATIC (BRECKINRIDGE) PLATFORM

Resolved, That the Platform adopted by the Democratic party at Cincinnati be affirmed, with the following explanatory Resolutions:

1. That the Government of a Territory organized by an act of Congress, is provisional and temporary; and during its existence, all citizens of the United States have an equal right to settle with their property in the Territory, without their rights, either of person or property, being destroyed or impaired by Congressional or Territorial legislation.

2. That it is the duty of the Federal Government, in all its departments, to protect, when necessary, the rights of persons and property in the Territories, and wherever else its Constitutional authority extends.

3. That when the settlers in a Territory having an adequate population, form a State Constitution, in pursuance of law, the right of sovereignty commences, and, being consummated by admission into the Union, they stand on an equal footing with the people of other States; and the State thus organized ought to be admitted into the Federal Union, whether its Constitution prohibits or recognizes the institution of Slavery.

4. That the Democratic party are in favor of the acquisition of the island of Cuba, on such terms as shall be honorable to ourselves and just to Spain, at the earliest practicable period.

5. That the enactments of State Legislatures to defeat the faithful execution of the Fugitive Slave Law are hostile in character, subversive of the Constitution, and revolutionary in their effect.

6. That the democracy of the United States recognize it as the imperative duty of this Government to protect the naturalized citizen in all his rights, whether at home or in foreign lands, to the same extent as its native-born citizens.

Whereas, one of the greatest necessities of the age in a Political, Commercial, Postal, and Military point of view, is a speedy communication between the Pacific and Atlantic coasts; therefore be it *Resolved*, That the Democratic party do hereby pledge themselves to use every means in Their power to secure the passage of some bill to the extent of the Constitutional authority of Congress for the Construction of a Pacific Railroad from the Mississippi River to the Pacific Ocean, at the earliest practicable moment.

CONSTITUTIONAL UNION (BELL-EVERETT) PLATFORM

Whereas, Experience has demonstrated that Platforms adopted by the partisan conventions of the country have had the effect to mislead and deceive the people, and at the same time to widen the political divisions of the country, by the creation and encouragement of geographical and sectional parties; therefore,

Resolved, That it is both the part of patriotism and of duty *to recognize no* political principle other than THE CONSTITUTION OF THE COUNTRY, THE UNION OF THE STATES, AND THE ENFORCEMENT OF THE LAWS, and that as representatives of the Constitutional Union men of the country in National Convention assembled, we hereby pledge ourselves to maintain, protect, and defend, separately and unitedly, these great principles of public liberty and national safety, against all enemies at home and abroad, believing that thereby peace may once more be restored to the country, the rights of the People and of the States reestablished, and the Government again placed in that condition, of justice, fraternity and equality, which under the example and Constitution of our fathers, has solemnly bound every citizen of the United States to maintain a more perfect union, establish justice, insure domestic tranquility, provide for the common defence [*sic*], promote the general welfare, and secure the blessings of liberty to ourselves and our posterity.

REPUBLICAN PARTY NATIONAL PLATFORM

Resolved, That we, the delegated representatives of the Republican electors of the United States, in Convention assembled, in discharge of the duty we owe to our constituents and our country, unite in the following declarations:

1. That the history of the nation, during the last four years, has fully established the propriety and necessity of the organization and perpetuation of the Republican party, and that the causes which called it into existence are permanent in their nature, and now, more than ever before, demand its peaceful and constitutional triumph.

2. That the maintenance of the principles promulgated in the Declaration of Independence and embodied in the Federal Constitution, "That all men are created equal; that they are endowed by their Creator with certain inalienable rights; that among these are life, liberty, and the pursuit of hap-

piness; that to secure these rights, governments are instituted among men, deriving their just powers from the consent of the governed," is essential to the preservation of our Republican institutions; and that the Federal Constitution, the Rights of the States, and the Union of the States, must and shall be preserved.

3. That to the Union of the States this nation owes its unprecedented increase in population, its surprising development of material resources, its rapid augmentation of wealth, its happiness at home and its honor abroad; and we hold in abhorrence all schemes for Disunion, come from whatever source they may; And we congratulate the country that no Republican member of Congress has uttered or countenanced the threats of Disunion so often made by Democratic members without rebuke and with applause from their political associates; and we denounce those threats of Disunion, in case of a popular overthrow of their ascendancy, as denying the vital principles of free government, and as an avowal of contemplated treason, which it is the imperative duty of an indignant People sternly to rebuke and forever silence.

4. That the maintenance inviolate of the rights of the States, and especially the right of each State to order and control its own domestic institutions according to its own judgment exclusively, is essential to the balance of powers on which the perfection and endurance of our political fabric depends; and we denounce the lawless invasion by armed force of the soil of any State or Territory, no matter under what pretext, as among the gravest of crimes.

5. That the present Democratic Administration has far exceeded our worst apprehensions, in its measureless subserviency to the exactions of a sectional interest, as especially evinced in its desperate exertions to force the infamous Lecompton Constitution upon the protesting people of Kansas; in construing the personal relation between master and servant to involve an unqualified property in persons; in its attempted enforcement, everywhere, on land and sea, through the intervention of Congress and of the Federal Courts of the extreme pretensions of a purely local interest; and in its general and unvarying abuse of the power intrusted [*sic*] to it by a confiding people.

6. That the people justly view with alarm the reckless extravagance which pervades every department of the Federal Government; that a return to rigid economy and accountability is indispensible [*sic*] to arrest the systematic plunder of the public treasury by favored partisans, while the recent startling developments of frauds and corruptions at the Federal metropolis, show that an entire change of administration is imperatively demanded.

7. That the new dogma, that the Constitution, of its own force, carries Slavery into any or all of the Territories of the United States, is a dangerous political heresy, at variance with the explicit provisions of the instrument itself, with contemporaneous exposition, and with legislative and judicial precedent; is revolutionary in its tendency, and subversive of the peace and harmony of the country.

8. That the normal condition of all the territory of the United States is that of freedom; That as our Republican fathers, when they had abolished Slavery in all our national territory, ordained that "no person should be deprived of life, liberty, or property, without due process of law," it becomes our duty, by legislation, whenever such legislation is necessary, to maintain this provision of the Constitution against all attempts to violate it; and we deny the authority of Congress, of a territorial legislature, or of any individuals, to give legal existence to Slavery in any Territory of the United States.

9. That we brand the recent re-opening of the African slave-trade, under the cover of our national flag, aided by perversions of judicial power, as a crime against humanity and a burning shame to our country and age, and we call upon Congress to take prompt and efficient measures for the total and final suppression of the execrable traffic.

10. That in the recent vetoes, by their Federal Governors, of the acts of the Legislatures of Kansas and Nebraska, prohibiting Slavery in those Territories, we find a practical illustration of the boasted Democratic principle of Non-Intervention and Popular Sovereignty, embodied in the Kansas-Nebraska bill, and a demonstration of the deception and fraud involved therein.

11. That Kansas should, of right, be immediately admitted as a State under the Constitution recently formed and adopted by her people, and accepted by the House of Representatives.

12. That, while providing revenue for the support of the General Government by duties upon imports, sound policy requires such an adjustment of these imposts as to encourage the development of the industrial interest of the whole country; and we commend that policy of national exchanges which secures to the working men liberal wages, to agriculture remunerative prices, to mechanics and manufactures an adequate reward for their skill, labor, and enterprise, and to the nation commercial prosperity and independence.

13. That we protest against any sale or alienation to others of the Public Lands held by actual settlers, and against any view of the Homestead policy which regards the settlers as paupers or suppliants for public bounty; and

we demand passage by Congress of the complete and satisfactory Homestead measure which has already passed the House.

14. That the Republican party is opposed to any change in our Naturalization Laws or any State legislation by which the rights of citizenship hitherto accorded to immigrants from foreign lands shall be abridged or impaired; and in favor of giving full and efficient protection to the rights of all classes of citizens, whether native or naturalized, both at home and abroad.

15. That appropriations by Congress for River and Harbor improvements of a national character, required by the accommodation and security of an existing commerce, are authorized by the Constitution, and justified by the obligations of Government to protect the lives and property of its citizens.

16. That a Railroad to the Pacific Ocean is imperatively demanded by the interest of the whole country; that the Federal Government ought to render immediate and efficient aid in its construction; and that, as preliminary thereto, a daily Overland Mail should be promptly established.

17. Finally, having thus set forth our distinctive principles and views, we invite the cooperation of all citizens, however differing on other questions, who substantially agree with us in their affirmation and support.

APPENDIX C

ABRAHAM LINCOLN'S INAUGURAL ADDRESS, MARCH 4, 1861

Fellow citizens of the United States:

In compliance with a custom as old as the government itself, I appear before you to address you briefly, and to take, in your presence, the oath prescribed by the Constitution of the United States, to be taken by the President "before he enters on the execution of his office."

I do not consider it necessary, at present, for me to discuss those matters of administration about which there is no special anxiety, or excitement.

Apprehension seems to exist among the people of the Southern States that by the accession of a Republican Administration, their property, and their peace, and personal security, are to be endangered. There has never been any reasonable cause for such apprehension. Indeed, the most ample evidence to the contrary has all the while existed, and been open to their inspection. It is found in all the published speeches of him who now addresses you. I do but quote from one of those speeches when I declare that "I have no purpose, directly or indirectly, to interfere with the institution of slavery in the States where it exists. I believe I have no lawful right to do so, and I have no inclination to do so." Those who nominated and elected me did so with full knowledge that I had made this, and many similar declarations, and had never recanted them. And more than this, they placed in the platform, for my acceptance, and as a law to themselves, and to me, the clear and emphatic resolution which I now read:

> *Resolved*, That the maintenance inviolate of the rights of the States, and especially the right of each State to order and control its own domestic institutions according to its own judgment exclusively, is essential to the balance of power on which the perfection and endurance of our political fabric depend; and we denounce the lawless invasion by armed force of

> the soil of any State or Territory, no matter under what pretext, as among the gravest of crimes.

I now reiterate these sentiments, and in doing so, I only press upon the public attention the most conclusive evidence of which the case is susceptible, that the property, peace and security of no section are to be anywise endangered by the now incoming Administration. I add too, that all the protection which, consistently with the Constitution and the laws, can be given, will be cheerfully given to all the States when lawfully demanded, for whatever cause—as cheerfully to one section, as to another.

There is much controversy about the delivering up of fugitives from service or labor. The clause I now read is as plainly written in the Constitution as any other of its provisions:

> No person held to service or labor in one State, under the laws thereof, escaping into another, shall, in consequence of any law or regulation therein, be discharged from such service or labor, but shall be delivered up on claim of the party to whom such service or labor may be due.

It is scarcely questioned that this provision was intended by those who made it, for the reclaiming of what are called fugitive slaves; and the intention of the law-giver is the law. All members of Congress swear their support to the whole Constitution—to this provision as much as to any other. To the proposition, then, that slaves whose cases come within the terms of this clause "shall be delivered up," their oaths are unanimous. Now, if they would make the effort in good temper, could they not, with equal unanimity, frame and pass a law, by means of which to keep good that unanimous oath?

There is some difference of opinion whether this clause should be enforced by national or by state authority; but surely that difference is not a very material one. If the slave is to be surrendered, it can be of little consequence to him, or to others, by which authority it is done. And should any one, in any case, be content that his oath shall go unkept, on a merely unsubstantial controversy as to *how* it shall be kept.

Again, in any law upon this subject, ought not all the safeguards of liberty known in civilized and humane jurisprudence to be introduced, so that a free man be not, in any case, surrendered as a slave? And might it not be well, at the same time, to provide by law for the enforcement of that clause in the Constitution which guaranties that "The citizens of each State shall be entitled to all privileges and immunities of citizens in the several States?"

I take the official oath to-day, with no mental reservations, and with no purpose to construe the Constitution or laws, by any hypercritical rules. And while I do not choose now to specify particular acts of Congress as proper to be enforced, I do suggest, that it will be much safer for all, both in official and private stations, to conform to, and abide by, all those acts which stand unrepealed, than to violate any of them, trusting to find impunity in having them held to be unconstitutional.

It is seventy-two years since the first inauguration of a President under our national Constitution. During that period fifteen different and greatly distinguished citizens, have, in succession, administered the executive branch of the government. They have conducted it through many perils; and, generally, with great success. Yet with all this scope for precedent, I now enter upon the same task for the brief constitutional term of four years, under great and peculiar difficulty. A disruption of the Federal Union heretofore only menaced, is now formidably attempted.

I hold that in contemplation of universal law, and of the Constitution, the Union of these States is perpetual. Perpetuity is implied, if not expressed, in the fundamental law of all national governments. It is safe to assert that no government proper ever had a provision in its organic law for its own termination. Continue to execute all the express provisions of our national Constitution, and the Union will endure forever—it being impossible to destroy it, except by some action not provided for in the instrument itself.

Again, if the United States be not a government proper, but an association of States in the nature of contract merely, can it, as a contract, be peaceably be unmade, by less than all the parties who made it? One party to a contract may violate it—break it so to speak; but does it not require all to lawfully rescind it?

Descending from these general principles, we find the proposition that, in legal contemplation, the Union is perpetual, confirmed by the history of the Union itself. The Union is much older than the Constitution. It was formed in fact, by the Articles of association in 1774. It was matured and continued by the Declaration of Independence in 1776. It was further matured and the faith of the then thirteen States expressly plighted and engaged that it should be perpetual by the Articles of Confederation in 1778. And finally, in 1787, one of the declared objects for ordaining and establishing the Constitution, was "*to form a more perfect union.*"

But if destruction of the Union, by one, or by a part only, of the States, be lawfully possible, the Union is *less* perfect than before the Constitution, having lost the vital element of perpetuity.

It follows from these views that no State, upon its own mere motion, can lawfully get out of the Union,—that *resolves* and *ordinances* to that effect are legally void; and that acts of violence, within any State or States against the authority of the United States are insurrectionary or revolutionary, according to circumstances.

I therefore consider that, in view of the Constitution and the laws, the Union is unbroken; and to the extent of my ability, I shall take care, as the Constitution itself expressly enjoins upon me, that the laws of the Union be faithfully executed in all the States. Doing this I deem to be only a simple duty on my part; and I shall perform it, so far as practicable, unless my rightful masters, the American people, shall withhold the requisite means, or, in some authoritative manner, direct the contrary. I trust this will not be regarded as a menace, but only as the declared purpose of the Union, that it *will* constitutionally defend, and maintain itself.

In doing this there needs to be no bloodshed or violence; and there shall be none unless it is forced upon the national authority. The power confided to me, will be used to hold, occupy, and possess the property and places belonging to the government, and to collect the duties and imposts; but beyond what may be necessary for these objects, there will be no invasion—no using of force against, or among the people anywhere. Where hostility to the United States, in any interior locality, shall be so great and so universal, as to prevent competent resident citizens from holding the Federal offices, there will be no attempt to force obnoxious strangers among the people for that object. While the strict legal right may exist in the government to enforce the exercise of these offices, the attempt to do so would be so irritating, and so nearly impracticable with all, that I deem it better to forego, for the time, the uses of such offices.

The mails, unless repelled, will continue to be furnished to all parts of the Union. So far as possible, the people everywhere shall have the sense of perfect security which is most favorable to calm thought and reflection. The course here indicated will be followed, unless current events, and experiences, shall show a modification, or change, to be proper; and in every case and exigency, my best discretion will be exercised, according to circumstances actually existing, and with a view and a hope of a peaceful solution of the national troubles, and the restoration of fraternal sympathies and affections.

That there are persons in one section, or another who seek to destroy the Union at all events, and are glad of any pretext to do it, I will neither affirm or deny; but if there be such, I need address no word to them. To those, however, who really love the Union, may I not speak?

Before entering upon so grave a matter as the destruction of our national fabric, with all its benefits, its memories, and its hopes, would it not be wise to ascertain precisely why we do it? Will you hazard so desperate a step, while there is any possibility that any portion of the ills you fly from, have no real existence? Will you, while the certain ills you fly to, are greater than all the real ones you fly from? Will you risk the commission of so fearful a mistake?

All profess to be content in the Union, if all constitutional rights can be maintained. Is it true, then, that any right, plainly written in the Constitution, has been denied? I think not. Happily the human mind is so constituted, that no party can reach to the audacity of doing this. Think, if you can, of a single instance in which a plainly written provision of the Constitution has ever been denied. If, by the mere force of numbers, a majority should deprive a minority of any clearly written constitutional right, it might, in a moral point of view, justify a revolution—certainly would, if such right were a vital one. But such is not our case. All the vital rights of minorities, and of individuals, are so plainly assured to them, by affirmations and negations, guaranties and prohibitions, in the Constitution, that controversies never arise concerning them. But no organic law can ever be framed with a provision specifically applicable to every question which may occur in practical administration. No foresight can anticipate, nor any document of reasonable length contain express provisions for all possible questions. Shall fugitives from labor be surrendered by national or by State authority? The Constitution does not expressly say. *May* Congress prohibit slavery in the territories? The Constitution does not expressly say. *Must* Congress protect slavery in the territories? The Constitution does not expressly say.

From questions of this class spring all our constitutional controversies, and we divide upon them into majorities and minorities. If the minority will not acquiesce, the majority must, or the government must cease. There is no other alternative; for continuing the government, is acquiescence on one side or the other. If a minority, in such case, will secede rather than acquiesce, they make a precedent which, in turn, will divide and ruin them; for a minority of their own will secede from them, whenever a majority refuses to be controlled by such minority. For instance, why may not any portion of a new confederacy, a year or two hence, arbitrarily secede again, precisely as portions of the present Union now claim to secede from it. All who cherish disunion sentiments, are now being educated in the exact temper of doing this. Is there such identity of interests among the States to compose a new Union, as to produce harmony only, and prevent renewed secession.

Plainly, the central idea of secession, is the essence of anarchy. A majority, held in restraint by constitutional checks, and limitations, and always changing easily, with deliberate changes of popular opinions and sentiments, is the only true sovereign of a free people. Whoever rejects it, does, of necessity, fly to anarchy or to despotism. Unanimity is impossible; the rule of a minority as a permanent arrangement, is wholly inadmissible; so that, rejecting the majority principle, anarchy, or despotism in some form, is all that is left.

I do not forget the position assumed by some, that constitutional questions are to be decided by the Supreme Court; nor do I deny that such decisions must be binding in any case, upon the parties to a suit, as to the object of that suit, while they are also entitled to very high respect and consideration, in all parallel cases, by all other departments of the government. And while it is obviously possible that such decision may be erroneous in any given case, still the evil effect following it, being limited to that particular case, with the chance that it may be overruled, and never become a precedent for other cases, can better be borne than could the evils of a different practice. At the same time the candid citizen must confess that if the policy of the government, upon vital questions, affecting the whole people, is to be irrevocably fixed by decisions of the Supreme Court, the instant they are made, in ordinary litigation between parties, in personal actions, the people will have ceased, to be their own rulers, having, to that extent, practically resigned their government into the hands of that eminent tribunal. Nor is there, in this view, any assault upon the court, or the judges. It is a duty, from which they may not shrink, to decide cases properly brought before them; and it is no fault of theirs, if others seek to turn their decisions to political purposes.

One section of our country believes slavery is *right*, and ought to be extended, while the other believes it is *wrong*, and ought not to be extended. This is the only substantial dispute. The fugitive slave clause of the Constitution, and the law for the suppression of the foreign slave trade, are each as well enforced, perhaps, as any law can ever be in a community where the moral sense of the people imperfectly supports the law itself. The great body of the people abide by the dry legal obligation in both cases, and a few break over in each. This, I think, cannot be perfectly cured; and it would be worse in both cases *after* the separation of the sections, than before. The foreign slave trade, now imperfectly suppressed, would be ultimately revived without restriction, in one section; while fugitive slaves, now only partially surrendered, would not be surrendered at all, by the other.

Physically speaking, we cannot separate. We cannot remove our respective sections from each other, nor build an impassable wall between them. A husband and wife may be divorced, and go out of the presence, and beyond the reach of each other; but the different parts of our country cannot do this. They cannot but remain face to face; and intercourse, either amicable or hostile, must continue between them. Is it possible then to make that intercourse more advantageous, or more satisfactory, *after* separation than *before*? Can aliens make treaties easier than friends make laws? Can treaties be more faithfully enforced between aliens, than laws can among friends? Suppose you go to war, you cannot fight always; and when, after much loss on both sides, and no gain on either, you cease fighting, the identical old questions, as to terms of intercourse, are again upon you.

This country, with its institutions, belongs to the people who inhabit it. Whenever they shall grow weary of the existing government, they can exercise the *constitutional* right of amending it, or their *revolutionary* right to dismember, or overthrow it. I can not be ignorant of the fact that many worthy and patriotic citizens are desirous of having the national constitution amended. While I make no recommendation of amendments, I fully recognize the rightful authority of the people over the whole subject, to be exercised in either the modes prescribed in the instrument itself; and I should, under existing circumstances, favor, rather than oppose, a fair opportunity being afforded the people to act upon it.

I will venture to add that, to me, the convention mode seems preferable, in that it allows amendments to originate with the people themselves, instead of only permitting them to take, or reject, propositions, originated by others, not especially chosen for the purpose, and which might not be precisely such, as they would wish to either accept or refuse. I understand a proposed amendment to the Constitution—which amendment, however, I have not seen, has passed Congress, to the effect that the federal government shall never interfere with the domestic institutions of the States, including that of persons held to service. To avoid misconstruction of what I have said, I depart from my purpose not to speak of particular amendments, so far as to say that, holding such a provision to now be implied constitutional law, I have no objection to its being made express, and irrevocable.

The Chief Magistrate derives all his authority from the people, and they have conferred none upon him to fix terms for the separation of the States. The people themselves can do this also if they choose; but the executive, as such, has nothing to do with it. His duty is to administer the present government, as it came to his hands, and to transmit it, unimpaired by him, to his successor.

Why should there not be a patient confidence in the ultimate justice of the people? Is there any better, or equal hope, in the world? In our present differences, is either party without faith of being in the right? If the Almighty Ruler of nations, with his eternal truth and justice, be on your side of the North, or on your of the South, that truth, and that justice, will surely prevail, by the judgment of this great tribunal, the American people.

By the frame of government under which we live, this same people have wisely given their public servants but little power for mischief; and have, with equal wisdom, provided for the return of that little to their own hands at very short intervals.

While the people retain their virtue, and vigilance, no administration, by any extreme of wickedness or folly, can very seriously injure the government, in the short space of four years.

My countrymen, one and all, think calmly and *well*, upon this whole subject. Nothing valuable can be lost by taking time. If there be an object to *hurry* any of you, in hot haste, to a step which you would never take *deliberately*, that object will be frustrated by taking time, but no good object can be frustrated by it. Such of you are as now dissatisfied, still have the old Constitution unimpaired, and, on the sensitive point, the laws of your own framing under it; while the new administration will have no immediate power, if it would, to change either. If it were admitted that you who are dissatisfied, hold the right side in the dispute, there still is no single good reason for precipitate action. Intelligence, patriotism, Christianity, and a firm reliance on Him, who has never yet forsaken this favored land, are still competent to adjust, in the best way, all our present difficulty.

In *your* hands, my dissatisfied fellow countrymen, and not in *mine*, is the momentous issue of civil war. The government will not assail *you*. You can have no conflict, without being yourselves the aggressors. *You* have no oath registered in Heaven to destroy the government, while *I* shall have the most solemn one to "preserve, protect and defend" it.

I am loth to close. We are not enemies, but friends. We must not be enemies. Though passion may have strained, it must not break our bonds of affection. The mystic chords of memory, stretching from every battle-field, and patriot grave, to every living heart and hearthstone, all over this broad land, will yet swell the chorus of the Union, when again touched, as surely they will be, by the better angels of our nature.

NOTES

PREFACE

1 *New York Times,* April 15, 1860.

CHAPTER 1. REPUBLICAN STORM RISING?

1 William H. Nimmick to *The Washington States and Union,* April 5, 1860, reprinted in the *New York Times,* April 12, 1860. Hereafter the *Times* will be cited as *NYT.*

2 Jackson gave his speech in Athens, Georgia, on July 7, 1860. It is printed in full in the *Southern Banner* (Athens, Georgia), July 26, 1860. I have relied on a digitized collection of Georgia newspapers for 1860. That collection can be found on Firefox at http://dig.galileo.usg.edu/MediaTypes/Newspapers.html?Welcome.

3 On January 5, 1860, the *Chicago Press and Tribune,* a Republican sheet, listed thirteen southern Democrats who, in December, had pledged secession on the floor of Congress should Republicans win in November. The list included senators Jefferson Davis of Mississippi, Clement C. Clay of Alabama, and James Chesnut of South Carolina as well as representative Roger Pryor of Virginia.

4 *NYT,* January 6, 1860.

5 *The National Era,* May 22, 1854, is quoted in Mark L. Berger, *The Revolution in the New York Party Systems, 1840–1860* (Port Washington, N.Y.: Kennikat Press, 1973), p. 36.

6 The Michigan Republican platform of July 6, 1854, is printed in the appendix to Hans L. Trefousse, "The Republican Party, 1854–1864," in Arthur M. Schlesinger Jr. (ed.), *History of U.S. Political Parties* (4 vols.; New York: Chelsea House and R. W. Bowker, 1973), Vol. II, pp. 1185–1188.

7 Here I emphatically disagree with the contention by James Oakes that by the time of Lincoln's election almost all Republicans insisted upon the abolition of slavery by one means or another. See his prize-winning *Freedom National: The Destruction of Slavery in the United States, 1861–1865* (New York: W. W. Norton, 2013).

8 The Hartford *Courant* is quoted in Bernard Mandel, *Labor: Free and Slave, Workingmen and the Anti-Slavery Movement in the United States* (New York: Associated Authors, 1955), p. 12. Thomas R. Williams is quoted in the *Pittsburgh*

Gazette, July 26, 1856. His fellow Republicans would choose Williams as one of the House prosecutors for Andrew Johnson's impeachment trial in the Senate.

9 Seward is quoted in James M. McPherson, *The Struggle for Equality: Abolitionists and the Negro in the Civil War and Reconstruction* (Princeton, N.J.: Princeton University Press, 1964), p. 25.

10 Speech of John Jay at Bedford, New York, October 8, 1856. Printed as a campaign pamphlet, Jay's speech was made available to me by Professor Kate Pierce when she was a graduate student at the University of Virginia.

11 The quotation is found in Seward's notorious "Irrepressible Conflict" speech at Rochester, New York, in October 1858. The speech is reprinted in Schlesinger, *History of U.S. Political Parties*, II, 1229–1238.

12 *Albany Evening Journal*, July 13, 1854, quoted in William E. Gienapp, *Origins of the Republican Party, 1852–1856* (New York: Oxford University Press, 1987), p. 83.

13 James W. Taylor to Hamilton Fish, November 11, 1854, Hamilton Fish Papers (Library of Congress); Edward L. Pierce to Salmon P. Chase, November 9, 1855, Salmon P. Chase Papers (Library of Congress).

14 Israel Washburn Jr. to J. L. Stevens, February 12, 1856, Israel Washburn Papers (Library of Congress); Edward Kent to Israel Washburn Jr., February 9, 1856, Israel Washburn Papers (Washburn Family Library, Norlands, Livermore, Maine).

15 The 1856 Republican national platform is printed in Schlesinger, *History of U.S. Political Parties*, II, 1203–1205.

16 Like the Republican pamphlet of John Jay's speech at Bedford, New York, on October 8, 1856, Kate Pierce brought this Michigan pamphlet to my attention when she was in the graduate program at the University of Virginia.

17 Russell Sage to Nathaniel P. Banks, May 31, 1856, Nathaniel P. Banks Papers (Library of Congress); Lyman Trumbull to Abraham Lincoln, June 15, 1856, Trumbull Family Papers (Illinois State Historical Library); T. M. Monroe to Daniel Ullmann, June 13, 1856, Daniel Ullmann Papers (New York Historical Society); Harry Bradley to Millard Fillmore, July 7, 1856, and John Wheeler to Fillmore, October 24, 1856, Millard Fillmore Papers (State University of New York at Oswego, microfilm edition).

18 Schuyler Colfax to Charles Heaton, May 21, 1856, Schuyler Colfax Papers (Northern Indiana Historical Society); James Kendall to John Fox Potter, July 8, 1856, John Fox Potter Papers (State Historical Society of Wisconsin); W. B. Thrall to Benjamin F. Wade, August 5, 1856, Benjamin F. Wade Papers (Library of Congress); Moses M. Davis to John Fox Potter, October 25, 1857, Potter Papers.

19 W. T. Nichols to Justin Morrill, August 23, 1856, Justin Morrill Papers (Library of Congress, microfilm edition).

20 This is the title of the final chapter in Gienapp's masterful *Origins of the Republican Party, 1852–1856*.

21 *Buffalo Express*, November 6, 1857, quoted in Joel H. Silbey, *The Partisan Imperative: The Dynamics of American Politics before the Civil War* (New York: Oxford University Press, 1985), pp. 134–135.

22 James D. Richardson (ed.), *Messages and Papers of the Presidents, 1789–1897* (10 vols.; Washington, D.C.: Government Printing Office, 1897), Vol. V, p. 479.

23 Unlike the congressional results in Illinois, Republicans won a small majority in statewide races and those for state legislative candidates.

24 Washington Hunt to John J. Crittenden, March 18, 1858, and John C. Lemon to Crittenden, April 15, 1858, John J. Crittenden Papers (Library of Congress).

25 S. B. Benton to John J. Crittenden, March 27, 1858, Crittenden Papers.

26 Benjamin D. Pettengill to Edwin D. Morgan, May 16, 1859, Edwin D. Morgan Papers (New York State Library); James Ashley to Salmon P. Chase, November 28, 1858, Chase Papers (Library of Congress).

27 Roy P. Basler (ed.), *The Collected Works of Abraham Lincoln* (9 vols.; New Brunswick, N.J.: Rutgers University Press, 1953), Vol. II, pp. 461–462. The entire "House Divided" speech is on pp. 461–468.

28 William Henry Seward to James Watson Webb, December 6, 1858, James Watson Webb Papers (Sterling Library, Yale University).

29 The "Irrepressible Conflict" speech is reprinted in Schlesinger, *History of U.S. Political Parties*, II, 1229–1238.

30 Circular dated May 25, 1859, in the Edwin D. Morgan Papers (New York State Library, Albany).

31 Nathan Sargent to Abraham Lincoln, June 13, 1859, Abraham Lincoln Papers (Library of Congress); I have used the digitized version of the Lincoln Papers available on the Library of Congress website.

32 Abraham Lincoln to Nathan Sargent, June 23, 1859, in Basler, *Collected Works of Lincoln*, III, 387–388.

33 *NYT*, December 10, 1859.

34 Ibid.

35 *Chicago Press and Tribune*, January 7, 1860.

36 *NYT*, December 23, 1859.

37 *Chicago Press and Tribune*, January 4, 1860.

CHAPTER 2. DEMOCRATS' TRIALS AND TRIBULATIONS

1 *Chicago Press and Tribune*, January 5, 1860.

2 *NYT*, January 6, 1860.

3 *National Intelligencer*, January 16, 1860.

4 Douglas was actually elected to a third House term in August 1847 before the state legislature elevated him to the Senate.

5 Ruffin quoted in Roy F. Nichols, *The Disruption of American Democracy* (New York: Macmillan, 1948), p. 80.

6 This was the headline of many newspaper stories. See, for example, the *Cleveland Herald*, August 26, 1857; the *Bangor Daily Whig and Courier*, September 4, 1857; and the *New Hampshire Statesman*, September 5, 1857.

7 *Memphis News* quoted in the *Weekly Raleigh Register*, September 16, 1857.

8 Lack of space prevents my going into more detail about this and other scandals under Buchanan's administration, save for what follows on the Covode Committee investigations. Years ago, when it appeared that the House of Rep-

resentatives might impeach Richard M. Nixon, John Doar, the special counsel for the House, asked a group of historians to prepare a study of how previous presidents had responded to charges of corruption and malfeasance. I was asked to prepare a brief section on Buchanan as well as a few other presidents. It is short but still more detailed than I can be here. It can be found in C. Vann Woodward (ed.), *Responses of the Presidents to Charges of Misconduct* (New York: Dell, 1974), pp. 85–96.

9 All the votes for Speaker and the partisan identification of the committee chairs appointed by Pennington can be found in Jeffrey A. Jenkins and Charles Stewart III, *Fighting for the Speakership: The House and the Rise of Party Government* (Princeton, N.J.: Princeton University Press, 2013), pp. 229–230, 351–353.

10 *NYT*, February 2, 1860.

11 Many newspapers quoted Covode's resolutions; here I have used the *Fayetteville Observer*, March 12, 1860. Buchanan's letter to Pittsburgh was occasioned by its centennial celebration of the British capture of the French Fort Duquesne and its renaming as Fort Pitt, which marked the founding of the city of Pittsburgh. In it, Buchanan lamented that "within a recent period" Americans had first heard "of the employment of money to carry elections." *Lowell Citizen and News*, April 3, 1860.

12 "Washington Correspondence," *New York Herald*, April 7, 1860.

13 Charleston tri-weekly *Courier*, April 3, 1860; *Cleveland Herald*, March 30, 1860; *Milwaukee Sentinel*, April 5, 1860.

14 *New York Herald*, April 5, 1860.

15 *Milwaukee Sentinel*, May 2, 1860; Richmond *Whig*, quoted in the *Virginia Free Press*, June 21, 1860.

16 *Milwaukee Sentinel*, March 22, 1860.

17 *New York Herald*, April 13, 1860.

18 *New Hampshire Statesman*, April 7, 1860.

19 A copy of the 1856 Democratic national platform can be found in Arthur M. Schlesinger Jr. (ed.), *History of U.S. Political Parties* (4 vols.; New York: Chelsea House and R. W. Bowker, 1973), Vol. I, pp. 557–561.

20 James D. Richardson (ed.), *Messages and Papers of the Presidents, 1789–1897* (10 vols.; Washington, D.C.: Government Printing Office, 1897), Vol. V, p. 431.

21 Ibid., 454. I have reversed the order of the first two quoted phrases from Buchanan's message.

22 *NYT*, December 23, 1859.

23 Stephen A. Douglas to James M. Scofield, March 1859, in Robert W. Johannsen (ed.), *The Letters of Stephen A. Douglas* (Urbana: University of Illinois Press, 1961), p. 440.

24 Douglas is quoted in Robert W. Johannsen, *Stephen A. Douglas* (New York: Oxford University Press, 1973), p. 569.

25 Stephen A. Douglas to John A. McClernand, February 21, 1858, and to Samuel Treat, February 28, 1858, in Johannsen, *Letters of Douglas*, 417–418.

26 This tale is best told in Nichols, *Disruption of American Democracy*, 216, 248.

27 *Chicago Press and Tribune*, January 11, 1860.

28 Johannsen, *Stephen A. Douglas*, 670, provides the critical excerpt from Douglas's speech.

29 *New York Herald*, February 25, 1859, quoted in Johannsen, *Stephen A. Douglas*, 696.

30 John Forney to Douglas, November 27, 1858, quoted in ibid., 698.

31 See the able summary of Douglas's essay in Johannsen, *Stephen A. Douglas*, 707–710.

32 *Chicago Press and Tribune*, January 5, 1860.

33 Richardson, *Messages and Papers of the Presidents*, V, 554–555.

34 *Ripley Bee* (Ohio), January 7, 1860.

35 *Chicago Press and Tribune*, January 2, 1860.

36 Both the Brown and the Davis resolutions are printed in the appendix to my essay "The Democratic Party, 1828–1860," in Schlesinger, *History of U.S. Political Parties*, I, 563–564.

37 On Davis's positions and his difference from Brown, see William J. Cooper Jr., *Jefferson Davis, American* (New York: Alfred A. Knopf, 2000), pp. 304–307.

38 Schlesinger, *History of U.S. Political Parties*, I, 564–565.

39 *NYT*, February 15, 1860.

40 *Southern Recorder* (Milledgeville, Georgia), April 24, 1860.

41 *New Orleans Bee*, March 5, 1860, in Dwight L. Dumond (ed.), *Southern Editorials on Secession* (New York: Century, 1931), pp. 48–50.

42 *Southern Banner* (Athens, Georgia), March 15, 1860. The editor of this Democratic sheet referred to the caucus resolutions as a blueprint for a platform at the Charleston convention that "equally ignore[d] the Squatter Sovereignty snare of Douglas and the impracticable and dangerous territorial 'slavecode' of Brown, Yancey, & Co." Yancey was William Lowndes Yancey of Alabama, of whom we will hear considerably more in the following chapter.

43 *NYT*, March 2, 1860.

44 *NYT*, March 13, 16, 1860.

45 Morton quoted in James Fuller, "The Election of 1860 and Political Realignment Theory: Indiana as a Case Study," in A. James Fuller (ed.), *The Election of 1860 Reconsidered* (Kent, Ohio: Kent State University Press, 2013), p. 210.

46 *NYT*, January 5, 1860; *Fayetteville* (N.C.) *Observer*, January 5, 1860.

47 *Southern Banner* (Athens, Georgia), March 15, 1860.

48 Public letter of John T. Morgan, *NYT*, April 11, 1860.

CHAPTER 3. DEMOCRATS' NOMINATIONS: ACT I

1 Robert P. Letcher to John J. Crittenden, April 2, 1860, John J. Crittenden Papers (Library of Congress, microfilm edition).

2 Charleston *Mercury*, quoted in *NYT*, March 1, 1860.

3 On Yancey's Alabama political milieu and Yancey himself, the key studies are J. Mills Thornton III, *Politics and Power in a Slave Society: Alabama 1820–1860* (Baton Rouge: Louisiana State University Press, 1978); William W. Freehling, *The*

Road to Disunion: Secessionists Triumphant, 1854–1861 (New York: Oxford University Press, 2007); and Eric Walther, *William Lowndes Yancey and the Coming of the Civil War* (Chapel Hill: University of North Carolina Press, 2006).

4 *New Orleans Bee*, January 18, 1860, in Dwight L. Dumond (ed.), *Southern Editorials on Secession* (New York: Century, 1931), p. 12.

5 *NYT*, March 10, 1860.

6 Athens, Georgia, *Southern Banner*, March 22, 1860.

7 *Cleveland Daily Herald*, April 24, 1860.

8 Athens *Southern Banner*, January 19, 1860.

9 The language about defending naturalized citizens' rights was included in all three platform proposals. It was intended as a criticism of Republicans in Massachusetts who had recently adopted a state constitutional amendment forbidding naturalized immigrants to vote for two years after they became citizens.

10 *New York Herald*, April 27, 1860.

11 "The Charleston Convention," *NYT*, April 28, 1860.

12 Roy F. Nichols, *The Disruption of American Democracy* (New York: Macmillan, 1948), p. 299.

13 Telegraphic dispatches in *New York Herald*, April 27, 1860.

14 Ibid.; "A Row among the Pennsylvanians," *NYT*, May 1, 1860.

15 Payne quoted in Robert W. Johannsen, *Stephen A. Douglas* (New York: Oxford University Press, 1973), p. 754.

16 William B. Hesseltine (ed.), *Three against Lincoln: Murat Halstead Reports the Caucuses of 1860* (Baton Rouge: Louisiana State University Press, 1960), p. 52. A reporter for the Cincinnati *Commercial*, Murat Halstead wrote unusually long and perceptive dispatches about all of the conventions held in 1860. He later gathered most of these into a book published in the summer of 1860 that Hesseltine edited and annotated a hundred years later.

17 Ibid., 54–55.

18 Ibid., 59.

19 Ibid., 60–61.

20 The breakdown of votes is given in ibid., 69.

21 Ibid., 74.

22 Ibid., 76, 83–84.

23 Ibid., 107.

24 *Milwaukee Daily Sentinel*, May 2, 1860.

25 "The Charleston Convention," *NYT*, May 1, 1860.

26 A. S. Seaton to Abraham Lincoln, Winona, Minn., April 24, 1860, Abraham Lincoln Papers (Library of Congress, American Memory digitized collection).

CHAPTER 4. THE THIRD WAY

1 See Raymond's speech to a Union meeting in Albany, New York, in *NYT*, January 17, 1860.

2 *NYT*, January 5, 1860.

3 *Pittsburgh Gazette* quoted in Michael Fitzgibbon Holt, *Forging a Majority: The Formation of the Republican Party in Pittsburgh, 1848–1860* (New Haven, Conn.:

Yale University Press, 1969), p. 284. It's been over fifty years since I first wrote and annotated the paragraph in which these quotations appear. I cite eleven different issues of the *Gazette* for that paragraph, and at this distance in time I have no idea which issues I here quote again.

4 *Pittsburgh Gazette*, November 2, 1860, quoted in Howard C. Perkins (ed.), *Northern Editorials on Secession* (2 vols.; New York: D. Appleton–Century, 1942), Vol. I, pp. 69–71.

5 *NYT*, January 5, 1860.

6 *Albany Evening Journal*, January 7, 1860. I accessed this paper at http://fultonhistory.com/newspapers5Disk3/Albany%20NY%20Journal5201860.

7 Anthony Kennedy to S. S. Nicholas, Baltimore, June 7, 1859, John J. Crittenden Papers (Library of Congress, microfilm edition).

8 S. A. Scroggs to John J. Crittenden, January 24, 1860, Crittenden Papers.

9 George Fisher to John J. Crittenden, Dover, Delaware, January 7, 1860, Crittenden Papers.

10 *NYT*, February 24, 1860.

11 *Southern Recorder* (Milledgeville, Georgia), May 15 and July 10, 1860.

12 *NYT*, March 27, 1860.

13 *New York Herald*, February 21, 1860.

14 *Baltimore American* quoted in the *Fayetteville Observer*, February 2, 1860.

15 *Nashville Southern Banner*, March 29, 1860, in Dwight L. Dumond (ed.), *Southern Editorials on Secession* (New York: Century, 1931), pp. 62–65.

16 William C. Rives to John J. Crittenden, Castle Hill, Albemarle County, Virginia, January 9, 1860, Crittenden Papers.

17 James Collins to J. J. Crittenden, New Albany, Indiana, February 2, 1860, ibid.

18 Joseph A. Randolph to John J. Crittenden, Trenton, January 30, 1860, ibid.

19 Hiram Ketchum to John J. Crittenden, New York City, May 7, 1860, ibid.

20 *Savannah Republican*, February 8, 1860, in Dumond, *Southern Editorials on Secession*, 27–29.

21 *Augusta Daily Chronicle and Sentinel*, February 13, 1860, ibid., 32–35.

22 Alexander H. H. Stuart to John J. Crittenden, Richmond, January 22, 1860, Crittenden Papers.

23 R. P. Letcher to J. J. Crittenden, Frankfort, March 1, 1860, ibid.

24 Jeremiah Clemens always referred to himself as Jere Clemens, and newspapers primarily identified him that way.

25 I've used the copy of the address in the Raleigh *Daily Register*, February 25, 1860.

26 William A. Graham to J. J. Crittenden, Hillsborough, North Carolina, February 27, 1860; and John P. Kennedy to Crittenden, Baltimore, March 5, 1860, Crittenden Papers.

27 Milledgeville *Southern Recorder*, April 24, 1860.

28 Ibid., April 17, 1860.

29 *NYT*, February 24, 1860.

30 Ibid., March 28, 1860.

31 Maryland Affairs, *NYT*, April 17, 1860.

32 James Collins to John J. Crittenden, New Albany, Indiana, February 2, 1860, Crittenden Papers.
33 S. S. Nicholas to John J. Crittenden, New York City, April 3, 1860, ibid.
34 Politics at Washington, *NYT*, April 18, 1860.
35 C. H. Bressler to John J. Crittenden, York, Pennsylvania, February 2, 1860, Crittenden Papers. Bressler believed that Crittenden could dissuade Republicans from even holding a national convention, let alone nominating their own candidate.
36 See the telegraphic dispatch from Baltimore in the *Chicago Press and Tribune*, May 11, 1860.
37 *Raleigh Register*, May 16, 1860.
38 Still in his early twenties, Halstead, who reported for the *Cincinnati Commercial*, attended all the nominating conventions in 1860 and later gathered his lengthy reports into a book. As was noted, it has been edited and annotated by historian William B. Hesseltine in *Three against Lincoln: Murat Halstead Reports the Caucuses of 1860* (Baton Rouge: Louisiana State University Press, 1960).
39 *NYT*, May 10, 1860; Washington *National Intelligencer*, May 11, 1850; Hesseltine, *Three against Lincoln*, 125.
40 Hesseltine, *Three against Lincoln*, 130.
41 Ibid., 129.
42 Convention report in Washington *National Intelligencer*, May 11, 1860.
43 *NYT*, May 11, 1860.
44 Harrison died in April 1841, a month after his inauguration. His entire cabinet except Secretary of State Daniel Webster resigned in September 1841 because they thought John Tyler, Harrison's successor, had lied to them.
45 *Bangor Whig and Courier*, April 3, 1860.
46 Boston *Daily Advertiser*, September 14, 1860.
47 Raleigh *Register*, May 23, 1860.
48 *Republican* quoted in the Fayetteville *Observer*, May 17, 1860.
49 Jackson *Semi-Weekly Mississippian*, May 22, 1860.
50 Lexington *Kentucky Statesman*, May 8, 1860, in Dumond, *Southern Editorials on Secession*, 75–77.
51 *New York Herald*, May 11, 1860.
52 *NYT*, May 11, 1860.
53 *NYT*, February 24, 1860.
54 *Chicago Press and Tribune*, May 12 and May 14, 1860. I have reversed the order in which these quotations appear in the two issues of the paper.
55 *NYT*, May 11, 1860.
56 Boston *Daily Advertiser*, May 15, 1860.

CHAPTER 5. REPUBLICANS CHOOSE AN "AVAILABLE" MAN

1 By 1860 Illinois had a considerably larger population than neighboring Indiana, as the popular vote totals from the 1860 election would show, but the allocation of House seats and thus of electoral votes in 1860 was based on the cen-

sus of 1850 that recorded Indiana as being the more populous. At the start of 1860 both Democrats and Republicans expected New Jersey to go Democratic in November. Hence it was rarely if ever included in Republican calculations of a path to victory.

2 Hawkins Taylor to Abraham Lincoln, Des Moines, Iowa, February 15, 1860, Abraham Lincoln Papers (Library of Congress, digital edition). All subsequent references to the Lincoln Papers refer to this digital edition.

3 Thurlow Weed to William H. Seward, March 15, 1858, quoted in Glyndon G. van Deusen (ed.), "Thurlow Weed's Analysis of William H. Seward's Defeat in the Republican Convention of 1860," *Mississippi Valley Historical Review* 34 (1947): 101.

4 I analyze the "Irrepressible Conflict" speech in Chapter 1. For the "Higher Law" speech, see Michael F. Holt, *The Rise and Fall of the American Whig Party: Jacksonian Politics and the Onset of the Civil War* (New York: Oxford University Press, 1999), pp. 489–493.

5 Samuel Galloway to Lincoln, Columbus, Ohio, March 15, 1860, Lincoln Papers.

6 Hawkins Taylor to Lincoln, Des Moines, Iowa, February 25, 1860, ibid.

7 Lyman Trumbull to Lincoln, Washington, April 24, 1860, ibid.

8 Herman Kreismann to Joseph K. C. Forest, Washington, April 14, 1860, ibid.

9 Lincoln was elected as a Whig to the Illinois state legislature in 1854, but he resigned that office before being sworn into it in order to compete within the legislature for a U.S. Senate seat that the Anti-Nebraska Democrat Lyman Trumbull ultimately won.

10 The address is printed in full in Roy P. Basler (ed.), *The Collected Works of Abraham Lincoln* (9 vols.; Brunswick, N.J.: Rutgers University Press, 1953), Vol. III, pp. 522–550. All subsequent quotations from it can be found on these pages.

11 Modern scholarship demonstrates that Lincoln's assertion that the founding generation expected slavery to die away was simply wrong. See, for example, George William Van Cleve, *A Slaveholders' Union: Slavery, Politics, and the Constitution in the Early American Republic* (Chicago: University of Chicago Press, 2010); and William J. Cooper Jr., "Where Was Henry Clay? President-Elect Abraham Lincoln and the Crisis of the Union," in Gary W. Gallagher and Rachel A. Shelden (ed.), *A Political Nation: New Directions in Mid-Nineteenth-Century American Political History* (Charlottesville: University of Virginia Press, 2012), pp. 126–140.

12 On this point, see Michael Burlingame, *Abraham Lincoln* (Baltimore: Johns Hopkins University Press, 208), Vol. I, p. 627.

13 *Chicago Press and Tribune*, March 14, 1860, quoted in William C. Harris, *Lincoln's Rise to the Presidency* (Lawrence: University Press of Kansas, 2007), p. 192.

14 Abraham Lincoln to Lyman Trumbull, April 29, 1860, in *Collected Works of Abraham Lincoln*, IV, 45.

15 Lincoln to Galloway, March 24, 1860, ibid., 33–34.

16 Fillmore garnered only 3.2 percent of Connecticut's vote in 1856.

17 Mark Delahay to Lincoln, Leavenworth, Kansas, April 7, 1860, Lincoln Papers.

18 Herman Kreismann to Huh, Washington, April 11, 1860, ibid.
19 David Davis to Lincoln, Urbana, Illinois, April 23, 1860, ibid.
20 Ibid.; Trumbull to Lincoln, April 24, 1860, ibid.
21 Hawkins Taylor to Lincoln, Keokuk, Iowa, December 27, 1859, ibid.
22 David Davis to Lincoln, April 23, 1860; and Nathan M. Knapp to Lincoln, Chicago, May 14, 1860, ibid.
23 William Butler to Lincoln, Chicago, May 14, 1860, ibid.
24 Lincoln to Trumbull, April 29, 1860, *Collected Works of Lincoln*, IV, 45–46.
25 Lincoln to Cyrus M. Allen, May 1, 1860, ibid., 46–47.
26 Lincoln to Robert M. Corwine, May 2, 1860, ibid., 47–48.
27 Harris, *Lincoln's Rise to the Presidency*, 197.
28 *Chicago Press and Tribune*, May 15, 1860, quoted in ibid., 200.
29 *Collected Works of Lincoln*, IV, 50.
30 William B. Hesseltine (ed.), *Three against Lincoln: Murat Halstead Reports the Caucuses of 1860* (Baton Rouge: Louisiana State University Press, 1960), pp. 159–160.
31 Charles C. Nourse to James Harlan, June 6, 1860, quoted in Burlingame, *Lincoln*, 605. Burlingame's chapter on the Chicago convention contains scores of quotations citing different reasons why Republicans must not nominate Seward.
32 The convention's credentials committee, however, awarded slightly less than double the number of electoral votes to the underrepresented slave states. Virginia got 23, not 30; Kentucky 23 not 24; Maryland 11, not 16; and Texas 6, not 8.
33 The platform is printed in Hesseltine, *Three against Lincoln*, 136–138. I have included it in Appendix B along with the other party platforms.
34 Hesseltine, *Three against Lincoln*, 159.
35 Davis quoted in Burlingame, *Lincoln*, 615.
36 Hesseltine, *Three against Lincoln*, 165–166.
37 Ibid., 166.
38 Ibid., 171.
39 Reply to the Committee of the Republican National Convention, May 19, 1860, *Collected Works of Abraham Lincoln*, IV, 51.
40 Abraham Lincoln to George Ashmun, Springfield, May 23, 1860, ibid., 52.
41 Hesseltine, *Three against Lincoln*, 176–177.
42. Thurlow Weed to William H. Seward, May 20, 1860, printed in van Deusen, "Weed's Analysis of Seward's Defeat at the Republican Convention of 1860."
43 Giddings to Lincoln, May 19, 1860, quoted in Burlingame, *Lincoln*, 627.
44 Henry R. Selden quoted in ibid.

CHAPTER 6. DEMOCRATS' NOMINATIONS: ACT II

1 William B. Hesseltine (ed.), *Three against Lincoln: Murat Halstead Reports the Caucuses of 1860* (Baton Rouge: Louisiana State University Press, 1960), p. 185.
2 Ibid., 221.
3 *Scioto Gazette*, June 26, 1860.

4 I have used the copy of the letter in the Jackson, Mississippi, *Semi-Weekly Mississippian*, May 22, 1860.

5 E. J. MeGehee to Editors, May 15, 1860, in Macon *Weekly Georgia Telegraph*, May 25, 1860.

6 Recall that South Carolina purposely forbid the men it sent to Richmond to go to Baltimore. The Floridians went there from Richmond as spectators, but they had not been accredited as delegates. They hoped they might be invited to participate, but their admission depended on the action of the full convention.

7 Both missives are printed in Robert W. Johannsen (ed.), *The Letters of Stephen A. Douglas* (Urbana: University of Illinois Press, 1961), pp. 492–493.

8 Hesseltine, *Three against Lincoln*, 215.

9 Ibid., 225.

10 "Presidential," *NYT*, June 22, 1860.

11 Hesseltine, *Three against Lincoln*, 229.

12 Ibid.

13 Ibid., 235–236.

14 Ibid., 254.

15 Ibid., 255.

16 "The Baltimore Convention," *NYT*, June 23, 1860.

17 Hesseltine, *Three against Lincoln*, 256.

18 All four national platforms in 1860 are printed in Appendix B.

19 Stephen A. Douglas to William H. Ludlow, R. P. Dick, R. C. Wickliffe, et al., June 27, 1860, in Johannsen, *Letters of Stephen A. Douglas*, 494–496.

20 *NYT*, June 27 and 30, 1860.

21 The other exceptions among the slave states were Missouri, with only two, and Maryland, with nine, of their elected delegates.

22 William C. Davis, *Breckinridge: Statesman, Soldier, Symbol* (Baton Rouge: Louisiana State University Press, 1974), p. 208.

23 Massachusetts Republican congressman Henry L. Dawes made the "dashing" comment about Breckinridge. Ibid., 196.

24 "The Baltimore Convention—The Democratic Candidates," *NYT*, June 25, 1860.

25 *New York Courier and Enquirer* quoted in the *Boston Daily Advertiser*, June 26, 1860.

26 My account relies entirely on Davis, *Breckinridge*, 224–227.

27 *Southern Banner* (Athens, Georgia), July 19, 1860.

28 *Dover Gazette and Stratford Advertiser*, June 30, 1860.

29 *New York Herald* quoted in the *Milwaukee Sentinel*, July 2, 1860.

30 Baltimore *Clipper* quoted in the *Virginia Free Press*, June 28, 1860.

31 Milledgeville, Georgia, *Southern Recorder*, July 10, 1860.

32 *Milwaukee Daily Sentinel*, June 25, 1860.

33 Ibid.

34 *Ripley Bee*, June 28, 1860.

35 New York *Tribune* quoted in the *Boston Daily Advertiser*, June 26, 1860.

36 *NYT*, June 26, 1860.

37. *NYT*, April 19, 1860.

CHAPTER 7. VARIEGATED CAMPAIGNS

1 For example, see the chapters on the 1860 election in Allan Nevins, *The Emergence of Lincoln: Prologue to Civil War, 1859–1861* (New York: Charles Scribner's Sons, 1950), pp. 261–317; and David M. Potter, *The Impending Crisis, 1848–1861*, completed and edited by Don E. Fehrenbacher (New York: Harper and Row, 1976), pp. 405–447.

2 Washington Hunt to John Bell, Newburgh, New York, August 19, 1860, John Bell Papers (Library of Congress, microfilm edition).

3 *Lowell Daily Journal and Courier*, September 5, 1860, in Howard C. Perkins (ed.), *Northern Editorials on Secession* (2 vols.; New York: D. Appleton-Century Company, 1942), Vol. I, pp. 29–31.

4 *New York Herald*, May 3, 1860.

5 James E. Harvey to Abraham Lincoln, Washington, June 25, 1860, and September 22, 1860, Lincoln Papers (Library of Congress); Schuyler Colfax to Lincoln, Washington, June 25, 1860, Lincoln Papers.

6 *Southern Banner* (Athens, Georgia), July 12, 1860.

7 *NYT*, May 17, 1860.

8 Macon *Weekly Georgia Telegraph*, July 20, 1860; *NYT*, May 11, 1860; Washington Hunt to John Bell, Lockport, New York, June 8, 1860, Bell Papers; *New York Herald*, August 8, 1860. Since the Constitution specified that the Senate would choose between only two vice presidential candidates, southern Democrats expected that the choice would be between only Lane and Hamlin, both sitting members of that body.

9 Douglas quoted in Nevins, *The Emergence of Lincoln: Prologue to Civil War*, 284.

10 "The Connecticut Election," *NYT*, March 29, 1860.

11 As quoted in Jon Grinspan, "'Young Men for War': The Wide Awakes and Lincoln's 1860 Presidential Campaign," *Journal of American History* 96 (September 2009): 361. All the information about the Wide Awakes in these paragraphs is taken from Grinspan's excellent article.

12 Seward quoted in ibid., 366.

13 Ibid., 357.

14 *New York Herald*, September 29, 1860.

15 Ibid., October 24, 1860.

16 Ibid., August 8, 1860.

17 Ibid., September 28, 1860.

18 Frederick *Examiner* reprinted in the *Southern Recorder* (Milledgeville, Georgia), July 17, 1860.

19 "Grand Bell Demonstration in Nashville," *New York Herald*, September 30, 1860.

20 Ibid., August 18, 1860.

21 I've used the copy of the address in the Washington *National Intelligencer*, August 10, 1860.

22 Curtis's speech is reprinted in the Milledgeville *Southern Recorder*, August 14, 1860.

23 "Grand Bell Demonstration in Nashville," *New York Herald*, September 30, 1860. Citing his advanced years, Crittenden had declined most of the many requests he received that summer to speak on Bell's behalf.

24 Milledgeville *Southern Recorder*, August 28, 1860.

25 *New York Herald*, August 8, 1860.

26 August 10, 1860.

27 Crittenden's speeches are reprinted in the Milledgeville *Southern Recorder*, August 28, 1860, and the *New York Herald*, September 30, 1860.

28 *New York Herald*, March 29, 1860.

29 Ibid., August 22 and October 3, 1860; extract from the *Herald* in the Athens *Southern Banner*, August 16, 1860.

30 Washington *Constitution*, September 6, 1860, in Perkins (ed.), *Northern Editorials on Secession*, I, 31–35.

31 Springfield *Daily Illinois Register*, September 28, 1860, in ibid., 42–44.

32 *NYT*, September 17, 1860; Montpelier *Vermont Patriot*, September 29, 1860.

33 *New York Herald*, June 18, 1860.

34 Joel H. Silbey, "The Surge of Republican Power: Partisan Antipathy, American Social Conflict, and the Coming of the Civil War," in Stephen E. Maizlish and John J. Kushma (eds.), *Essays on American Antebellum Politics, 1840–1860* (College Station: Texas A&M University Press, 1982), p. 217. Silbey cites several Democratic papers in the footnote for this quotation, so it is impossible to be certain which paper it came from. The lead newspaper cited, however, is a September 21, 1860, issue of the *New York Herald*.

35 George Curtis made this charge in his Massachusetts speech cited above.

36 Washington *National Intelligencer*, August 10, 1860.

37 *Weekly Raleigh Register*, June 27, 1860.

38 Milledgeville *Southern Recorder*, May 15, 1860, and June 29, 1860.

39 Clemens's public letter is printed in ibid., July 31, 1860.

40 Ibid., August 7, 1860.

41 *Charleston Tri-Weekly Courier*, September 11, 1860.

42 Athens *Southern Banner*, July 19, 1860.

43 Ibid., August 9, 1860.

44 Jackson *Semi-Weekly Mississippian*, May 22, 1860.

45 Columbia *Daily South Carolinian*, August 3, 1860, in Dwight L. Dumond (ed.), *Southern Editorials on Secession* (New York: Century, 1931), pp. 157–158.

46 *Nashville Union and American*, October 12, 1860, in ibid., 181–184.

47 Athens *Southern Banner*, July 10 and 19, 1860.

48 Lexington *Kentucky Statesman*, May 8, 1860, in Dumond, *Southern Editorials on Secession*, 75–77.

49 Ibid.

50 Milledgeville *Southern Recorder*, August 28, 1860.

51 Ibid., July 10, 1860.

52 Forty years ago the historian William J. Cooper Jr. astutely identified this

back-and-forth arguing about which party and candidates better defended slavery and southern rights as a persistent theme of antebellum southern politics in his *The South and the Politics of Slavery, 1828–1856* (Baton Rouge: Louisiana State University Press, 1978). Subsequently William W. Freehling labeled the phenomenon "loyalty politics" in his *The Road to Disunion, Volume One: Secessionists at Bay, 1800–1854* (New York: Oxford University Press, 1990).

53 *Weekly Raleigh Register*, September 5, 1860.

54 *Charleston Tri-Weekly Courier*, September 11, 1860.

55 Watts's letter to the editor of the *Montgomery Post* reprinted in the *Fayetteville Observer*, August 9, 1860.

56 *New York Herald*, June 27, 1860.

57 *Weekly Raleigh Register*, October 10, 1860; Jackson *Semi-Weekly Mississippian*, October 26, 1860.

58 Stephen A. Douglas to Nathaniel Paschal, July 4, 1860, and Douglas to Charles Lanphier, July 5, 1860, in Robert W. Johannsen (ed.), *The Letters of Stephen A. Douglas* (Urbana: University of Illinois Press, 1961), pp. 497–498.

59 James E. Harvey to Abraham Lincoln, Saratoga Springs, July 27, 1860, and George G. Fogg to Lincoln, New York City, August 18, 1860, Lincoln Papers. Fogg was the secretary of the Republican national campaign committee that was headquartered in New York.

60 Springfield *Republican*, July 28, 1860, quoted in Robert W. Johannsen, *Stephen A. Douglas* (New York: Oxford University Press, 1973), p. 781.

61 Ibid., 788–789.

62 Ibid., 789–790; Nevins, *Emergence of Lincoln*, 294.

63 Richard W. Thompson to Abraham Lincoln, Washington, June 12, 1860, Lincoln Papers.

64 All four national party platforms in 1860 are reproduced in Appendix B.

65 Elihu B. Washburne to Lincoln, Washington, May 20, 1860, and Lyman Trumbull to Lincoln, Washington, May 22, 1860, Lincoln Papers (Library of Congress, digital edition).

66 Alexander K. McClure to Lincoln, Chambersburg, Pennsylvania, June 16, 1860, and William M. Reynolds to Lincoln, Lancaster, Pennsylvania, July 23, 1860, ibid.

67 James E. Harvey to Lincoln, Washington, June 25, 1860, ibid.

68 Charles Ray to Lincoln, Chicago, June 27, 1860, ibid.

69 Richard W. Thompson to Abraham Lincoln, Washington, June 12, 1860, ibid.

70 Carl Schurz to Lincoln, New Albany, Indiana, August 22, 1860, ibid.

71 Schuyler Colfax to Lincoln, South Bend, Indiana, July 6, 1860, ibid.

72 Joseph Medill to Lincoln, Chicago, July 29, 1860, ibid.

73 Russell Errett to Joseph Medill, Pittsburgh, July 24, 1860, ibid.

74 James E. Harvey to Lincoln, Washington, June 25, July 4, and September 22, 1860; John P. Sanderson to David Davis, Philadelphia, August 27, 1860, ibid.

75 Both Allan Nevins and David Potter in their previously cited chapters on the 1860 election make this point about superior Republican fund-raising.

76 *Cincinnati Commercial*, October 18, 1860, in Perkins, *Northern Editorials on Secession*, I, 53–57.

77 *New York Herald*, September 19, 1860, ibid., 35–37.

78 Springfield *Daily Illinois Register*, September 28, 1860, ibid., 42–44.

79 I learned this fact about New York Democrats' ballots in 1860 from my late friend, the historian William E. Gienapp, who died far too young.

80 See the bibliographical postscript in Daniel W. Crofts, *Lincoln & the Politics of Slavery: The Other Thirteenth Amendment and the Struggle to Save the Union* (Chapel Hill: University of North Carolina Press, 2016), for a withering refutation of the argument that most Republicans sought abolition by 1860.

81 Eric Foner, *Free Soil, Free Labor, Free Men: The Ideology of the Republican Party before the Civil War* (New York: Oxford University Press, 1970), p. 118.

82 Abraham Lincoln to Hon. George Robertson, Springfield, August 15, 1855, in Roy P. Basler (ed.), *Collected Works of Lincoln* (9 vols.; Brunswick, N.J.: Rutgers University Press, 1953), Vol. II, pp. 317–319. Crofts, *Lincoln & the Politics of Slavery*, 71, brought this strikingly important letter to my attention. He notes that almost all students of the pre–Civil War years have failed to appreciate its significance.

83 Basler, *Collected Works of Lincoln*, II, 461.

84 *Hartford Evening Press*, October 26, 1860, in Perkins, *Northern Editorials on Secession*, I, 64–66.

85 See Crofts's stunningly insightful chapter "Mutual Misconceptions" in his *Lincoln & the Politics of Slavery*, 83–105.

86 *NYT*, April 14, 1860.

87 Ibid., May 11, 1860.

88 Foner, *Free Soil, Free Labor, Free Men*, 212–213.

89 Schuyler Colfax to Abraham Lincoln, Washington, June 25, 1860, Lincoln Papers. Democrats opposed Kansas statehood because it would be another Republican state, not because it was another free state.

90 Michael Burlingame, *Abraham Lincoln* (Baltimore: Johns Hopkins University Press, 2008), p. 613. Burlingame cites an excerpt from the *World* in the July 13, 1860, issue of *The Liberator* for this quotation.

91 *Newark Advocate*, July 20, 1860.

92 *Fayetteville Observer*, October 28, 1860.

93 Joshua Giddings to Abraham Lincoln, Jefferson, Ohio, June 19, 1860, Lincoln Papers.

94 The circular is in the Lincoln Papers.

95 *Hartford Evening Press*, October 25, 1860, in Perkins, *Northern Editorials on Secession*, I, 60–63.

96 *Milwaukee Daily Sentinel*, November 3, 1860.

CHAPTER 8. AMERICA VOTES

1 Michael F. Holt, *The Political Crisis of the 1850s* (rev. ed.; New York: W. W. Norton, 1982), pp. 250–251.

2 See Table 12 in William E. Gienapp, "Who Voted for Lincoln?" in John L.

Thomas (ed.), *Abraham Lincoln and the American Political Tradition* (Amherst: University of Massachusetts Press, 1986), p. 81.

3 Table 13, ibid., 82; James L. Huston, *The Panic of 1857 and the Coming of the Civil War* (Baton Rouge: Louisiana State University Press, 1987), demonstrates that Democratic conversions to the People's Party were concentrated in coal-mining and iron-making counties.

4 Lowell, Massachusetts, *Daily Citizen and News*, October 12, 1860.

5 *Chicago Press and Tribune*, October 10, 1860, quoted in William C. Harris, *Lincoln's Rise to the Presidency* (Lawrence: University Press of Kansas, 2007), p. 237.

6 *NYT*, October 12, 1860.

7 "The Presidency—The Forlorn Hope of the Democracy," ibid.

8 Cleveland *Herald*, October 12, 1860.

9 Jackson *Semi-Weekly Mississippian*, October 12, 1860.

10 Montgomery *Weekly Advertiser* and Atlanta *Confederacy*, quoted in Robert A. Johannsen, *Stephen A. Douglas* (New York: Oxford University Press, 1973), p. 799.

11 Ibid., p. 798.

12 Douglas quoted in Allan Nevins, *The Emergence of Lincoln: Prologue to Civil War, 1859–1861* (New York: Charles Scribner's Sons, 1950), p. 295.

13 Johannsen, *Stephen A. Douglas*, 798.

14 Ibid., 800–801.

15 Ibid., 801–802.

16 Harris, *Lincoln's Rise to the Presidency*, 242.

17 In New Jersey Lincoln's opponents had constructed a fusion electoral ticket composed of three Douglas men, two Breckinridge men, and two Bell men. All of Lincoln's opponents voted for the three Douglas men, but Douglas's friends scratched the names of enough Bell and Breckinridge men from the tickets they turned in that they ran behind electors on the Republican ticket. Hence the three Douglas electors, who garnered a clear majority of the popular vote, won election, but the other four votes were awarded to the top four vote-receiving Republican electors. For this information, I have relied on the special note on New Jersey's 1860 election in Walter Dean Burnham, *Presidential Ballots, 1836–1892* (Baltimore: Johns Hopkins University Press, 1955), p. 933.

18 Johannsen, *Stephen A. Douglas*, 803.

19 Tables IV and V in Ollinger Crenshaw, "Urban and Rural Voting in the Election of 1860," in Eric F. Goldman (ed.), *Historiography and Urbanization: Essays in American History in Honor of W. Stull Holt* (Baltimore: Johns Hopkins University Press, 1941), p. 66.

20 Table 8 in Peyton McCrary, Clark Miller, and Dale Baum, "Class and Party in the Secession Crisis: Voting Behavior in the Deep South, 1856–1861," *Journal of Interdisciplinary History* 8 (Winter 1978): 451.

21 See the many tables in Chapter 7 of Daniel W. Crofts, *Reluctant Confederates: Upper South Unionists in the Secession Crisis* (Chapel Hill: University of North Carolina Press, 1989). Unfortunately, as Professor Crofts told me by letter, he

made no attempt to disaggregate the Douglas and Breckinridge votes for these estimates of how slaveholders and nonslaveholders voted in the three states he studied so superbly. Crofts also estimated what proportions of slaveholders and nonslaveholders failed to vote at all in 1860, but here I have cited only his estimates for those who did vote.

22 Here I have used the estimates by Walter Dean Burnham in the U.S. Census Bureau's *Historical Guide to Statistics of the United States.*

23 Philadelphia *North American and United States Gazette,* November 7, 1860.

24 Minnesota and Oregon achieved statehood only after the 1856 election.

25 Pittsburgh *Gazette,* January 1, 1858; Michael F. Holt, *Forging a Majority: The Formation of the Republican Party in Pittsburgh, 1848–1860* (New Haven, Conn.: Yale University Press, 1969), pp. 287–288.

26 Charles M. Allen to Abraham Lincoln, November 8, 1860, Lincoln Papers.

27 Carl Schurz to Lincoln, November 7, 1860, ibid.

28 Medill quoted in Michael Burlingame, *Abraham Lincoln* (2 vols.; Baltimore: Johns Hopkins University Press, 2008),Vol. I, p. 682.

29 All of these quotations can be found in ibid., I, 681–682. Burlingame identifies an 1880 recollection of James K. Moorhead, Pittsburgh's Republican congressman during the Civil War, for Lincoln's statement that he personally believed that "I have been elected primarily on the cry of Honest Old Abe."

30 August Belmont to John Forsyth, November 22 and December 19, 1860, in *Letters, Speeches, and Addresses of August Belmont* (privately printed, 1890), pp. 23–24, 38.

31 *New York Herald,* November 8, 1860.

32 *Cincinnati Gazette* reprinted in the *Chicago Tribune,* November 15, 1860.

33 Salmon P. Chase to Abraham Lincoln, November 7, 1860, Lincoln Papers.

34 Adams and Seward are quoted in Eric Foner, *Free Soil, Free Labor, Free Men: The Ideology of the Republican Party before the Civil War* (New York: Oxford University Press, 1970), pp. 140, 223.

35 Philadelphia *North American and United States Gazette,* November 7, 1860, in Howard C. Perkins (ed.), *Northern Editorials on Secession* (2 vols.; New York: D. Appleton-Century Company, 1942), Vol. I, pp. 80–82.

36 *NYT,* November 7, 1860.

37 *Boston Advertiser,* November 7, 1860.

38 Charleston *Tri-Weekly Courier,* November 8, 1860.

39 Jackson *Semi-Weekly Mississippian,* November 9, 1860.

40 Ibid.

41 *Daily Constitutionalist* (Augusta, Georgia), November 16, 1860, and the *New Orleans Bee,* November 19, 1860, in Dwight L. Dumond (ed.), *Southern Editorials on Secession* (New York: Century, 1931), pp. 242–250.

42 Fitzhugh quoted in William L. Barney, *The Road to Secession: A New Perspective on the Old South* (New York: Praeger, 1972), p. 203; Edmund Ruffin, *Anticipation of the Future* (Richmond, 1860), p. viii, quoted in Margaret Cooper, "Memminger and the Virginia Politicians" (seminar paper, University of Virginia, 1975), p. 7.

43 Charlottesville *Review*, November 23, 1860, in Dumond, *Southern Editorials on Secession*, 261–263.

44 *Greensborough Patriot*, October 4, 1860.

45 Leroy P. Graf and Ralph W. Haskins (eds.), *The Papers of Andrew Johnson, Volume 4, 1860–61* (Knoxville: University of Tennessee Press, 1976), p. 43.

46 Roy P. Basler (ed.), *Collected Works of Lincoln* (9 vols.; Brunswick, N.J.: Rutgers University Press, 1953), Vol. IV, p. 138.

47 *Chicago Tribune*, November 15, 1860.

48. Zachariah Chandler to Lyman Trumbull, Detroit, November 15, 1860, Lyman Trumbull Family Papers (Illinois State Historical Society).

49 These quotations from Weed's *Albany Evening Journal* are taken from draft chapters of my advisee John R. Kirn's PhD dissertation. The revised and completed version is John R. Kirn, "Voters, Parties, and Legislative Politics in New York State, 1846–1876" (PhD diss., University of Virginia, 2003).

50 Thurlow Weed to Preston King, December 10, 1860, in Harriet W. Barnes (ed.), *The Life of Thurlow Weed, Including his Autobiography and a Memoir* (2 vols.; Boston: Houghton, Mifflin, 1884), Vol. 2, p. 309.

BIBLIOGRAPHIC ESSAY

The literature on the presidential election of 1860 and the run-up to it is far too vast to attempt to assess here. I've therefore confined this note to works that influenced me when writing the book, although I have intentionally omitted secondary works I cite in notes simply as a source for quoted material. Nor do I here attempt to list all of the individual newspapers and manuscript collections I cited. The notes to the text suffice for that purpose.

Let me begin with a book that influenced me in two very different ways: James Oakes, *Freedom National: The Destruction of Slavery in the United States, 1861–1865* (New York: W. W. Norton, 2013). On the one hand, it alerted me to the seminal importance of Republicans' rejection of Southerners' and Roger B. Taney's claim that the Constitution recognized a property right in slaves. On the other, I found its assertions that "however long it took, and by whatever particular means, the destruction of slavery was inscribed in the Republican electoral victory in November 1860" so profoundly wrongheaded about the intentions of most Republican voters in 1860 that it helped provoke my decision to write this book in order to challenge it.

Every biography of the four candidates, almost every study of Lincoln, and every general history of the period has something to say about the 1860 election. Of the latter, David M. Potter, *The Impending Crisis 1848–1861* (New York: Harper and Row, 1976), and Allan Nevins, *The Emergence of Lincoln: Prologue to Civil War, 1859–1861* (New York: Charles Scribner's Sons, 1950), contain especially useful portraits of the election, although both portray it as two separate contests, one in the North and the other in the South. Older, though still useful, studies of the election include Emerson D. Fite, *The Presidential Campaign of 1860* (New York: Macmillan, 1911); Reinhard Luthin, *The First Lincoln Campaign* (Cambridge, Mass.: Harvard University Press, 1944); and Olinger Crenshaw, *The Slave States in the Election of 1860* (Baltimore: Johns Hopkins University Press, 1945). A far more recent collection of essays focused on the contest is James Fuller (ed.), *The Election of 1860 Reconsidered* (Kent, Ohio: Kent State University Press, 2013).

Most of my research in newspapers was in digitized collections available to me in the University of Virginia's Alderman Library. Aside from digitized versions of the *New York Times* and the *Chicago Tribune*, two multi-paper digitized sources were also quite valuable. One, published by the Gale Company, collects "Nineteenth Century U.S. Newspapers" from a number of cities and towns. The other, assembled by the University System of Georgia, presents historical newspapers from a number of

Georgia towns. It can be accessed at http://dig.galileo.usg.edu/MediaTypes/Newspapers.html?Welcome.

I also relied on two exceptionally valuable printed collections of newspaper commentary about the election and its aftermath: Dwight L. Dumond (ed.), *Southern Editorials on Secession* (New York: Century, 1931); and Howard C. Perkins (ed.), *Northern Editorials on Secession* (2 vols.; New York: D. Appleton-Century, 1942).

Other printed primary sources that I drew on in preparing this book are Glyndon G. Van Deusen (ed.), "Thurlow Weed's Analysis of William H. Seward's Defeat in the Republican Convention of 1860," *Mississippi Valley Historical Review* 34 (1947); *Letters, Speeches, and Addresses of August Belmont* (privately printed, 1890); James D. Richardson (ed.), *Messages and Papers of the Presidents 1789–1897, Volume V* (Washington, D.C.: Government Printing Office, 1897); Roy P. Basler (ed.), *The Collected Works of Abraham Lincoln* (9 vols.; New Brunswick, N.J.: Rutgers University Press, 1951); William B. Hesseltine (ed.), *Three against Lincoln: Murat Halstead Reports on the Caucuses of 1860* (Baton Rouge: Louisiana State University Press, 1960), which was indispensable in following what occurred at the four nominating conventions; Robert W. Johannsen (ed.), *The Letters of Stephen A. Douglas* (Urbana: University of Illinois Press, 1961); and the documentary appendices to Michael F. Holt, "The Democratic Party, 1828–1860" in Volume I and Hans Trefousse, "The Republican Party, 1854–1864" in Volume II of Arthur M. Schlesinger Jr. (ed.), *History of U.S. Political Parties* (4 vols.; New York: Chelsea House and R. W. Barker, 1973).

A digitized version of the Abraham Lincoln Papers, which contain Lincoln's incoming correspondence, is available from the Library of Congress. I also used its microfilm editions of the John Bell Papers and the John J. Crittenden Papers, as well as a few other collections I read at the library itself when researching earlier projects. I identify those collections when I cite them in the text. The major collection of Stephen A. Douglas Papers is at the University of Chicago.

So far as secondary works are concerned, all biographies and many other studies of Abraham Lincoln say something about his first election to the White House. Those studies are far too numerous even to list, let alone recapitulate. In my opinion, the two best single-volume biographies are David Donald, *Lincoln* (New York: Simon and Schuster, 1995), and Richard Carwardine, *Lincoln: A Life of Purpose and Power* (New York: Alfred A. Knopf, 2006). In preparing this book, however, I found the following far more useful: William C. Harris, *Lincoln's Rise to the Presidency* (Lawrence: University Press of Kansas, 2007); Michael Burlingame, *Abraham Lincoln: A Life* (2 vols.; Baltimore: Johns Hopkins University, 2008); and Daniel W. Crofts, *Lincoln & the Politics of Slavery: The Other Thirteenth Amendment and the Struggle to Save the Union* (Chapel Hill: University of North Carolina Press, 2016). Though now over sixty years old, Don E. Fehrenbacher, *Prelude to Greatness: Lincoln in the 1850s* (Stanford, Calif.: Stanford University Press, 1962), remains invaluable in laying out the strategy behind Lincoln's famous "House Divided" speech in 1858 and demonstrating that Douglas's so-called Freeport Doctrine arguing that territorial residents could prohibit slavery despite the *Dred Scott* decision was simply repeating what Douglas had said on several previous occasions.

There are also biographies of the other three presidential candidates in 1860, although their usefulness in preparing this study varied considerably. Joseph Howard Parks, *John Bell of Tennessee* (Baton Rouge: Louisiana State University Press, 1950), is thin on the election, perhaps because so few letters in the Bell Papers concern it. William C. Davis, *Breckinridge: Statesman, Soldier, Symbol* (Baton Rouge: Louisiana State University Press, 1974), was far more useful. Nonetheless, I learned more about Breckinridge's precocious rise in Kentucky politics in the early 1850s from Harry August Volz III, "Party, State, and Nation: Kentucky and the Coming of the American Civil War," (PhD dissertation, University of Virginia, 1982). Best of all the biographers for my purposes were Robert W. Johannsen, *Stephen A. Douglas* (New York: Oxford University Press, 1973), and James L. Huston, *Stephen A. Douglas and the Dilemmas of Democratic Equality* (New York: Rowan and Littlefield, 2007). I particularly relied on Johannsen for Douglas's travel itinerary and the substance of his campaign speeches during 1860.

Several good biographies of other central players in my story are also available. For William Henry Seward, the front-runner for the Republican nomination in 1860, see Glyndon G. Van Deusen, *William Henry Seward* (New York: Oxford University Press, 1967), and Walter Stahr, *Seward: Lincoln's Indispensable Man* (New York: Simon and Schuster, 2012). For the key player in organizing the Constitutional Union Party, see Albert D. Kirwan, *John J. Crittenden: The Struggle for the Union* (Lexington: University of Kentucky Press, 1962). I based much of my narrative of the founding of the Constitutional Union Party on Kirwan's excellent volume as well as the Library of Congress microfilm edition of the John J. Crittenden Papers. For diametrically different appraisals of James Buchanan, the Republicans' chief target in the election, see Philip Shriver Klein, *President James Buchanan* (University Park, Penn.: Penn State University Press, 1962), and Jean H. Baker, *James Buchanan* (New York: Times Books, 2004).

The rise of the Republican Party is covered in most of the books previously mentioned in this note. David Potter's *The Impending* Crisis, for example, devotes consecutive individual chapters to the *Dred Scott* decision, the Lecompton constitution controversy, and the Lincoln-Douglas debates. Eric Foner, *Free Soil, Free Labor, Free Men: The Ideology of the Republican Party before the Civil War* (New York: Oxford University Press, 1970), is the standard history of the party's belief system in the 1850s. William E. Gienapp, *The Origins of the Republican Party, 1852–1856* (New York: Oxford University Press, 1987), is a brilliant analysis of the party's birth and career up through the 1856 presidential election. Of great value to that story as well is James L. Huston, *The Panic of 1857 and the Coming of the Civil War* (Baton Rouge: Louisiana State University Press, 1987). Most of my account in the first chapter, however, is based on research I did for the following of my previous publications: *Forging a Majority: The Formation of the Republican Party in Pittsburgh, 1848–1860* (New Haven, Conn.: Yale University Press, 1969); *The Political Crisis of the 1850s* (rev. ed.; New York: W. W. Norton, 1983); *The Rise and Fall of the American Whig Party: Jacksonian Politics and the Onset of the Civil War* (New York: Oxford University Press, 1999); and "Making and Mobilizing the Republican Party, 1854–1860," in Robert F. Engs and Randall M. Miller (eds.), *The Birth of the Grand Old Party: The Republicans' First Generation* (Philadelphia: University of Pennsylvania Press, 2002).

The ordeal of the Democratic Party during Buchanan's presidency is also discussed in most general histories of the period. Absolutely the best study of that topic is Roy F. Nichols, *Disruption of American Democracy* (New York: Macmillan, 1948). For the story of Stephen Douglas's foes among southern Democrats, see William J. Cooper Jr., *Jefferson Davis: American* (New York: Alfred A. Knopf, 2000), and William W. Freehling, *The Road to Disunion: Secessionists Triumphant, 1854–1861* (New York: Oxford University Press, 2007). Cooper is also indispensable in limning the differences between Davis's and Albert Gallatin Brown's versions of a federal slave code. Freehling's volume, in turn, provided much of the background information about developments within southern state Democratic parties between the Charleston and Baltimore conventions.

Of published works on the Constitutional Union Party, the Kirwan biography of Crittenden was most helpful to me. But I also relied heavily on the final chapter of the final doctoral dissertation written under my supervision: Sean P. Nalty, "'We Are Going to Destruction as Fast as We Can': Slavery, the Rule of Law, and the Constitutional Union Party, 1849–1861" (PhD dissertation, University of Virginia, 2013).

For the election campaigns, election returns, and analyses of those returns, I relied on the following: Jon Grinspan, "'Young Men for War': The Wide Awakes and Lincoln's 1860 Presidential Campaign," *Journal of American History* 96 (September 2009): 357–378; Walter Dean Burnham, *Presidential Ballots, 1836–1892* (Baltimore: Johns Hopkins University Press, 1955); Olinger Crenshaw, "Urban and Rural Voting in the Election of 1860" in Eric F. Goldman (ed.), *Historiography and Urbanization: Essays in American History in Honor of W. Stull Holt* (Baltimore: Johns Hopkins University Press, 1941); Peyton McCrary, Clark Miller, and Dale Baum, "Class and Party in the Secession Crisis: Voting Behavior in the Deep South, 1856–1861," *Journal of Interdisciplinary History* 8 (Winter 1978): 429–457; Daniel W. Crofts, *Reluctant Confederates: Upper South Unionists in the Secession Crisis* (Chapel Hill: University of North Carolina Press, 1989); and William E. Gienapp, "Who Voted for Lincoln," in John L. Thomas (ed.), *Abraham Lincoln and the American Political Tradition* (Amherst: University of Massachusetts Press, 1986). Though I do not cite it, Richard Franklin Bensel provides an intriguing portrait of how votes were actually cast around the time of the 1860 election in his *The American Ballot Box in the Mid-Nineteenth Century* (New York: Cambridge University Press, 2004). For evidence that Jefferson Davis, for one, hoped that Democrats would drop both John Breckinridge and Stephen Douglas in 1860 and unite instead behind former president Franklin Pierce, see Michael F. Holt, *Franklin Pierce* (New York: Times Books, 2010).

For my brief remarks on the secession crisis, I relied, in addition to the books by Crofts and Freehling listed above, on David M. Potter, *Lincoln and His Party in the Secession Crisis* (New Haven, Conn.: Yale University Press, 1941); J. Mills Thornton II, *Power and Politics in a Slave Society, 1800–1860* (Baton Rouge: Louisiana State University Press, 1978), which is also particularly good on William L. Yancey's role in the run-up to the Charleston and Baltimore Democratic conventions; Russell Mc-

Clintock, *Lincoln and the Decision for War: The Northern Response to Secession* (Chapel Hill: University of North Carolina Press, 2008); and William J. Cooper Jr., *"We Have the War upon Us": The Onset of the Civil War, November 1860 to April 1861* (New York: Alfred A. Knopf, 2012). These books constitute only the tip of the iceberg of the vast literature on southern secession and the northern response to it.

INDEX